VOID

Library of
Davidson College

Ireland and EC Membership Evaluated

EC Membership Evaluated Series
Series Editor: Carl-Christoph Schweitzer, The University of Bonn

The Netherlands and EC Membership Evaluated
ed. Menno Wolters and Peter Coffey

Federal Republic of Germany and EC Membership Evaluated
ed. Carl-Christoph Schweitzer and Detlev Karsten

Ireland and EC Membership Evaluated
ed. Patrick Keatinge

The United Kingdom and EC Membership Evaluated
ed. Simon Bulmer

Denmark and EC Membership Evaluated
ed. D. Lyck

France and EC Membership Evaluated
ed. François Dreyfus and Jacques Morizet

Spain and EC Membership Evaluated
ed. Amparo Almarcha and Alfonso Ortega

Italy and EC Membership Evaluated
ed. Francesco Francioni

Portugal and EC Membership Evaluated
ed. José de Silva Lopes

Greece and EC Membership Evaluated
ed. Stavros Theofanides

Belgium, Luxembourg and EC Membership Evaluated
ed. M.A.G. van Meerhaeghe

Ireland and EC Membership Evaluated

Edited by Patrick Keatinge

St. Martin's Press
New York

© Patrick Keatinge 1991

All rights reserved. For information, write:
Scholarly and Reference Division,
St. Martin's Press, Inc., 175 Fifth Avenue, New York, NY 10010

First published in the United States of America in 1991

Printed in Great Britain

ISBN 0–312–06094–7

Library of Congress Cataloging-in-Publication Data

Ireland and EC membership evaluated / edited by Patrick Keatinge.
   p. cm. — (EC membership evaluated series)
  Includes index.
  ISBN 0–312–06094–7
  1. European Economic Community — Ireland. I. Keatinge, Patrick,
1939–   . II. Series.
HC241.25.I748 1991
341.24′22—dc20

90-24899
CIP

Contents

List of contributors — ix

Series Introduction — xi

The Europe-12 — xv

Preface — xvi

Editor's introduction — xviii

PART I: ECONOMIC POLICY

1. Introduction to Part I — 3
   Rory O'Donnell

2. The internal market — 7
   Rory O'Donnell

3. Agricultural policy — 42
   Andy Conway

4. Regional policy — 60
   Rory O'Donnell

5. Monetary policy — 76
   Rory O'Donnell

6. Competition policy — 90
   Rory O'Donnell

7. Industrial policy — 97
   Rory O'Donnell

8. Transport policy — 104
   Tom Ferris

9. Energy policy — 114
   Rory O'Donnell

10. Environmental policy — 119
    Rory O'Donnell

11	Fiscal/taxation policy *Rory O'Donnell*	126
12	Technology policy *Rory O'Donnell*	136

PART II: FOREIGN RELATIONS

13	Introduction to Part II *Patrick Keatinge*	147
14	Foreign policy *Patrick Keatinge*	149
15	Security policy *Patrick Keatinge*	160
16	External trade policy *Rory O'Donell*	165
17	Development policy *Helen O'Neill*	172

PART III: POLITICAL AND LEGAL SYSTEMS

18	Introduction to Part III *Brigid Laffan*	185
19	Sovereignty and national identity *Brigid Laffan*	187
20	Government and administration *Brigid Laffan*	190
21	The political process *Brigid Laffan*	197
22	The political system assessed *Brigid Laffan*	206
23	The legal system *Paul McCutcheon*	209

PART IV: SOCIAL, EDUCATIONAL AND CULTURAL POLICIES

24	Introduction Part IV *Brigid Laffan*	233
25	Manpower policy and vocational training *Brigid Laffan*	236

26	Women *Brigid Laffan*	244
27	Industrial relations *Brigid Laffan*	252
28	Consumer law *Brigid Laffan*	256
29	Education *Dermot Scott*	260
30	Culture and media policy *Fintan O'Toole*	270

PART V: CONCLUSIONS

31	Weighing up gains and losses *Patrick Keatinge, Brigid Laffan, Rory O'Donnell*	279

Glossary of Irish names 292

Index 293

List of contributors

Andy Conway, Ph.D. worked for many years with the Agricultural Institute in Ireland, where he was Head of the Agricultural Economics Department. In 1988 he established **Cera**, a private research consultancy firm. He has engaged in studies relating to a range of topics, including farm production, growth and adjustment in the farm sector, agricultural and environmental policy and rural development.

Tom Ferris, M.A., F.C.I.T., is a Senior Economist in the Department of Tourism and Transport. He contributed to *The Single European Market and the Irish Economy* (Anthony Foley and Michael Mulreany (eds.), 1990). He is a member of the Council of the Chartered Institute of Transport and Chairman of its Membership Committee.

Patrick Keatinge, Ph.D. is an Associate Professor in Political Science at Trinity College Dublin, where he teaches international politics. His publications include *A Place Among the Nations: Issues of Irish Foreign Policy* (1978), *A Singular Stance: Irish Neutrality in the 1980s* (1984), and many articles on Irish foreign policy.

Brigid Laffan, Ph.D. is a Lecturer in Politics at University College Dublin. She is author of numerous articles on European Integration in *The Journal of Common Market Studies*, *Administration*, and *Irish Political Studies*. She has contributed to *Making European Policy Work* (H. Siedentopf and J. Ziller (eds.), 1988), and published *Ireland and South Africa: Government Policy in the 1980s* (1988).

Paul McCutcheon, LL.M., is a Lecturer in Law at the University of Limerick. He is co-author with R. Byrne of *The Irish Legal System* (2nd ed. 1989), and is author of *The Larceny Act* (1989), and 'The Irish Supreme Court, European Political Cooperation and the Single European Act', *Legal Issues of European Integration* (1988).

Rory O'Donnell, Ph.D. is a Senior Research Officer at the Economic and Social Research Institute in Dublin. He previously worked for the

National Economic and Social Council, where he prepared the report on *Ireland in the European Community: Performance, Prospects and Strategy* (1989). He has published *Adam Smith's Theory of Value and Distribution: A Reappraisal* (1990), and articles on regional policy in the European Community.

Helen O'Neill is a Statutory Lecturer in Economics and Director of the Centre for Development Studies in University College Dublin. She has written four books and many articles in the field of international economics and economic development. She has served on the Economic and Social Committee of the EC, and is currently Vice-President of the European Association of Development Research and Training Institutes.

Fintan O'Toole is a columnist with *The Irish Times* and the literary advisor to the Abbey Theatre, Dublin. He has published *The Politics of Magic: The Work and Times of Tom Murphy* (1987), *No More Heroes: A Radical Guide to Shakespeare* (1989), and *A Mass for Jesse James* (1990).

Dermot Scott is Head of Office *ad interim* of the European Parliament Office for Ireland, and has published many articles on the European Community and Ireland.

Series introduction

This volume is one in a series entitled *European Community Membership Evaluated*. The series comprises eleven volumes and examines the gains and losses of European Community (EC) membership for each of the twelve states.

Over the entire period since the first steps in European integration were taken, with the formation of the European Coal and Steel Community, the impact of membership upon the individual states has been both a matter of importance to, and an issue for evaluation by, the political parties, interest groups, government, elites, researchers and, increasingly, the public at large. The renewed dynamism of the EC in the period following the signing of the Single European Act in 1986, and in the approach of the completed internal market by the end of 1992, have raised awareness of EC membership to new heights.

It is against this backdrop that the project leading to this series was undertaken. Policy-makers and the European electorate alike require the information to make informed judgements about national gains and losses (or costs and benefits) arising from EC membership.

— How far have the EC's economic policies brought gains?
— Does EC membership impose constraints on the powers of national and regional/local government, or on the legal system?
— What have been the effects of the hitherto somewhat disparate EC activities in the social, cultural and educational policy areas?
— What are the gains and losses of foreign policy co-operation among the member-states?
— How pronounced are the specific national interests of the individual member-states?

In order to answer questions such as these, each volume brings together a team of specialists from various disciplines. Although the national teams are composed predominantly of academics, the series is aimed at a readership beyond the confines of the education world. Thus each volume seeks to present its findings in a manner accessible to *all* those affected by, or interested in, the EC. Extensive footnoting of academic literature is avoided, although some guidance is offered on the legal bases of EC policies; a bibliography at the end of each study gives guidance on narrower sectoral impact studies and on further reading.

A distinctive feature of the series as a whole is that a common framework has been followed for all eleven studies. This is aimed at facilitating comparison between the national studies. No systematic international comparative study of this kind has been attempted before. Indeed, for some member-states there exists no study of the impact of EC membership. The absence of such a series of studies initially seemed rather surprising. However, as the project progressed, the reasons for this became clearer. It is by no means easy to find a common framework acceptable to the academic traditions of all the member-states *and* all the policy areas and academic disciplines involved.

The project co-ordinators experienced these tensions in a striking way. Their international 'summit meetings' meant reaching compromises acceptable to all the diverse academic traditions of the countries involved. Then the individual national contributors had to be convinced of the merits of the international compromises! These negotiations brought many insights into precisely the type of problem faced by EC policymakers themselves! Hence academic perfectionism has been subordinated to some extent to pragmatism and the wish to address a wider readership.

In some countries, for instance the Netherlands, Great Britain, Portugal and the Federal Republic of Germany, up to thirty scholars of various disciplines make up the national team. In other countries, such as Ireland, a team numbers less than ten authors. In the latter *one* author deals with several parts of a subject-group or even with the whole of a subject-group. In either case, however, authors have assured comparability by making cross-references to subsections of policies.

The basic principle of the project has been to assess the gains and losses of EC membership for the individual state, with the hypothetical alternative in mind of that state leaving the EC. This alternative may be deemed to be somewhat simplistic but it is far more manageable than making assumptions about where individual states would be, had they not joined the EC in the first place. Such speculation is virtually impossible scientifically and would undermine efforts to make the findings accessible to a wider readership. The terms 'benefits', 'gains' and 'positive effects', and 'costs', 'losses' and 'negative effects', respectively, are used synonymously.

The activities of the EC, together with the foreign policy co-operation process EPC (European Political Co-operation), are grouped under four broad headings in the project (see Table A). *Economic policy* covers a range of EC policies: from the internal market to the Common Agricultural Policy but also including environmental policy. *Foreign relations* comprise not only European Political Co-operation but also the EC's external trade policy and security policy. *Social and educational policy* brings together the rather disparate measures taken in a range of areas, some of which are now coming to be regarded as forming the 'social dimension' of the EC. Finally, the subject area *political and legal system* refers not to EC policies but rather to the EC's impact upon the principles and practices of government (for a list see Table A at the end of this Introduction).

Each of the EC policy headings is assessed following a common approach. The objectives of the EC policy, and the accomplishments thus far, are assessed against the equivalent set of national policy goals and legislation, many of them common to all countries, some of them are obviously national ones. The idea, then, is to arrive at a 'balance sheet', both at the level of the individual policy area or sector and, at the macro level, for the member-state as a whole. Drawing up the individual sectoral balance sheets has to involve a rather flexible approach. The 'mix' of quantitative and qualitative assessments varies according to the subject matter. There can be no quantitative data on how far foreign policy co-operation has brought gains to national foreign policy; figures may be available, however, on the impact of EC trade policy on national trade patterns. In the case of quantitative data it is important to note that very little, if any, primary statistical research was involved in the project. In consequence, quantitative assessments generally present available evidence from previous studies; they follow no consistent methodological approach, while qualitative assessments are often arrived at for the first time. One further point must be made with regard to the common approach of the project: it is clear that the importance of individual EC policy areas varies from one member-state to another.

It follows, therefore, that the weighting, and in some cases the categorization, of EC policy areas will vary between the national studies. To assign the same weight to fisheries policy in the British and Luxembourg cases, for instance, would be irrational. Some national policy goals and national interests are related to specific interests of some member countries. For instance, the German question and the problem of Northern Ireland are specific to the Federal Republic, Ireland and the United Kingdom respectively.

The whole project has been brought to fruition under the auspices of Europe-12 — Research and Action Committee on the EC. Created in 1986, Europe-12 brings together academics of all disciplines and from all member-states, as well as policy-makers and senior politicians. It aims to inform the policy debate through collaborative research and to raise public awareness of the important issues raised by European integration.

As with any such project a large number of acknowledgements must be made. A number of the participants took on the additional task of horizontal co-ordination, i.e. seeking to ensure consistency of approach across the national studies. For *economic policy* this was undertaken by Detlev Karsten, Bonn, and Peter Coffey, Amsterdam; for *foreign relations* by Carl-Christoph Schweitzer, Bonn, and Rudolf Hrbek, Tübingen; for contributions on *the political and legal system* by Francesco Francioni, Siena, and K. Kellermann, The Hague; finally, for *social and educational policies* by

Bernard Henningsen, Munich and Brigitte Mohr, Bonn. Sadly, Guenther Kloss, a co-ordinator of the British volume, died during the preparation of the series.

Last but by no means least, we are indebted to the Commission of the EC and to those bodies supporting the project: the German foundations, Stifterverband für die Deutsche Wissenschaft, Essen; Bosch GmbH, Stuttgart; Ernst Poensgen-Stiftung, Düsseldorf; as well as the Government of the Saarland and the Federal Ministry for Science and Technology, Bonn. The British and German Studies were made possible by the support of the Anglo-German Foundation for the Study of Industrial Society, London.

Carl-Cristoph Schweitzer
Bonn

Table A: Project's categorization of EC policies and structures

I	**Economic policy**	
	Internal market policy	Agricultural policy
	Competition policy	Environmental policy
	Industrial policy	Fiscal/taxation policy
	Technology policy	Monetary policy
	Transport and communications policy	Regional policy
	Energy policy	External trade policy
II	**Foreign relations**	
	Foreign policy co-operation	Development policy
	Security policy	
III	**Political and legal system**	
	Sovereignty	National legal system
	Parliamentary control of the executive	Judicial procedures
	Electoral system	Maintenance of public order
	Political parties	Protection of fundamental rights
	Regional and local government	State organization
	Policy-making process	
IV	**Social, educational and cultural policies**	
	Manpower (employment/ unemployment)	Consumer protection
	Movement of labour and migrant workers	Education and training
	Industrial relations	European identity and cultural policies
	Social security and health	
	Equal treatment of men and women	Media policy

Note: This list was a schematic guideline for the project; not every sub-section will be dealt with individually and the sequence is purely illustrative.

The Europe-12

Hon. Presidents:
Lord Jenkins of Hillside
Chancellor of the University of Oxford, Oxford
H.E. Emilio Colombo,
Minister Rome

Board:
Chairman: Minister Dr Ottokar Hahn,
Saarland, Bonn and Brussels
Vice-Chairmen:
Prof. Dr Hélène Ahrweiler,
Recteur et Chanceller Universités de Paris, Paris
Enrico Baron, MEP,
Vice-President European Parliament Brussels–Madrid
Piet Dankert, MEP,
Vice-President European Parliament, Edam–Brussels
Dr Garret FitzGerald,
former Prime Minister, Dublin
Niels Anker Kofoed, MP,
former Minister, Copenhagen
Dr Hans Stercken, MP,
Chairman Bundestag Foreign Affairs Committee, Bonn
Franz Ludwig Graf von Stauffenberg, MEP,
Representative of the President of the European Parliament, Lord Plumb

Senior Economic Advisory Group (in being):
Dr Otto Graf Lambsdorff, MP,
former Minister of Economics, National Chairman FDP, Bundestag Bonn
Staatssekretär a. D. Dr D.K. Rohwedder,
Chairman, Hoesch AG, Dortmund
Co-ordinator of Committees:
Prof. Dr C.C. Schweitzer,
University of Bonn, Political Science

Steering Committee:
Spokesman: Dr Renate Hellwig, MP,
Deutscher Bundestag, Bonn, Sub-Committee Europe
Dr Peter Baehr,
Netherlands Scientific Council, The Hague
Prof. Dr P.D. Dagtoglou,
University of Athens, Law
W. Dondelinger, MP,
Chairman Foreign Affairs Committee, Luxembourg
Prof. Dr Francesco Francioni,
University of Siena, Law
Fernand Herman, MEP,
Chairman Institutional Committee, EP, Brussels
Dr J. Silva Lopes, MP,
Caixa Geral de Depositos, Lisbon, Economics
Antony J. Nicholls, MA,
Senior Fellow, St Anthony's College, Oxford
Dr Hans-J. Seeler, MEP,
Committee on External Ec. Relations, EP, Hamburg
Georges Sutra de Germa, MEP,
Vice-Chairman, Institutional Committee, EP, Pezenas, France
Prof. Count L. Ferraris,
Council of State, Rome

Research Committee:
Prof. Dr Simon Bulmer, Prof. G. Kloss,
University of Manchester, European Studies
Gerry Danaher,
Secretary Irish National Economic and Social Council, Dublin
Prof. Dr Cesar Draz
University of Madrid, Political Science
Prof. Dr Grotanelli de Santi,
University of Siena, Law and Political Science
Prof. Dr R. Hrbek,
University of Tübingen, Political Science
Prof. Dr Detlev Karsten,
University of Bonn, Economics
Prof. Dr M.A.G. van Meerhaeghe
University of Gent. Economics
Prof. Dr Stavros Theofanides,
Pantelos School of Pol. Science, Athens, Economics
Prof. Dr Christian Tomuschat,
University of Bonn, International Law

Media Advisers:
Ralf Goll,
Gesellschaft für Kommunikation und Markentechnik, Frankfurt
Prof. Dr E.G. Wedell,
Chairman, European Media Centre, University of Manchester
Hon. Secretary:
Dr Rosemary Allen,
Oxford

Preface

The approach adopted by the contributors to this volume of the EC Membership Evaluated series broadly follows that of the common framework adopted at the outset of the Europe-12 project. However, the size of the Irish research team was deliberately restricted in order to reduce the psychological, financial and temporal costs of co-ordination.

After a brief historical introduction by the editor, Part I examines the broad range of economic policies affected by EC membership. For Ireland, four of these policy sectors deserve particular attention and have thus been treated more extensively; these include the internal market, monetary policy, regional policy (Rory O'Donnell), and agricultural policy (Andy Conway). The remaining economic sectors have been summarised by Rory O'Donnell, assisted by Tom Ferris on transport policy.

Part II is concerned with the diverse activities which come under the heading of Foreign Relations. Two of these, external trade policy and development policy (Rory O'Donnell and Helen O'Neill respectively) are susceptible to economic analysis, but foreign policy and security policy (Patrick Keatinge) necessarily require a more impressionistic approach.

The effects of membership on the political and legal system, explored in Part III, have been less clear cut but may be no less significant than some of the quantifiable economic changes. After examining the general question of sovereignty and national identity, and the more specific executive and representative aspects of government, Brigid Laffan attempts an overall assessment of the impact of the EC on the Irish political system; Paul McCutcheon does likewise for the legal system.

Brigid Laffan (with Dermot Scott on education policy, and Fintan O'Toole on culture) also reviews the various aspects of social policy in Part IV. In the final part of the volume, she joins Patrick Keatinge and Rory O'Donnell in attempting an overall 'balance sheet' of the impact of EC membership on Ireland. The three main contributors then relate their conclusions to the new agenda of EC integration, at a time of considerable change in the European and world political and economic systems.

The major political institutions in Ireland are generally referred to by their Irish names, and this practice has been followed in the text. For the convenience of non-Irish readers a glossary of these terms can be found at the end of this volume.

Patrick Keatinge

Editor's introduction

Ireland joined the European Community in 1973 alongside the United Kingdom and Denmark as part of the Community's first enlargement. The original decision to apply for membership had been made much earlier, in 1961, but the application made no progress so long as French opposition to British membership remained.

Compared to its partners, the Irish state possesses several distinctive characteristics. Apart from the special case of Luxembourg, it is the smallest political unit, of three-and-a-half million people. Its level of economic development was the lowest of the Nine in the 1970s, and although somewhat higher than that of Greece and Portugal it remains well below the community average. As with the latter two countries, a geographical location on the periphery of the Community's industrial centre is the source of particular difficulties in adapting to integration.

Indeed the decision to apply for membership was by no means an easy one. Although the links between Ireland and continental Europe have distant roots (MacNiocaill and O'Tuathaigh, 1984), for most of the modern era Ireland's orientation towards the English-speaking world has been much more substantial. Emigration to North America, Australia and Britain persisted beyond the achievement of statehood in 1921. So too did an extremely high level of economic dependence on the United Kingdom, and attempts to achieve self-sustained development during the 1930s had only limited effects. Even the legal basis of independent statehood was contested in the inter-war period. The manner in which independence was effectively demonstrated, through the policy of neutrality during the Second World War, only served to insulate Ireland from the trauma experienced by most West European societies; thus what proved elsewhere to be an important political motivation for integration was absent in the Irish case. After 1945 the preoccupation with Anglo-Irish relations continued, with little change in economic dependence and irredentist attitudes regarding Northern Ireland, which remained in the United Kingdom.

On the other hand, the very failure to move beyond this unsatisfactory state of affairs, a failure which was painfully felt in continuing emigration and economic stagnation in the mid-1950s, encouraged a gradual openness to new directions (Hederman, 1983). Faced with the need to adapt to the post-war liberalization of trade, and more particularly confronted by the reorganization of West European economic relationships following the agreement on the EEC in 1957, the Irish Government could no longer simply drift in the wake of decisions taken elsewhere. Although British decisions were still the most immediate external consideration, the United Kingdom's response to the EEC, the creation of the European Free Trade Association (EFTA) in 1960, was not followed by Ireland. EFTA made no provision for agriculture, whereas the EEC for all its hazards addressed what was for Ireland a critical issue. Thus when the British, for quite different reasons, changed their mind and turned towards the EEC in 1961 the Irish Government could present its own application to join as a realistic, and even necessary, gamble.

Yet 1961 proved to be only the half-way house on what has aptly been described as the 'tortuous path' to EC membership (Maher, 1986). Neither public debate nor the EEC's reaction to the Irish application proceeded very far before President de Gaulle vetoed British membership. Nevertheless, two problems were already apparent. The first was the question of whether Ireland was serious about the open-ended political obligations of membership; unlike the other applicants or the original members, the state had stayed aloof from the parallel system of West European security, NATO. However, since neither Ireland's neutrality nor the political aspirations of the EEC were clearly defined, this question proved to be less pressing than that of the compatability of a relatively underdeveloped economy with much wealthier economies. The Government's response throughout the 1960s lay in a policy of reducing tariff barriers and building an industrial base by encouraging foreign investment.

Thus when EC enlargement again became a live issue at the Hague summit in December 1969, Ireland was better prepared to negotiate entry. In particular – and in marked contrast to all the other applicant countries – there was a strong political consensus advocating membership (Salmon, 1981: 197). The Fianna Fáil Government was supported by the largest opposition party, Fine Gael, and apprehensions concerning the effect on Irish industry were more than compensated by expectations of significant gain from the Common Agricultural Policy (CAP). In a referendum in May 1972, the accession treaty was approved by a majority of 83 per cent to 17 per cent in a turnout of 71 per cent.

But entry to the EC coincided with a significant deterioration in the broader international environment. The collapse of the Bretton Woods System in 1971 and the first oil crisis of 1973 were only the more dramatic opening events in what proved to be a general pattern of recession and inflation, associated with an underlying trend of considerable technological change. While the prospects of political détente between the superpowers and a consequent diminution of military confrontation in Europe had been raised in the early 1970s, political relationships were also seriously disturbed by the end of the decade. These negative influences were matched by changes closer to home. The stresses of rapid social transformation, especially rapid urbanization and a questioning of traditional sources of authority such as the Catholic Church, were more widespread than in the 1960s. Also, the unexpected emergence of sustained political violence in Northern Ireland raised issues of national identity which only ten years previously seemed to have been consigned to the balladeer's songbook.

As Ireland passed beyond the transitional stage of EC membership in the early 1980s these malign trends were still evident, almost to the point of caricature. Nothing seemed to work very well, whether at the global, European or national level. Assessments of the country's first ten years in the EC, even where they on balance arrived at a favourable conclusion, reflect a strong sense of disappointment (Coombes, 1983; Drudy and McAleese, 1984; Lee, 1989). The original opponents of membership returned to the attack in the debate on the Single European Act (Crotty, 1988). They remained in the minority in a referendum in 1987, which approved the SEA by 69.9 per cent to 30.1 per cent, but a turnout of only 44.1 per cent suggests the Community's relevance had diminished for the general public.

The remaining years of the 1980s presented a rather different picture, with improvements in general economic trends and in the international political system as a whole. A renewed impetus in West European integration has been evident in the Community's programme to complete the internal market by 1993, the very structure of the post-1945 partition of Europe is being altered, and the Irish economy itself has been showing signs of recovery. The evaluation of gains and losses of EC membership attempted in this volume thus takes place against a more optimistic background than that experienced at any time since Ireland joined the Community.

Nevertheless, for a country like Ireland certain questions are bound to persist, in good times and bad. Can a small, dependent economy adjust successfully to the demands of a very large market? What are the effects of membership of a major diplomatic coalition on a small, peripheral state's foreign relations? How does integration impinge on a relatively young political system which is used to an idiosyncratic mix of administrative centralism and local loyalties? Does EC membership reach beyond the sphere of economic management to affect a society which by West European standards is in many respects impoverished? It is on answers to questions such as these that Irish perceptions of the gains and losses of membership will ultimately be based.

Bibliography

Coombes, D. (ed.) (1983), *Ireland and the European Communities: Ten Years of Membership*, Dublin: Gill and Macmillan.
Crotty, R. (1988), *A Radical's Response*, Dublin: Poolbeg.
Drudy, P.J. and McAleese, D. (eds) (1984), *Ireland and the European Community*, Cambridge: Cambridge University Press.
Hederman, M. (1983), *The Road to Europe: Irish Attitudes 1948–61*, Dublin: Institute of Public Administration.
Lee, J. (1989), *Ireland 1912–1985: Politics and Society*, Cambridge: Cambridge University Press.
MacNiocaill, G. and O'Tuathaigh, M.A.G. (1984), 'Ireland and Continental Europe: the historical dimension', in P.J. Drudy and D. McAleese, *Ireland and the European Community*, Cambridge: Cambridge University Press.
Maher, D. (1986), *The Tortuous Path: The Course of Ireland's Entry into the EEC 1948–73*, Dublin: Institute of Public Administration.
Salmon, T.C. (1981), 'Ireland', in C. and K. Twitchett (eds), *Building Europe: Britain's Partners in the EEC*, London: Europa.

PART I: ECONOMIC POLICY

Chapter 1

Introduction to Part I

Rory O'Donnell

The Community's economic policy

The Treaty of Rome, signed by Belgium, France, Germany, Italy, Luxembourg and the Netherlands in 1957, expressed the determination to 'lay the foundations of an ever closer union among the peoples of Europe'. In the face of problems on both the political and military fronts the means chosen to achieve this aim was economic — the establishment of a European Economic Community. The central element of this was to be the creation of a common market — an integrated market without obstacles to the movement of goods, persons, services and capital. Another important feature of the Treaty was agreement to adopt a common policy in the spheres of agriculture and transport, and to devise a system to ensure that competition in the common market was not distorted. In addition, it was agreed that member-states would approximate their laws and co-ordinate their economic policy to the extent necessary to ensure the proper functioning of the common market and to attain other objectives of the Treaty.

By the time Ireland joined in 1973 the Community's economic policy contained additional areas. Nevertheless, the initial agenda — the common market, the Common Agricultural Policy, competition policy (and to a lesser extent, transport and energy policy) — continued to form the core of Community economic policy. Indeed, some of the additional economic policies were developed because they were considered necessary to achieve the central economic objective of a common market. This can certainly be said of fiscal or taxation policy, some elements of which entered the Community agenda early on. It is partly true also of monetary policy. While some saw monetary union as necessary for a genuine common market, it was equally true that it would greatly deepen the degree of integration and require political as well as economic institutions and developments. Faced with its full implications member-states have several times shied away from monetary union — even if that did limit the common market.

Community industrial and regional policy were not adopted because they were directly necessary for a common market, but they can be traced to original Treaty aims. They were viewed as necessary if the achievement of the common market was not to create excessive economic and social disruption and not to be threatened by national, regional or industrial resistance. Since then, they have developed beyond this pragmatic role and, while some would wish to relegate them to it again, they seem destined to form an integral and permanent part of the Community's economic policy. The Community's technology and environmental policies developed somewhat later, in response to problems which were not perceived at the outset. The development of a Community technology policy reflects the fact that for the Community, if not for certain ideologues, the common market is an instrument for the achievement of common aims, and not an end in itself.

These new policies — reflecting greater focus on original objectives — received formal status in the Community in the revision of the Treaty of Rome introduced by the Single European Act of 1987. Overall, the development of the Community's economic policy agenda can be seen to reflect a growing — but in some cases very grudging — recognition that market integration is inseparable from monetary, regional, technological, industrial and even fiscal integration.

Ireland's economic objectives and policy

Ireland was in an economic and political union — the United Kingdom of Great Britain and Ireland — for the 120 years up to 1921, and the severe economic difficulties experienced during this period were instrumental in creating the desire to secede from that union. The economic policy goals of the independent Irish state, apart from those shared by all European states, were the industrialization of the country, and increased agricultural production based on the maximum number of family farms. For over three decades these goals were pursued by industrial protectionism and supply of agricultural produce to the large British market.

In the 1950s this policy of protectionism was re-evaluated when it failed to prevent severe balance-of-payments crises, rising unemployment and large-scale emigration. It was decided that further industrialization and greater prosperity required export-led growth and greater participation in the international economy. On moving towards free trade, the state undertook intensive study of the strengths and weaknesses of indigenous manufacturing and established an industrial policy with a wide range of incentives for both Irish and newly arriving foreign firms. This industrial policy has been at the centre of Irish economic policy ever since.

The initial success of this new approach in creating manufacturing employment and export markets other than the United Kingdom was an important determinant of the decision, in the early 1960s, to seek membership of the EC. The eventual decision to join, taken in 1972, was strongly supported in a referendum — but very different views of the likely effects of membership were expressed by representatives of interest groups, such as farmers and trade unions.

Ireland's experience since the major reductions in protection in 1965 and 1973, and her policy interests within the Community, have been greatly conditioned by the fact that while the incentives for attraction of foreign direct investment were very successful, those aimed at indigenous industry had much less impact. Indeed, by 1972 official expectations of the effects of membership of the Community had shifted somewhat, in the light of the failure of indigenous manufacturing industry, built up behind protective tariffs, to achieve significant export sales. This was reflected in an increasing emphasis on new, and especially foreign-owned, industry and in the issues raised by Ireland in the formal negotiations on accession.

The costs and benefits of EC membership — methods of investigation

In order to assess the benefits and losses to Ireland of membership of the EC three things are, theoretically, necessary. First, it is necessary to have some measure or idea of the effects of EC membership on Ireland. The second requirement is closely related to the first; in order to identify the effects of EC membership it is necessary to form some view of what would have happened in the absence of integration. This view can vary from the very simplest — that nothing would have changed — through the simple idea that variables would have developed along pre-existing trends, to a much more complicated specification of likely economic developments in the absence of integration. This view of how things would have developed in the absence of integration is known as the *anti-monde*. Some *anti-monde* will be explicit or implicit in any serious description of the effects of EC membership on any given country. Even where these two demanding requirements have been met, there is a third. In order to turn an analysis of the effects of EC membership into an assessment of costs and benefits it is necessary to attach some welfare weights to each of the effects of integration. Even in the simplest case this is a difficult and, in the view of many, a fruitless exercise. International trade and economic integration will benefit some and harm others; in this situation there are formidable conceptual and practical problems in deriving a measure of aggregate national welfare gain or loss.

In this study most effort is devoted to identifying the effects on the Irish economy of membership of the EC market. This necessarily involves some view of what would have happened if Ireland had not joined. Brief consideration is then given to whether the effects identified were gains or losses to Ireland.

Structure of economic policy entries

The application of the above approach reveals that four Community policies emerge as having been of overwhelming significance for Ireland to date. These are internal market policy, agricultural policy, monetary policy and regional policy. Consequently, at an early stage in the Europe-12 project a decision was made by the Irish research team that a balanced and accurate view of the gains and losses to Ireland required that these four policy areas be allocated a large share of the space devoted to economic policy. Indeed, such was the significance of the internal market on the Irish economy that a further decision was made to provide a detailed analysis of its effects. The Irish team believe that these decisions are confirmed by results which emerge in the eleven chapters on economic policy subjects.

These decisions, and the resulting structure of this section of the volume, reflect judgments on the effects of Community membership to date. In the future, indeed in the near future, other EC policies, such as fiscal and taxation policy, are likely to be of increasing significance. This is reflected in our comments on the likely future gains and losses to Ireland.

Chapter 2
The internal market
Rory O'Donnell

Introduction

It has been argued in the previous section that the internal market was the aspect of Community policy which had much the greatest impact on Ireland. One of the major economic policy goals of the independent Irish state was the industrialization of the country. For over three decades (early 1930s to mid-1960s) this objective was pursued by a policy of industrial protectionism and reliance on native capital and entrepreneurship. In the late 1950s policy-makers became disillusioned with this approach and adopted a more outward looking economic strategy. This involved a progressive lowering of protection and an emphasis on export growth — to be achieved in part by foreign firms attracted to Ireland. It follows that membership of the EC was the logical outcome of the economic and political policies pursued by successive Irish governments since the 1950s.

In the Introduction to this section we briefly discussed the methodological problems which confront any attempt to assess the gains and losses from EC membership. We noted that in this volume most of our investigative effort is devoted to identifying the *effects* of EC membership, which — in this chapter — means the effects of Ireland's membership of the EC *internal market*. We begin by identifying the possible effects of EC membership, as derived from economic theory, and proceed to assemble the evidence we require to make an assessment. This involves a review of Ireland's overall economic performance, and a fairly detailed analysis of changes in patterns of trade, production, employment, specialization and firm size since 1973. In the final section we summarize all the evidence and offer an interpretation of Ireland's experience in the internal market.

The effects of economic integration: orthodox trade theory

In attempting to ascertain the impact of EC membership on Ireland the first task is to identify the possible effects. The likely or possible effects of economic integration are revealed by the economic theories of trade and integration. Consequently, some reference to these theories is necessary. In this section and the following one we provide a brief explanation of the major orthodox and more recent theories of international trade. Our purpose is to identify propositions about the gains and losses from trade and EC membership. A more detailed account of these theories, with references and application to Ireland can be found in NESC (1989).

Orthodox or traditional trade theory explains the pattern of trade between two countries by reference to their relative endowments of resources such as labour, capital and land. Without international trade, each country must produce the full range of goods it wishes to use in consumption or investment. When trade is allowed then the theory predicts that the country which has relatively abundant labour will find it advantageous to concentrate on labour-intensive goods and to purchase capital-intensive goods abroad — where they are produced more cheaply. Likewise, the capital-rich country will find that it cannot produce labour-intensive goods as cheaply as the labour-rich country, and will purchase them abroad rather than produce them. Thus each country exports those commodities which utilize best its most abundant input. Indeed, each country specializes completely in the products to which it is most suited — and acquires the other products through trade. Thus the traditional theory of trade says that the pattern of trade reflects the differences between countries' endowments of labour and capital.

This trade between countries is known as *inter-industry* trade, because each country imports and exports very different products of *different* industries. The international pattern of production which is involved is called *inter-industry specialization*.

The orthodox economic analysis of integration consists largely of the application of this trade theory to different models or stages of integration such as a *customs union* and a *common market*. In a customs union member countries agree to eliminate tariffs and quotas on trade among themselves, and to adopt a common external tariff. A common market goes beyond a customs union in that it entails free movement of *factors of production*, capital and labour, as well as free movement of *goods*.

Trade creation and trade diversion

The orthodox theory of trade, described above, usually compares autarky (no-trade) with complete free trade. The formation of a customs union or a common market is not a move to *complete* free trade, since the countries forming the union exclude other countries by maintaining, or increasing, tariffs against them. This complicates the analysis of the gains from trade. As well as 'trade created' as the member countries specialize, there is, against this, 'trade diverted', as trade with non-members is reduced or stopped altogether. For example, if Ireland had joined the EC when the British application was refused, both Ireland and the EC countries would gain by specializing in particular lines and this would imply new trade flows. But, at the same time, Ireland might now buy from France some products which it previously bought from Britain, and which would be cheaper to buy from Britain, but for the new tariff against British goods. This new trade with France would be 'diverted' and reduces the net gains from forming the common market. Whether the formation of the common market increases or decreases total welfare depends on the relative size of the 'trade created' and 'trade diverted' and early studies of the EC focused precisely on these magnitudes (Robson, 1987).

Overall then, orthodox trade theory leads us to expect that Ireland's membership of the EC would have altered the pattern of goods produced and traded in Ireland. The theory would predict that Ireland would specialize in those activities most favoured by its relative abundance of labour, capital and land. Consequently, the removal of tariff barriers with other EC countries would lead to a run down of some industries and a build up of others.

The effects of economic integration: beyond orthodox trade theory

Improving technical efficiency

A possibility not included in the orthodox trade theory is that, prior to the opening of trade, firms employ inefficient practices and processes. By inefficient practices and processes we mean that more output could be achieved with the same inputs. The assumption of technical efficiency is part of the reason why the gains from integration are so narrowly defined in the conventional theory. Those who have studied the process of European integration are in no doubt that the assumption of technical efficiency must be dropped; in other words, they feel certain that prior to trade liberalization many firms in various Community countries were not maximizing the output they achieved from the inputs they used (Pelkmans, 1984).

It follows from this line of thinking that European industrial market integration could have a 'cold shower' effect on the behaviour of industrial firms. They could respond to increased international competition by increasing their efficiency. This would lead to a reduction in costs of production which would constitute a gain to society. Pelkmans argues that 'the "welfare" consequences of an improvement of technical efficiency after the reduction of protection seem likely to be many times larger than the rather trivial gains from improving price-efficiency' (Pelkmans, 1984: 26).

It is very difficult to measure this technical inefficiency and hence to quantify the beneficial effect of market integration. Nevertheless, some consideration must be given to the possibility that one of the major effects of EC membership on Ireland was the effect of foreign competition on the efficiency of Irish firms.

Introducing economies of scale

One of the major innovations in recent approaches to the analysis of economic integration is the inclusion of *economies of scale*. Economies of scale exist where the cost of producing a good is *lower* the larger is the scale of production. Remarkably, the conventional approach to trade, and most orthodox economics, is premised on the assumption that cost of production is either constant or *increasing* as output increases. However, there is much evidence to show that manufacturing and some kinds of agriculture experience economies of scale and that these economies of scale play a significant role in international trade.

Surprising as it may seem, including economies of scale in the analysis has significantly altered economists' views on the likely effects of trade and integration (Krugman, 1987). The reason is that once economies of scale are introduced into the analysis then other new phenomena must be allowed in also. Where economies of scale exist it is unrealistic to view each industry consisting of very many small producers, as is assumed in traditional theory. Instead, industries with economies of scale tend to be highly concentrated, i.e. dominated by a few firms. It follows that in analysing the effects of integration, attention must be given to the size structure of firms and industries and the market power of corporations. This subject is known in economics as market structure or *industrial structure*.

Another concept of considerable significance in new approaches to trade is that of *product differentiation*. This arises because much international trade between industrialized countries now involves two-way exchange of very similar goods. Such trade is known as *intra-industry* trade (IIT), because it occurs *within* a given industry and involves specialization *within* industries rather than *between* them. Theoretical argument shows that the presence of economies of scale, and the associated market power of firms, encourages product differentiation and intra-industry trade.

The four phenomena, *economies of scale*, *industrial structures*, *intra-industry trade* and *product differentiation* are linked in ways which allow for a very wide variety of outcomes from the integration process. Here we ignore the theoretical analysis of these interactions and merely state some of the possibilities which should be considered in identifying the effects on Ireland of EC membership. The following hypotheses can be found in the literature on European integration (see NESC, 1989: chapter 3).

Integration

The level of *intra*-industry trade and specialization, as opposed to *inter*-industry specialization, will be higher the higher is the degree of economic integration.

Size of country

There are two competing hypotheses concerning the size of a country and the level of intra-industry trade. The first, known as the Dreze standardization hypothesis, says that small countries will tend to specialize in relatively *standardized* products (i.e. the level of IIT will be lower than in larger countries). A contrary hypothesis is that small countries will import intermediate products and achieve large-scale production by specializing in highly *differentiated* versions of products for the world market. It would clearly be of considerable interest to know which, if any, of these hypotheses applies in the Irish case.

The costs of adjusting to free trade

Another important proposition is that adjustment to free trade will be both quicker and easier when trade expansion takes the form of intra-industry rather than inter-industry trade. This probable difference in the costs of adjusting to free trade is one reason to study the level of intra-industry trade. It has been argued that because most of the post-war increase in trade in the developed world, and especially in the EC, has been intra-industry trade, it has been relatively free of adjustment problems. Indeed, the predominance of intra-industry trade in European integration to date was cited in a major EC study, the Cecchini Report, as one reason to expect few reallocative and redistributive effects from the completion of the internal market currently under way (Emerson *et al.*, 1988).

Integration increases industrial concentration

One very important proposition concerning industrial structure has emerged in modern research on economic integration. It has been argued that the reduction of barriers to trade should bring about an increase in the concentration of industry. The idea is that access to foreign markets increases the incentives for large-scale producers in each country to drive out marginal producers by increasing capacity and thereby lowering cost (Owen, 1983).

Furthermore, firms which are threatened by the low cost of the dominant producers will presumably search for counter-strategies such as product differentiation, product innovation, process innovation, and mergers or take overs. But most of these strategies also imply a slow but steady reorganization of industry towards large-scale production, with weeding out of fringe producers. Pelkmans' conclusion therefore is that 'there are solid reasons to expect a Customs Union to lead to a rise in domestic producer concentration over time, while the number of sellers may or may not remain the same' (Pelkmans, 1984).

Empirical research confirms the accuracy of this prediction for the Six after the formation of the Community, and more recent work shows that the growth of trade between 1963 and 1978 further increased the size of production units in Germany, Italy, and the United Kingdom. It is clearly of some significance whether the increase in trade prompted a similar process of concentration in Ireland.

Conclusion

Given these possible effects of integration it is necessary to study not only the changing pattern of trade and employment in Ireland after 1973, but also the *nature* of Ireland's *specialization* (as revealed by statistics on intra-industry trade) and the changing size structure of firms and industries in Irish manufacturing industry.

However, a study of the facts alone will not reveal what effects membership of the EC had on Ireland. The reason is that the facts of economic performance since 1973 were the result, not just of Ireland's integration into the European economy, but of a host of other forces also — such as trends in the world economy, technical change and economic policies adopted by Irish governments. This problem arises in any attempt to identify the effects of integration; but it arises very acutely in the case in hand. The reason is that Ireland's accession to the EC in 1973 coincided with a major and prolonged change in the world economic climate resulting from international monetary instability and the oil crisis. Thus 1973 was a turning point for all countries, and this makes it especially difficult to identify the effects of Community membership on Ireland.

The Irish economy in the EC: overall economic performance

As a preliminary to our study of changes in the pattern of trade,

Table 2.1 *Average annual growth rates of real product, various periods, 1960–86*

	1960–73	1973–9	1979–86
Gross Domestic Product (GNP)	4.4	4.1	1.5
Gross National Product (GNP)	4.3	3.4	−0.3
GNP adjusted for terms of trade	4.8	2.2	0.2
Gross National Disposable Income (GNDI)	4.9	2.8	0.3
Population	0.6	1.5	0.7
GNDI per head	4.2	1.2	−0.4

Sources: K.A. Kennedy *et al.*, *The Economic Development of Ireland in the Twentieth Century* (1988) and A. Punch, 'Real gross national disposable income adjusted for terms of trade 1970–84', *Quarterly Economic Commentary* (ESRI), April 1986. The difference between GDP and GNP arises from the inclusion in the latter of the outflow of net factor payments, while GNDI includes transfer payments received from abroad as well as the terms of trade adjustment.

production, employment and changes in the size structure of Irish industry we summarize Ireland's overall economic performance since accession to the EC in 1973. Ireland adopted Community rules and procedures progressively over a five-year transition period from 1973 to 1978.

Economic growth 1973–9

Ireland's entry to the EC in 1973 coincided with a major slowdown in economic growth in all OECD countries. However, Ireland's recovery from the recession of 1974–5 was very strong and, as a result, the annual average rate of growth of real Gross Domestic Product (GDP) was 4.1 per cent in the period 1973–9 — only slightly lower than the 4.4 per cent achieved in the period 1960–73. However, it is widely agreed that the decline in the growth of GDP does not convey an adequate picture of the change in economic conditions and performance which occurred after 1973. For a number of reasons the rate of growth of real product *available for consumption or investment* declined much more sharply.[1] These influences have been quantified by a number of researchers and can be used to present a thumbnail sketch of overall economic performance before and after Ireland's entry to the EC (see Table 2.1). We are concerned first with the contrast between the period 1960–73 and the period immediately after accession, 1973–9. The average annual growth rate of real gross national disposable income (GNDI) fell from 4.9, before 1973, to 2.8 after. The final row in Table 2.1 relates the growth of real product to the rate of growth of population in order to reveal the growth of GNDI *per head*. Faster population growth after 1973 implied an even greater fall in the growth rate of real product per head of population.

However, when these growth rates of output and employment are compared with those of other EC countries, the Irish economy is seen to have performed relatively well in the period 1973 to 1979.

Turning from real to financial indicators, Ireland's experience was not so strong. The attempt to maintain growth in the face of international recession inevitably involved increased government borrowing. Rapidly increasing deficits pushed the overall exchequer borrowing requirement to almost 16 per cent of GNP in the mid-1970s and early 1980s. These trends in economic growth and the public finances were, to a considerable extent, reflected in the balance of payments. The second half of the 1970s saw a worsening trend in the current account deficit.

Economic performance, 1979–present

The overall economic performance since the end of the transition period was markedly worse than in the years from 1973 to 1978. This contrast is summarized in Table 2.1 which shows first, that there was much slower growth of domestic product and, second, that this was reduced to virtual stagnation, or even contraction, of disposable income per head by increased factor payments abroad.

The period 1980 to 1988 was one of balance-of-payments adjustment, from the very large deficits in 1980, 1981 and 1982, to small surpluses in 1987 and 1988. Most of this adjustment was achieved on the trade account, by means of a huge decline in home demand aided by some improvement in the terms of trade. This adjustment in the balance of payments was not initially matched by an equivalent adjustment in the overall public sector deficit. However, since 1987 considerable progress has been made in correcting the public finances.

Phases of economic experience

At a number of places in this volume we identify two phases in Ireland's economic experience in the Community. One phase, from accession in 1973 through the transition period to 1979, was a period of vigorous economic growth by international standards. A second phase, from 1979 to 1986, was characterized by very poor economic performance on almost all counts. However, we should also identify a third phase — or at least the first signs of a distinctive phase of economic performance. That third phase has occurred in 1987, 1988 and 1989 and has been characterized by a resumption of economic growth and very positive evolution of many important determinants and indicators of economic performance.

Given the very sharp contrast between Ireland's economic experience in the 1970s and (most of) the 1980s there is something to be gained from examining these two periods separately. However, when we look beyond the outcome for growth, consumption and employment, we see that economic performance in the 1970s and 1980s were, in fact, very closely connected. One obvious connection between the two phases is the state of the public finances. Another is the balance of payments. But we will see that the performance of industry and agriculture in the two periods also contain important continuities. Most important of all, the effects of *integration into the EC* on the Irish economy did not differ so much in the 1970s and the 1980s; or, any difference in integration effects in the two decades, was a difference of *degree* not of *kind*. Consequently, our approach suggests that in seeking to identify the effects of economic integration attention should not be focused primarily on the contrasting macroeconomic characteristics of the 1970s and 1980s.

In order to identify the effects of membership we must now ask which of the possible effects, listed and explained above, have actually materialized in the Irish case. Since the internal market has removed many tariff and non-tariff barriers to trade in *manufactured* goods, but has left in place most barriers to trade in *services*, our main focus is on the effects of the EC internal market on manufacturing in Ireland. In the remaining sections we examine, in turn, each of the possibilities listed earlier concerning trade, employment, output, the cold shower effect, intra- versus inter-industry specialization and changes in industrial structures. Our final task is to combine our findings under all of these headings and present an interpretation and evaluation of Ireland's membership of the EC internal market.

Trade

In this section we examine the changing geographical and commodity composition of Ireland's foreign trade.

Increased level of trade

As would be expected, the removal of tariff barriers with EC states brought about changes in trading behaviour. Both exports and imports increased considerably as a per cent of GDP during the transition period to full membership – and indeed, continued to increase until the early 1980s. Because of the small scale of the home market, the importance of agriculture, and the lack of other natural resources, Ireland has, for a very long time, been a trading country. Tables 2.2 and 2.3 show exports and imports as a per cent of GDP in each Community country in 1960, 1973 and 1988. These tables show that even in 1960 Ireland was a very open economy by comparison with most Community countries. Secondly, these tables show the remarkable increase in the openness of the Irish

Table 2.2 *Exports of goods and services, per cent of GDP*

	1960	1973	1988
Ireland	32	38	65
Germany	19	22	29
France	15	18	22
Italy	14	19	20
Netherlands	48	47	54
Belgium	38	56	69
Luxembourg	87	88	103
United Kingdom	21	24	25
Denmark	32	29	29
Greece	9	14	23
Spain	10	14	20
Portugal	18	27	35
EUR 12	20	23	27

Source: Annual Economic Report 1988–89, European Commission.

Table 2.3 *Imports of goods and services, per cent of GDP*

	1960	1973	1988
Ireland	37	45	55
Germany	16	19	24
France	13	18	22
Italy	14	21	19
Netherlands	46	44	51
Belgium	39	53	66
Luxembourg	74	77	96
United Kingdom	22	26	28
Denmark	33	30	29
Greece	17	25	31
Spain	8	16	20
Portugal	24	34	42
EUR 12	19	23	27

Source: Annual Economic Report 1988–89, European Commission.

economy since that date. Imports, as a per cent of GDP, reached a high level earlier but have not increased as rapidly as exports.

These tables reveal a striking contrast between the extremely trade dependent economies of Ireland, Belgium and the Netherlands, on the

Table 2.4 *Commodity structure of Irish exports (percentage shares)*

	Food, drink, tobacco	Raw materials fuels	Manufactures		Total
			Chemicals machinery	Other	
SITC	0+1	2+3+4	5+7	6+8	0–9
Year					
1955	68.0	8.1	3.0	9.3	100
1960	65.0	10.0	4.4	14.6	100
1972	45.6	7.0	15.1	25.7	100
1978	40.2	4.8	25.8	24.3	100
1984	25.5	7.0	42.6	20.6	100
1988	25.6	5.1	44.3	21.5	100

Source: *Statistical Abstract of Ireland* and *Trade Statistics of Ireland*, CSO.

one hand, and the rest of the Community, on the other. The most significant contrast is that between Ireland and Denmark, since these two economies have considerable structural similarities (peripheral location, small population and substantial reliance on grassland agriculture) and they joined the EC in the same year.

Changing patterns of trade

Although Ireland had a free trade agreement with the United Kingdom since 1965, accession to the EC in 1973 did imply major changes in Ireland's trade regime and trade policy. A detailed account of these changes, and their effects on the geographical pattern of Irish trade, can be found in Chapter 16, on external trade policy. There it is demonstrated that the trend towards *geographical* diversification of Ireland's trade, evident in the 1960s, continued after EC accession.

The *commodity* composition of Irish trade has also changed considerably. Table 2.4 shows that, despite the buoyancy of Irish agricultural exports in the early years of EC membership, the value of food, drink and tobacco exports was soon overtaken by the value of manufactured exports. The table divides total manufactured exports into two sub-sections in order to highlight the remarkable growth of exports by the chemicals and engineering industries (SITC, sections 5 + 7). The period from 1979 to the present has seen a continuation of these patterns of change — but at a much more dramatic rate. And although the share of food, drink and tobacco exports may have stabilized, the share of chemicals and machinery has continued to rise, accounting for almost 45 per cent of all exports in 1988!

It has often been noted that Irish manufactured products have a high import content. Consequently, it is not surprising that the increased share of manufacturers, in Irish GDP and exports, should be reflected in increased manufactured imports. An examination of the commodity structure of Irish imports would confirm that this has indeed occurred, although, on the whole, changes in the structure of imports are less pronounced. The high import content of Irish exports of chemicals and electronic machinery means that the balance-of-payments contribution of these manufactured exports is considerably less than that of agricultural or service sector exports.

In his recent study of the determinants of Irish imports FitzGerald found no significant independent effect of EC membership on the evolution of total Irish imports (1987). Despite this, it should not be inferred that there was no such effect. It simply means that no EC effect, *independent of the variables already used to explain imports*, could be detected. Among the major determinants of the very large increase in manufactured imports, was the Irish economy's increased orientation towards exporting. This was, in turn, largely a result of EC membership, both directly — through falling trade barriers — and indirectly — through the increase in foreign direct investment in Ireland.

The experience of manufacturing industry since 1973

Overall performance

The growth of manufactured output was somewhat slower after accession in 1973 than it had been from 1960 to 1973. Table 2.5 provides a summary of the overall performance by showing the growth rates of output, employment and productivity. The somewhat slower growth of output, combined with faster productivity growth, meant that employment in manufacturing increased very little indeed in the years after EC accession.

Restructuring of the manufacturing sector

The slowing of output growth in manufacturing after 1973, and the very slow growth of employment should not be read as evidence of stagnation in this part of the Irish economy. In fact, major changes were underway in the years after 1973. The restructuring of the manufacturing industry can be seen by considering the changes in the distribution of employment *between* sectors and *within* sectors. Table 2.6 shows total employment and share of total employment in each sector in the years 1973 and 1981.

Table 2.5 *Growth rates of manufacturing output, employment and output per head*

	Output	Employment	Productivity
1950–60	3.1	0.8	2.3
1960–73	6.5	2.3	4.0
1973–9	5.1	0.8	4.3
1979–86	4.1	−2.7	7.0

Source: Adapted from K.A. Kennedy *et al.*, *The Economic Development of Ireland in the Twentieth Century* (1988). Based on *Census of Industrial Production* and *Industrial Inquiries*.

Table 2.6 *Manufacturing employment by sector*[1]*, 1973 and 1981*

Sub-sector	1973		1981	
	Aggregate employment	Share %	Aggregate employment	Share %
Food	46,856	21.3	47,318	19.8
Drink and tobacco	10,790	4.9	10,860	4.5
Textiles	22,885	10.4	19,388	8.1
Clothing and footwear	24,887	11.3	18,326	7.7
Wood and furniture	10,788	4.9	11,699	4.9
Paper and printing	14,498	6.6	16,965	7.1
Chemicals and plastics	11,253	5.1	13,979	5.8
Glass and cement	15,532	7.1	17,735	7.4
Metals and engineering	42,504	19.3	57,702	24.1
Other manufacturing	17,127	7.8	21,282	8.9
Grant-aided services	2,544	1.2	3,802	1.6
Total	219,664	100.0	239,056	100.0

Sources: IDA Employment Survey Files published in Ruane (1984).
[1] Data in this table are those collected in the IDA employment surveys taken on 1 January 1973, and 1 January 1981. The total survey figures *differ from CSO total manufacturing figures*.

Changes in the distribution of employment *between* sectors after EC membership were not substantial. There was a relative and absolute decline in textiles, clothing and footwear; traditional sectors which faced severe competition as tariff protection was reduced. The other noteworthy feature of these data is the increased share of metals and engineering; this sector includes firms producing electronics and office equipment, both of which have increased enormously.

Table 2.7 *Components of manufacturing employment change by sector, 1973–81*

Sub-sector	Job gains	Job losses	Net change in employment
Food	11,610	11,148	+462
Drink and tobacco	1,653	1,583	+70
Textiles	8,207	11,704	−3,497
Clothing and footwear	5,626,	12,187	−6,561
Wood and furniture	5,052	4,141	+911
Paper and printing	6,303	3,836	+2,467
Chemicals and plastics	6,259	3,533	+2,726
Glass and cement	5,164	2,961	+2,203
Metals and engineering	30,956	15,758	+15,198
Other manufacturing	9,518	5,363	+4,155
Grant-aided services	1,833	575	+1,258
Total	92,181	72,789	+19,392

Sources: as for Table 2.8.

However, when the pattern of employment *within* sectors is examined much more dramatic changes are revealed. Table 2.7 shows job *gains* and job *losses* in each sector between the years 1973 and 1981. Although the net change in employment in all the firms surveyed was only 19,392, this figure was the result of 72,789 job losses and the generation of 92,181 jobs. The implication of this is that although the net change in manufacturing employment after 1973 was well below what was expected and hoped for, it should not be inferred from this that the manufacturing sector was stagnant. There was, in fact, a very profound change in the structure of the sector. Our task is to identify precisely what that change was, for it must be seen as the single most important effect of EC membership.

Trends in manufacturing output and employment

In the period after accession there was considerable variation in the output performance of different sectors of industry. Figures 2.1 and 2.2 show an index of the volume of production and employment in various sectors in the years after 1973. Our immediate interest is in performance from accession to around the end of the 1970s. It is possible to distinguish between sectors, such as chemicals and metals and engineering, which grew considerably, and others, like clothing, footwear, textiles, paper and printing, and wood and furniture, which declined or grew very little indeed. These figures make clear that the output performance of industry in the period immediately after accession was

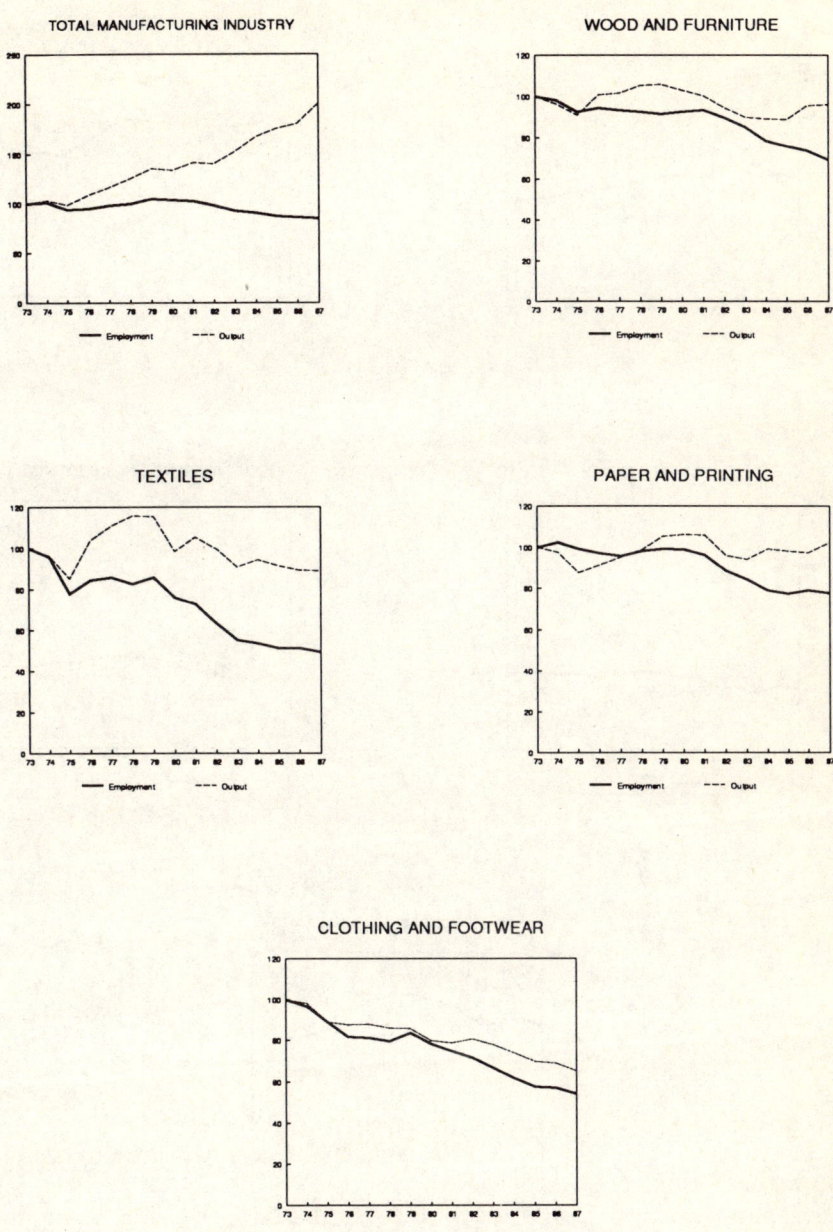

Figure 2.1 *Employment and output in Irish manufacturing industry (1980 = 100)*

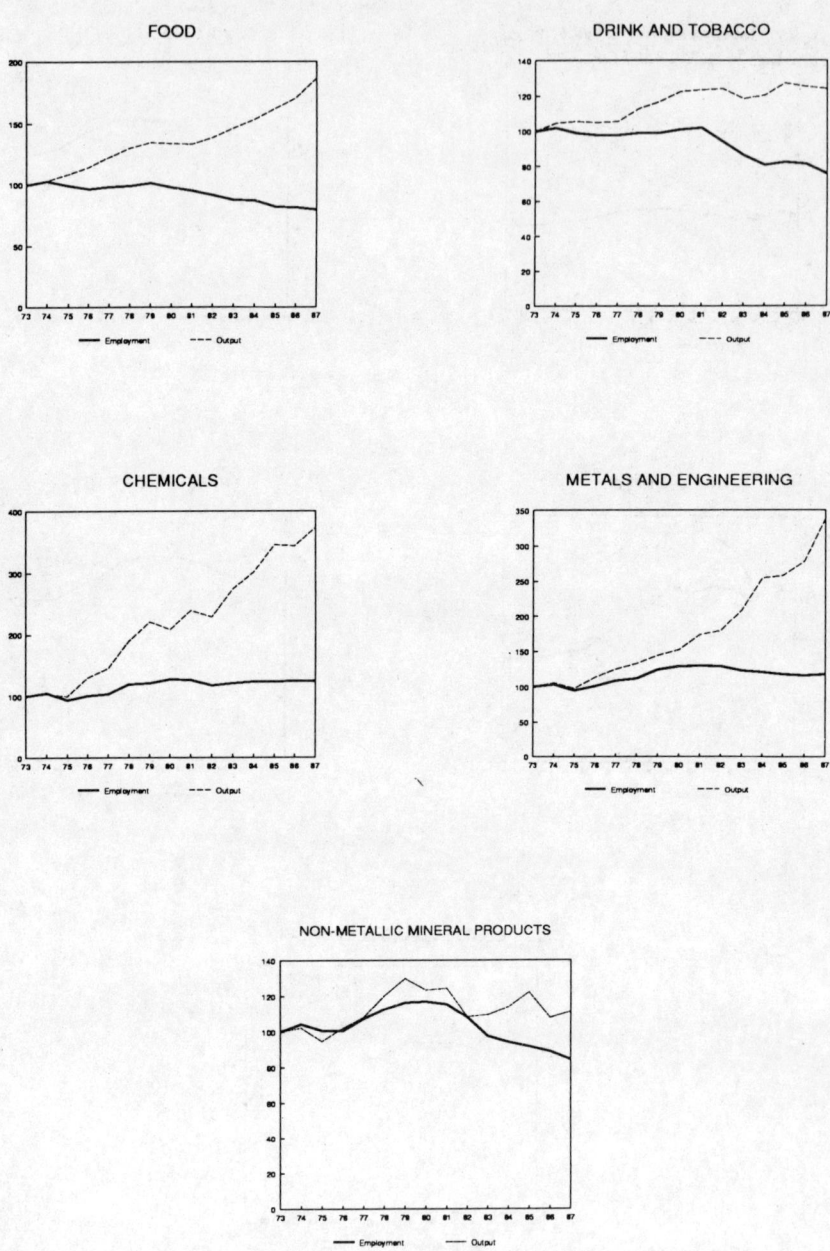

Figure 2.2 *Employment and output in Irish manufacturing industry (1980 = 100)*

dominated by the recession of 1974/5, when output of industry as a whole fell. But, it is also clear that the impact of recession, of integration, and of whatever other forces were at work, were very varied — falling much more heavily on those sectors suffering long-run decline.

However, most sectors of manufacturing contain *sub-sectors* which vary considerably in capital or labour intensity, level of technological sophistication, international or domestic orientation, size of firm, etc. From what has been said in our brief survey of the theory of integration we expect these characteristics to influence the way in which a sub-sector responds to economic integration. Consequently, in order to identify the impact of integration on Irish manufacturing industry, it is necessary to look in even more detail at output, employment and productivity since 1973.

Three groups of manufacturing industry

After this exercise, it is possible to identify three groups of industries — each characterized by a different response to Ireland's integration into the EC and to other changes in the economic environment of the 1970s. Furthermore, the different characteristics of these groups allows us to understand the very different experience of the 1980s. Consequently, this classification of industries plays and important role in our interpretation of the effects of EC membership on the Irish economy.

1. FOREIGN-OWNED, GRANT-AIDED, EXPORT-ORIENTED FIRMS

These firms are found in: pharmaceuticals; chemicals; electronic and data-processing equipment; instrument engineering. Firms in these sectors experienced rapid growth of both output and employment based on export markets, which reflects high investment in these sub-sectors, strongly influenced by both EC membership and industrial policy incentives (see Chapter 7 on industrial policy).

2. INDUSTRIES IN WHICH THE DOMESTIC MARKET IS NATURALLY
   PROTECTED

These industries are of two types. First, *large scale*: paper and printing; drink and tobacco; food (parts of — especially milk and beef products); non-metallic minerals.

In these industries employment was increased, or at least maintained, during the 1970s. Output also increased somewhat, but productivity growth was slow. In general, the poor output performance of these industries after accession was a *reversal* of the trends which prevailed before 1973. The source of the natural protection from international competition differed from one industry to another. In food it arose from being located close to the source of the major material input — Irish milk and beef producers — and from the nature of the processing undertaken. In drink and tobacco protection from international competition would seem to have arisen because the Irish market has traditionally been dominated by a few firms with considerable market power (O'Malley, 1981).

Second, *fragmented*: metal articles; mechanical engineering; electrical engineering (parts of); wood and furniture. These industries serve very local markets and consist of many small producers. The most significant fact about them is that the number of enterprises and workers *increased* considerably during the 1970s and output grew in the very buoyant demand conditions. Indeed, given the difficulties experienced by much of indigenous manufacturing, the growth in these industries was a substantial part of the overall growth of the economy during the transition period.

3. INTERNATIONALLY TRADED, RELATIVELY LARGE SCALE

This group of industries is comprised of: textiles; clothing; footwear; leather; chemicals (parts of); motor vehicles and parts; electrical engineering; shipbuilding; bread, biscuits and flour confectionery; sugar, cocoa, chocolate; fruit and vegetable processing. These relatively large-scale activities showed both output and employment decline in the 1970s. For some of them it was a continuation of a trend that began in the mid- to late 1960s; in others, decline was a new phenomenon. After the removal of tariff protection import penetration was rapid and, in the highly competitive environment, the larger Irish producers were eliminated from these industries.

Thus we have a thumbnail sketch of how the most sensitive sector of the Irish economy — manufacturing — responded to Ireland's EC membership. We will presently supplement these data on employment and output with a further analysis of trade statistics and the size of structure of manufacturing industry in Ireland. However, we first complete the basic picture by reporting how manufacturing industry fared after the end of the transition period to full EC membership.

Manufacturing industry after the transition period

The growth of output and employment which characterized Irish manufacturing during the transition period was brought to an abrupt halt by the recession of 1980—1. Total manufacturing *output* decreased only very slightly in 1980 (and again in 1982) before resuming an upward trend; but *employment* began a steep fall which continued for several years and has not been reversed.

The changes in the sectoral shares of total manufacturing employment which were identified for the period 1973 to 1981 continued in the 1980s — but at a much faster rate. Clothing and footwear continued to lose their share of employment while metals and engineering increased its share. However, *all* sectors lost employment during the 1980s. To understand what was happening it is useful to trace how the sectors and sub-sectors in each of our three groups fared in the period since 1980.

CATEGORY 1: FOREIGN-OWNED, GRANT-AIDED, EXPORT-ORIENTED

Firms in these sectors maintained their rapid growth of output and exports in the 1980s, with the sub-sector 'office and data processing equipment' surpassing electrical and instrument engineering and chemicals. Most of these sub-sectors also increased employment somewhat, but a very large fall in employment in man-made fibres is clear evidence of job losses in relatively new, grant-aided, foreign-owned firms.

CATEGORY 2: INDUSTRIES IN WHICH THE DOMESTIC MARKET IS
NATURALLY PROTECTED

Reliance on the domestic market left these industries extremely vulnerable to the events which unfolded after 1980. The severe international recession, followed by prolonged depression of domestic demand, caused contraction of both output and employment in most sectors in this category. This was true of both the large-scale industries (e.g. employment in drink and tobacco fell by 25 per cent between 1980 and 1987) and the fragmented sectors (e.g. employment in 'metal articles' fell by over 32 per cent in the same period).

CATEGORY 3: INTERNATIONALLY TRADED, RELATIVELY LARGE SCALE

The long-run decline of these sectors continued — but at a more rapid rate in the 1980s than in the 1970s. This decline is confirmed by the employment figures in Table 2.8 which shows the change in employment in some relevant sub-sectors. The figures reveal that these sub-sectors, generally considered to be in danger as protection was reduced and finally eliminated — though they showed definite signs of decline in the 1970s — suffered an even more dramatic contraction during the 1980s. In these sub-sectors there are fewer signs of recovery in the generally improved economic conditions since 1987.

We have now examined the changes in Ireland's trade behaviour and the pattern of manufacturing output and employment, which followed accession to the EC in 1973. According to traditional trade theory these are the main variables in which to find the effects of economic integration

Table 2.8 *Employment in declining industries 1980 and 1987*

Industry sector or sub-sector	NACE code	Numbers employed in 1980 (000s)	Numbers employed in 1987 (000s)	Percentage change
Motor vehicles, parts	35	6.6	2.7	−59.1
Other transport	36	5.7	4.1	−28.1
Bread, biscuit, flour confectionery	419	9.4	7.0	−25.5
Sugar, cocoa, choc. etc.	420−1	6.6	5.0	−24.2
Woollen industry	431	3.2	1.8	−43.8
Knitting industry	436	5.1	4.0	−21.6
Other textiles	432−4 437−9	8.1	4.8	−40.7
Leather and leather goods	44,451	4.8	1.6	−66.6
Clothing	453−6	15.6	12.5	−19.9

Source: CSO, *Industrial Employment, Earnings and Hours Worked.*

— and some remarkable changes have certainly been revealed. However, we noted at the outset that newer, and more realistic, theories of trade suggest that other variables be examined also. We now proceed to consider the 'cold shower effect', intra-industry trade and specialization, and the size structure of manufacturing industry. With these data, and the more conventional ones, assembled, we proceed to offer an interpretation of the effects of the EC internal market on Ireland.

Increased technical efficiency

Measuring the 'cold shower' effect

We noted above that it is impossible to quantify the improvement in technical efficiency induced by the integration of the European market. Pelkmans, who has undertaken extensive study of European market integration, relies on the fact that the persistence of technical inefficiency in the relatively insulated Western European economies was a cause of grave concern in the early 1950s. There is particularly strong evidence of this in the traditionally sheltered French and Italian economies. It has been argued that French manufacturing industry was strongly sheltered from foreign competition, and that domestic firms colluded in maintaining a non-competitive environment in which they could all take high profit margins. Others have noted the archaic distribution systems which prevailed in France, Italy and Belgium, and which almost certainly inhibited trade and thereby protected both high-margin but inefficient producers and traditional high-margin distributors (Owen, 1983).

Pelkmans has no doubt that in the EC of the Six, and especially in France and Italy, the 'cold shower' of industrial market integration has been extremely effective. Indeed, he noted that both France and Italy made substantial trade gains after the formation of the EC and considers that:

Given the relatively higher technical efficiency of the German economy in the 1950s, *the conclusion of a drastic increase in technical efficiency induced by the competitive threats and opportunities of the common market seems to be the only plausible explanation* (there are, of course, other indications pointing in the same direction). (Pelkmans, 1984; emphasis in original)

The Irish case

Given that the Irish economic structure in 1973 was one that had developed behind high protective barriers it is likely that considerable inefficiencies existed. But there is no sure way of measuring this or the improvements in efficiency brought about by the 'cold shower' of international competition. However, the official studies of Irish manufacturing industry conducted by the Committee on Industrial Organization and the Committee on Industrial Progress and other bodies in the 1960s, should probably be seen in the same light as the evidence cited by Pelkmans and others. In other words, they did not, and indeed could not, choose *between* different Irish industries on the basis of identifying comparative advantage, but instead, *within* each industry they could and did draw attention to the inefficiencies in production, management and marketing, which would render Irish firms vulnerable in a free trade environment. In addition, our study of the evolution of manufacturing since 1973 in the rest of this chapter will give some idea, however suggestive, of the impetus to increased efficiency provided by reductions in tariffs. Unfortunately, it is not possible to provide a more systematic investigation of the 'cold shower' effect than this.

Intra-industry trade and specialization

The economic theory surveyed briefly at the outset produces a number of hypotheses about the effects of economic integration on a country's economy. It will be noted that the idea of intra-industry trade and intra-industry specialization features in several of these hypotheses. In this section we report trends in the level of Ireland's intra-industry trade in order to evaluate these hypotheses. While it will not be possible to test these hypotheses formally here, some idea of their validity in the Irish case can be gained, and this certainly adds to our knowledge of the effects of EC membership on Ireland.

Measuring intra-industry trade

The essence of intra-industry trade is the international exchange of very similar products. It has been observed that much of the enormous growth in international trade since the Second World War has been of this sort. This intra-industry trade has been explained by the fact that firms, and therefore countries, specialize in slightly different versions or types of product *within* a given industry. Where intra-industry specialization exists we commonly find each country both exporting and importing any particular product, for example, radios or motor cars. Since intra-industry trade and specialization implies simultaneous exchange by countries of products of the same industry, all measures of intra-industry trade involve examination of the relative size of the imports and exports of a particular industry. The standard measure of intra-industry trade is that proposed by Grubel and Lloyd in 1975. Where imports of a particular type of product exactly match exports of the same good then the Grubel Lloyd index of intra-industry trade has its highest value, 1. Where there are exports of a product but no imports (or vice versa) then the index takes the value 0, and trade is entirely *inter*-industry. The index of intra-industry trade varies between 0 and 1 depending on the extent to which imports of particular goods are matched by exports of similar goods.

McAleese calculated the level of intra-industry for Ireland and found a pronounced increase over the period 1964 to 1977. The index for total merchandise trade rose from 0.48 in 1964, to 0.52 in 1971, and further to 0.63 in 1977. The level of IIT rose in thirty-three out of the forty-three separate commodity divisions for which he calculated the index. Like many researchers in other countries he found that trade in manufactured goods showed an even more rapid increase in intra-industry trade.

The author has recently calculated the level of IIT for 1980 and 1986. The detailed results are presented and discussed in *Ireland in the European Community: Performance, prospects and strategy* (NESC, 1989). The most striking feature of these calculations is the fact that the steady upward trend in IIT observed by McAleese has been reversed in the 1980s. The index for total merchandise trade has fallen from 0.63 in 1977, to 0.50 in 1980, and 0.52 in 1986. Indeed, even the level of intra-industry trade in *manufactured* goods has fallen from 0.66 in 1977, to 0.60 in 1986. Since the measure of *intra*-industry trade is the inverse of the level of *inter*-industry trade these results imply that the level of inter-industry trade has increased.

Why IIT has not continued to increase

Our task is to interpret this trend in our assessment of the effects of EC membership on the Irish economy. While considerable further research would be required to reach a definitive analysis and interpretation, its identification provides important new information on the Irish economy and in this chapter we tentatively suggest an interpretation. In order to interpret these developments it is necessary to look at the disaggregated calculations of the level of IIT.

The reduction in the index of IIT is certainly evidence of more inter-industry trade. But inter-industry trade and inter-industry specialization are not a problem, in and of themselves. It all depends on whether the country is specializing *in*, or being specialized *out*, of a particular industry. On inspection, it can be seen that both processes have been occurring in Irish manufacturing industry. In a number of sub-sectors, drink and tobacco, organic chemicals, and office and data processing machinery, the falling level of IIT reflects Ireland's growing trade *surplus*. Such is the imbalance of recorded exports over imports in office machinery and organic chemicals that these sub-sectors have relatively low levels of IIT. In a number of other sectors, fertilizers, plastics, segments of machinery and transport equipment, clothing, footwear, travel goods, textiles and parts of food, the falling level of intra-industry trade reflects a growing trade *deficit*. The developments in these sectors bear some of the hallmarks of an adverse *inter-industry* adjustment, that is, Ireland has been specialized *out* of these industries.

Trade with developed and less-developed countries

Theory predicts that trade between developed industrial economies will show a higher index of IIT than trade between developed and less-developed economies. The reason is that while developed countries tend to exchange similar products (*intra*-industry trade), less-developed countries tend to exchange raw materials or standardized goods for highly manufactured products (*intra*-industry trade). Consequently, it is worth asking whether the fall in the level of IIT in Ireland in the 1980s is explained by the decline of industries like textiles, clothing and footwear, in the face of competition from newly industrializing countries.

The Irish data conform to what is expected, and what has been found in other countries: namely, trade with developed industrial economies shows a far higher index of IIT than trade with less-developed countries (NESC, 1989). In general this would tend to imply that Ireland's trade with less-developed countries could have caused greater *adjustment problems* than trade with developed countries. However, it is not easy to ascribe the increased inter-industry trade in textiles, clothing and footwear, and the effective specialization of Ireland *out* of these industries, to competition from less-developed economies that are specializing into these industries. Imports from such countries still constitute a small percentage of total Irish imports of these products — though a considerably higher percentage than for imports in general. Ireland's trade with less-developed countries is discussed in more detail in Chapter 16, on external trade policy.

The size structure of manufacturing industry

Introduction

It will be recalled that one of the most interesting hypotheses of the new theories of trade and integration is the prediction that integration will bring about concentration within each industry. In order to investigate whether this has occurred in the Irish case we must examine the changing size structure of manufacturing industry. Ideally, we would wish to investigate the size structure of both *establishments* and of *firms*. This would allow us to consider both economies of scale in production (which would encourage the formation of large *establishments*) and economies of scale in other activities, such as marketing, finance, R&D, etc. (which would encourage the formation of large *firms*). Unfortunately the data which are available refer to establishments only.[2]

Industrial structure in Irish manufacturing

In their recent study of small-scale manufacturing industry Kennedy and Healy (1985) summarized the development of the size structure of Irish manufacturing as follows: from the late 1920s to the late 1960s the employment share of establishments with less than fifty employees declined considerably. But the share of establishments in the size ranges from 50 to 500 employees remained remarkably stable. Consequently, the chief long-term change in the period to the late 1960s has been the gain in the share of establishments with more than 500 employees at the expense of those with less than 50. In the early to mid-1970s this process of concentration went into reverse. In particular, the share of employment in the largest size category (more than 500) declined. It will be seen below that this reversal of the concentration process continued and, indeed, quickened in the late 1970s and the 1980s.

Limitations of space preclude a detailed analysis of the data which demonstrates the de-concentration of Irish manufacturing industry in the 1970s and 1980s. A more detailed account can be found in NESC (1989). Here we illustrate the general trend by reference to a single sector, metals and engineering. While no one sector can adequately represent all of manufacturing, this sector does contain sub-sectors of all three types identified above: grant-aided foreign-owned firms, sub-sectors reliant on the domestic market and relatively large-scale activities open to international competition.

In the late 1950s metals and engineering was a sector which had 31 per

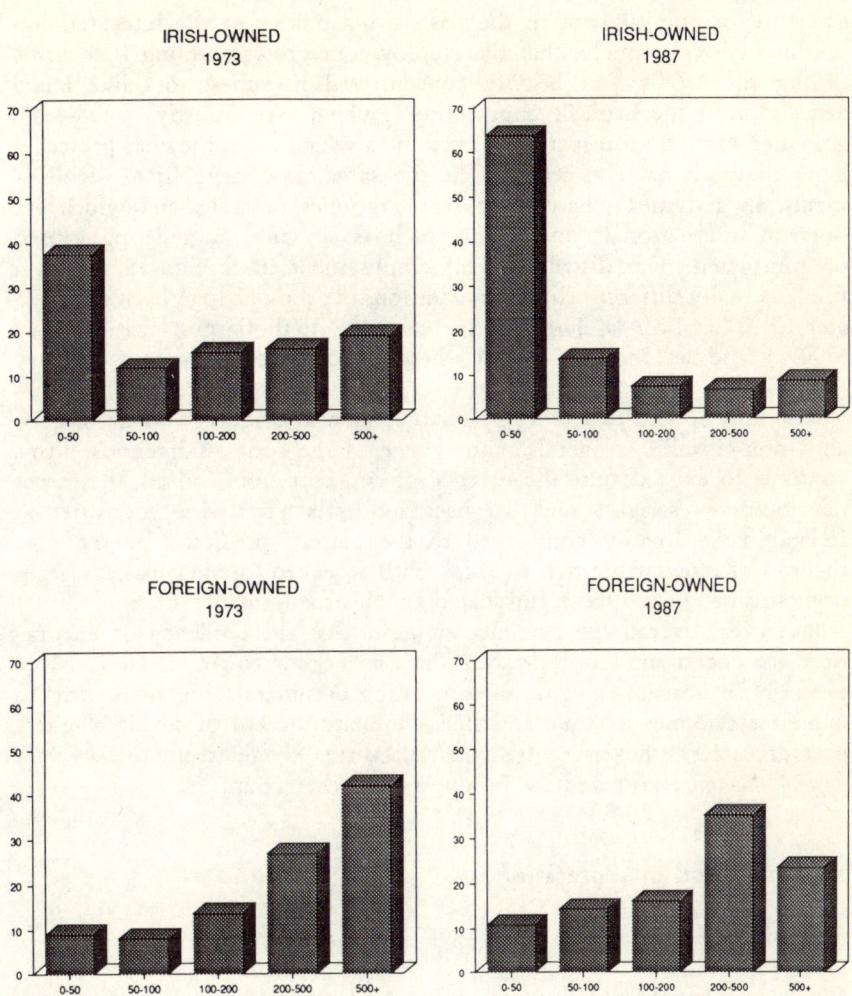

Figure 2.3 *Size structure of engineering industry (per cent of employment in each size category)*

cent of its employment in establishments with more than 500 employees, and a further 23 per cent in the size category 200–500. This made it a considerably more concentrated sector than manufacturing in general. Between 1958 and 1968 employment in the sector became even more concentrated in large establishments, with over 60 per cent in firms with more than 200 employees. Figure 2.3 shows developments since 1973 for the foreign and Irish-owned firms separately. The change in the size structure of employment in the Irish firms reinforces the interpretation outlined above: namely, that the employment growth among Irish firms during the 1970s was heavily concentrated in sub-sectors like metal articles and mechanical engineering, which are mostly small-scale activities serving local markets in products which are somewhat protected from international competition. At the same time large Irish establishments, in activities where there are economies of scale, and which are open to international competition (such as electrical engineering) closed or contracted. The distribution of employment in foreign firms has a fundamentally different shape. In addition, the only change between 1973 and 1987 has been a slight fall in the share of the largest size category (500+) and an increase in the share of the second largest category (200—500).

It should be said that in a few sectors, such as drink and tobacco, glass and non-metallic minerals and paper, large-scale indigenous firms continue to exist despite the reversal of concentration. Indeed, the recent developments suggest that the beef and milk processing industries in Ireland have broadly conformed to the pattern predicted by the new theories of integration: that is, faced with access to foreign markets larger domestic producers have eliminated or absorbed smaller firms.

However, overall the evidence suggests that the tendency of integration to encourage concentration has *not* occurred in Ireland. More precisely, instead of integration stimulating dominant indigenous firms to exploit economies of scale and thus eliminate the tail of smaller higher-cost producers, the larger Irish manufacturers would seem to *have been part of the tail* eliminated by producers in other countries.

Summary and interpretation

Summary of the evidence

We have now examined some of the evidence which economic theory suggests is relevant in seeking to identify the effects of the EC internal market on Ireland. This has confirmed that Ireland's foreign trade has altered both its geographical and commodity structure in the years since accession to the EC. We have studied the changing pattern of employment in manufacturing industry — noting that there was substantial, but undramatic, change in the distribution of employment *between* broad sectors of industry, but a quite remarkable level of job loss and job gain *within* many sectors of manufacturing. In addition, we have traced the evolution of output and employment from the mid-1960s to 1987 and identified three broad types of response to free trade and to other changes in the economic environment. These three responses allow us to categorize individual sub-sectors into three groups: (1) grant-aided, export-oriented, foreign-owned; (2) sectors that benefit from an element of natural protection; and (3) relatively large-scale sectors open to intense international competition. We have traced the different employment and output experience of these three groups in the 1970s and the 1980s.

Next we considered the possibility that the removal of tariff protection induced an increase in efficiency in Irish firms. Despite the impossibility of quantifying improvements in technical efficiency, we found some evidence to support the strong a priori assumption that there was considerable inefficiency prior to free trade, and a distinct improvement in response to the 'cold shower' of international competition.

The relative significance of inter- and intra-industry trade is an important indicator of the pattern of specialization which a country has adopted in the international economic system. Our study of this subject revealed a considerable increase in the index of IIT in Ireland in the 1960s and 1970s. However, in the 1980s the level of IIT has fallen or, in many cases, stopped increasing. This reflects the evolution of large trade surpluses in some sectors (such as electronic machinery, inorganic chemicals and drink and tobacco) and large trade deficits in other sectors (such as clothing, textiles, much of engineering and parts of food).

Finally, we have reported trends in the size structure of manufacturing industry in Ireland. From the late 1920s to the late 1960s there was a strong tendency towards an increasing concentration of employment in larger establishments. In the early to mid-1970s this process of concentration went into reverse. This reversal of the concentration process continued and, indeed, quickened in the late 1970s and the 1980s — when most large-scale indigenous firms in internationally traded sectors disappeared.

Interpretation

In studies of the development of the international trading system great stress is put on the fact that the growth of trade has mainly, though by no means exclusively, entailed specialization *within* industries, rather than *between* them. This pattern of international specialization has a number of advantages. One of the most important of these is that specialization within industries involves firms moving into particular products and processes, whereas specialization between industries involves running down whole sectors and building up others. The performance of the Irish manufacturing sector during the 1970s was such that these trends may seem to have applied to Ireland also. In particular, the very slight changes in the distribution of employment between sectors, the changing geographic and commodity composition of Irish exports, and the increased level of IIT, seemed to indicate an adjustment in which resources were reallocated to specific *firms* and *products* within each industry.

However, the longer view which can now be taken, and the broader collection of evidence which has been assembled here, indicate that developments in Irish manufacturing require further interpretation before they can be compared with the experience of other European countries in the initial stage of economic integration.

The performance of indigenous industry can broadly be seen in the second and third groups summarized above. There were very large job losses in all those industries which were exposed to international competition (group 3). In the 1970s these difficulties were offset by increased employment in indigenous firms in the second group — especially metal articles, mechanical engineering and wood and furniture. The definite downward trend in the exposed indigenous industries (group 3) would seem to indicate that there was an *inter*-industry adjustment occurring; that is, a process in which Ireland specializes *into* some industries and *out* of others, and which therefore implies the run down of some whole industries and build-up of others. Specifically, there is strong evidence of an inter-industry specialization *into* sectors such as organic chemicals, pharmaceuticals, office and data processing equipment and parts of food processing, such as meat and milk products. This occurred simultaneously with a process of inter-industry specialization *out of* industries such as clothing, footwear, textiles, transport equipment, travel goods, fertilizers, animal and vegetable fats, and parts of the food industry such as fruit and vegetable processing, biscuit and confectionery, and the large-scale indigenous segments of metals and engineering, chemicals, and wood and furniture.

This interpretation of Ireland's experience is strengthened and added to when changes in the industrial structure are considered. Recall the trend observed in several countries: that growth of trade induced a concentration of industry. Indeed, it was even argued that firms threatened by the low cost of dominant producers will search for counter-strategies, which themselves imply a slow but steady reorganization of industry towards large-scale production with weeding out of fringe producers. A study of the changing size structure of manufacturing in Ireland shows that the exact reverse was occurring in the exposed indigenous sectors of Irish manufacturing industry in the period after accession. The proportion of employment in medium to large firms has declined dramatically, and this process was occurring even in the 1970s. The segments of metals and engineering, and chemicals, which are included in group 3 (those industries under severe competitive pressure) are precisely the *large-scale* activities in which the larger Irish firms declined disproportionately. Furthermore, much of the *increased* employment in indigenous industry was in the highly fragmented sectors, metal articles, mechanical engineering, and wood and furniture. Together these developments constitute a distinct adjustment from one set of industries to another.

The sharp decline of manufacturing employment in the 1980s, the quickened pace of change in the size structure of indigenous firms, and the decline of the index of IIT, all suggest that in the early 1980s a pattern of severe adjustment *between* industries emerged to dominate the adjustment *within* industries which seemed prevalent in the 1970s. If this interpretation of the evidence is accepted then the question which remains is: what is the explanation for these changes and, in particular, what role should Ireland's membership of the EC be accorded in analysis of them? Our contention will be that the developments in both the 1970s and the 1980s should be seen, in part, as effects of Ireland's economic integration into the European economy.

Explanation: the sequence of integration effects

It is possible to interpret the entire experience of indigenous Irish manufacturing, since accession, in terms of the response of firms to economic integration. Although some complicating factors will be considered presently, we now outline this interpretation, since it plays an important role in our overall assessment of the effects of EC membership on Ireland.

The most immediate effect of economic integration was almost certainly the 'cold shower' effect. There can be little doubt that the removal of inefficient practices accounted for some of the rationalization observed in the period after accession. Where job losses reflected improved efficiency, in response to the shock of competition, then firms could produce the same output at lower cost and would, indeed, have improved their position. The next effect of integration on firms is likely to have been specialization on particular products *within* their own industry. Indeed, the message of much of the literature on the growth of trade following the formation of the EC, is that this specialization within the industry often *completes* the process of adjustment.

But if the firms' basic scale was too small relative to their competitors, or if they suffered other competitive disadvantages (both of which seem to be true of Irish manufacturing industry in the 1970s), then the breathing space offered by removal of inefficiency, and by an element of specialization on particular products, would only have been temporary. Consequently, competitive pressure for further adjustment inevitably built up. Where this further pressure forced contraction of output and employment, the adjustment to intensified international competition tended to become the process of long-run decline, inherent in international specialization *between* industries. The reason was that, in industries where economies of scale existed, contractions of employment (except where they remove basic inefficiency or introduce new technologies), and contraction of output, tended to *raise* costs rather than *lower* them. Consequently, such 'adjustments', rather than re-establishing competitiveness on a new basis, were the start of a process of attrition. What we observed in the 1980s was precisely *further* contraction or elimination of many of the indigenous firms in exposed and relatively large-scale activities. Thus the experience of Irish manufacturing industry since accession can be seen to be consistent with a sophisticated and realistic understanding of how trade and integration can work where there are initial differences in the level of development, technology and scale of production. The analysis of the Irish experience in these terms suggests that some of the severe problems of manufacturing industry in Ireland in the period 1980 to 1986 should be seen as effects of economic integration, unredressed by counteracting policies.

Other explanatory factors

There are two elements to the story being told here about the experience of Irish manufacturing in the EC internal market. One concerns the pattern of adjustment which has occurred; the other concerns the *timing* of that adjustment. We have suggested that the pattern and timing of adjustment are explained by Ireland's integration into the EC internal market. In both cases it is necessary to mention other explanatory factors. In particular, we must take account of Ireland's developmental policies, both before and after accession. There can be little doubt that Irish developmental policy failed to address some of the major barriers facing indigenous manufacturing. This problem did not exist only, or especially, in the period 1973 to 1980, but the changed trading and growth environment in those years brought to light the consequent weakness of the manufacturing base.

The developmental policy pursued in the period 1973 to 1980 and before was not, of course, the ultimate cause of the weakness of Irish manufacturing. But for various reasons it failed to overcome the basic constraints to industrialization (see NESC, 1982 and 1989). It has been argued that the earlier policy of industrial protectionism left a legacy of undersized firms, involved mainly in the final assembly of products for sale on the small home market (Kennedy *et al.*, 1988). On moving towards free trade, the state undertook intensive study of the strengths and weaknesses of indigenous manufacturing and established an industrial policy with a wide range of incentives. While the incentives for attraction of foreign direct investment were very successful, those aimed at indigenous industry had much less impact.

Indeed, in its operation, if not in its intention, industrial policy strongly favoured new foreign-owned enterprises over older and indigenous firms (see the chapters on regional policy and industrial policy). To this extent it not only failed to overcome the obstacles facing indigenous industry, but actually encouraged Ireland's subsequent specialization out of many industries and into others. The result was a manufacturing sector which was not well placed to grasp the opportunities or withstand the threats posed by the free trade. From inadequate scale stemmed other weaknesses, such as low levels of R&D and innovation. It is this structure, encouraged — or at least not successfully alerted — by past and contemporary industrial policy that was so thoroughly challenged by free trade. This is the challenge that is documented in our study of industrial output and employment, intra-industry trade and adjustment, and industrial structure. Indeed, it has recently been said that 'The poor performance of the large indigenous firms emerges as a major factor inhibiting Irish industrialization' (Kennedy *et al.*, 1988).

A second factor which may have some role in explaining the run down of much indigenous industry, and its replacement by foreign firms in a narrow range of sectors, is the uneven growth of domestic demand. During the 1970s Ireland pursued an expansionary fiscal policy which was frequently pro-cyclical. The resulting severe imbalances in both the public finances and international payments dictated that deflationary macroeconomic policies be pursued throughout the 1980s. In this period of prolonged depression a major contraction of indigenous manufacturing industry occurred. It seems likely that the uneven pattern and timing of Ireland's growth, when compared with that of its major trading partners, did something to encourage the adjustment between industries identified above.

Timing of adjustment

We have argued that in the early 1980s a pattern of severe adjustment between industries emerged to dominate the adjustment *within* industries which seemed prevalent in the 1970s, and that this partly explains the severe difficulties in manufacturing industry between 1980 and 1986. What can explain the timing of these changes?

A realistic view shows that there are many reasons why the effects of economic integration on the patterns of production, employment and trade could take a considerable number of years to work themselves out. First, we noted the hypothesis that specialization *within* industries will tend to be both quicker and easier than specialization *between* industries. Second, one of the more immediate effects of reducing tariff protection is to shake out basic inefficiencies; the resulting gain in efficiency can postpone further adjustments for a time. Third, in the Irish case integration occurred first with the United Kingdom, then with the EC-nine (six of whom had already integrated since 1958), and finally with Greece, Spain and Portugal. It should be noted that the United Kingdom had very similar prices of labour, capital and materials to Ireland — whereas the economies and societies of the EC-six differed much more. An implication of this is that as integration widens and deepens, a country may experience more disruptive adjustment in the pattern of production and employment because greater *differences* between countries come into play. Fourth, it was argued earlier that in industries where there are economies of scale then costs will become *more* and not less important — despite the presence of non-price determinants of competitive advantage. Fifth, in the 1970s the EC Common External Tariff provided some measure of protection to sections of European industry — particularly clothing and textiles. Sixth, internal EC tariffs were reduced in stages during the transition period 1973 to 1978.

Finally, a factor which must be considered when discussing the contrast between Ireland's economic experience in the 1970s and the 1980s is the change in the exchange rate regime resulting from the decision to join the European Monetary System in 1979. This fundamental change in regime altered both the *level* and *volatility* of Ireland's exchange rate. It is likely that this had some effects on Ireland's economic performance and, in particular, on manufacturing industry, after 1979. This issue is explored in the chapter on EC monetary policy, below (Chapter 5).

The balance sheet

We stated in the Introduction (Chapter 1) that an assessment of the costs and benefits of Ireland's membership of the EC internal market required three things: first, a measure of the effects of EC membership on Ireland; second, some view of what would have happened in the absence of integration; and, third, some judgment of the welfare significance of the gains and losses experienced. The major part of this chapter has been devoted to the first of these tasks. We have identified what actually happened since 1973 and discussed whether these developments can be seen as *effects* of integration into the internal market or whether they require other explanations. By attempting to identify *why* things developed as they did we are implicitly suggesting what would have happened had Ireland not joined the internal market. In other words, we are implicitly constructing an *anti-monde*.

What happened and failed to happen

We have identified that membership of the EC internal market had its greatest effect on manufacturing. Manufacturing in Ireland underwent a very substantial inter-industry adjustment. This adjustment consisted of the running-down of many traditional industries, the virtual disappearance of most indigenous firms in large-scale internationally traded sectors and their replacement by foreign-owned grant-aided export-oriented firms in a narrow range of high-technology sectors.

The significance of this pattern of specialization lies not in the fact that entry into the EC market caused substantial loss of jobs in certain manufacturing sectors — this was to be expected and has been experienced elsewhere — but in the degree to which it changed the *structure* of indigenous manufacturing industry. Two things are significant about this aspect of Ireland's pattern of specialization. First, it would seem to differ from that experienced elsewhere (see OECD, 1988). Second, this change in the structure undermined the leading firms in industries where innovative activity or scale are significant, and thus probably reduced the ability of indigenous manufacturing to generate industrial growth. In consequence, the very pronounced specialization which has occurred in the Irish economy since accession to the EC has not provided a foundation for indigenous economic development.

Explanation

Our overall assessment of the gains and losses depends on how we explain these developments. In our judgment the developments summarized in this chapter were caused by three forces. First, they were undoubtedly caused in part by Ireland's integration into the EC internal market. We say this because the developments observed are consistent with a sophisticated view of how free trade works when there are significant initial differences in economic structures and levels of development. Second, economic *policy* almost certainly played an important role in shaping developments in manufacturing industry in Ireland. Four types of policy were relevant: Irish developmental and industrial policy (see Chapters 7 and 12), Irish demand management policy, EC budgetary and regional policy (see Chapter 4), and EC and Irish monetary policy. The third major factor which explains the developments surveyed in this chapter is the structure of Irish manufacturing industry in the early 1970s. This conditioned how free trade would affect Ireland, and strongly influenced the content of Irish industrial policy and these — as we have seen — were major forces determining what happened.

Overall gains and losses

The developments documented in this chapter reveal considerable difficulties since Ireland joined the EC internal market. Despite the difficulties, our overall judgment is that the benefits have outweighed the costs. Three considerations underlie this conclusion. First, it is based on a realistic assessment of the policies which would be available to Ireland, and the external economic forces which would still be very powerful, were Ireland outside the Community. Second, integration into the internal market should not be seen as the only cause of the adverse developments documented in this chapter. A recent NESC study, *Ireland in the European Community: Performance, prospects and strategy*, and several earlier reports, have identified major failures in Irish policy-making.

These played an important role in the poor overall performance since 1973. Most importantly, it cannot be said that Ireland adopted the policies it did — or, more accurately, failed to developed policies — *because of its membership of the EC*. Consequently, it cannot be argued that Irish policy-making would have been better if Ireland had remained outside the Community, or it had left it at any time.

Third, the EC internal market has brought to light fundamental weaknesses in the Irish economy and society. But it cannot be said that membership of the Community was the *cause* of these structural problems. The problems of industrial under-development and a poor rural economy based on commodity production have their origin elsewhere. Indeed, these problems have on many other occasions given rise to crises of employment and emigration, similar to that experienced in the 1980s. Furthermore, they have given rise to economic and social crisis *even under a regime of protection* — as, for example, in the 1950s. It is these structural weaknesses, rather than the question of EC free trade versus protection, which need to be analysed and addressed by both national and Community policy.

Notes

1. A number of factors account for this. First, Gross *National* Product (GNP) grew more slowly than Gross *Domestic* Product — because of greatly increased net factor outflows. Second, deterioration of the terms of trade, because of the oil price increase, reduced the purchasing power of Ireland's GNP. Third, Ireland received transfers from the EC.
2. Information on the size structure of Irish manufacturing industry is available from the *Census of Industrial Production* (CIP) and the IDA's Employment Surveys. The CIP data go back to 1929 but contain a certain discontinuity in 1979 due to a change of coverage. The IDA data go back only as far as 1973, but distinguish between indigenous and foreign firms. In the following discussion we draw on both sources.

Bibliography

Emerson, M. *et al.* (1988), 'The economics of 1992', *European Economy*, no. 35. Brussels: European Commission, March.

FitzGerald, J.D. (1987), *The Determinants of Irish Imports*, General Research Series, no. 135. Dublin: ESRI.

Kennedy, K.A., Giblin, T. and McHugh, D. (1988), *The Economic Development of Ireland in the Twentieth Century*, London: Routledge.

Kennedy, K.A. and Healy, T. (1985), *Small Scale Manufacturing Industry in Ireland*, General Research Series, no. 125. Dublin: ESRI.

Krugman, P.R. (1987), *Strategic Trade Policy and the New International Economics*, Cambridge, Mass.: MIT.

O'Malley, E. (1981), 'The decline of Irish industry in the nineteenth century',

Economic and Social Review, vol. 13, no. 1, October.
Owen, N. (1983), *Economies of Scale, Competitiveness and Trade Patterns Within the European Community*, Oxford: Clarendon Press.
Pelkmans, J. (1984), *Market Integration in the European Community*, The Hague: Martinus Nijhoff.
Robson, P. (1987), *The Economics of International Integration*, 3rd edn, London: Allen and Unwin.
Ruane, F. (1984), 'Manufacturing industry', in *The Economy of Ireland – Policy and Performance*, 4th edn, ed. J.W. O'Hagen, Dublin: IMI.

Official

NESC, 1989, Report No. 88, *Ireland in the European Community: Performance, prospects and strategy*, Dublin: National Economic and Social Council.
NESC, 1982, Report No. 64, *A Review of Industrial Policy*, Dublin: National Economic and Social Council.
OECD, 1988, *Structural Adjustment and Economic Performance*, Paris: Organisation for Economic Cooperation and Development

Chapter 3
Agricultural policy
Andy Conway

Introduction

The formulation and implementation of agricultural policies is a dynamic process. Even when policy objectives do not change, changes in the economic and political context shift the emphasis to different aspects of the objectives which requires adaptation of policy measures. This is reflected in the changes in the CAP since accession in 1973 and in the changes in domestic policies before membership. In order to see the impact on agricultural policy in Ireland, policy objectives and measures before membership are examined and changes due to expected membership and consequent on membership are discussed. The change in the policy formulation process, due to the institutional changes brought about by EC membership, are also discussed.

The impact on the pattern of development in the agricultural sector is examined by looking at quantitative trends, both before and since 1973 and relating them to changes in policy. The impact is shown in terms of changes in both volume and value. While there is no way of telling what really would have happened in the event of non-membership, the question is explored on the basis of available analysis.

Agriculture in Ireland

Its importance

Ireland refers to the Republic of Ireland, excluding Northern Ireland which is part of the United Kingdom. Agriculture in Ireland is relatively important, accounting for 10 per cent of Gross Domestic Product. In 1987 the EC-12 had 8 per cent of its civilian employment engaged in agriculture compared with 15 per cent for Ireland. This percentage is as high as in Spain and, within the EC, is only exceeded in Portugal and Greece. In 1970 the corresponding figures were 14 per cent for EC-12 and 27 per cent for Ireland.

Table 3.1 *Share in the value of gross agricultural output*

Sub-sector	1972 %	1980 %	1988 %
Cattle	32.5	42.7	39.5
Pigs	10.3	8.0	4.2
Sheep	4.0	3.5	4.4
Horses	1.2	0.5	2.4
Poultry	2.4	2.9	2.9
Total livestock	50.3	57.7	53.4
Milk	23.5	32.3	33.5
Hen eggs	2.0	1.3	0.8
Total livestock products	26.3	34.1	34.6
Crops (including turf)	15.3	15.8	11.9
Gross agricultural output	100.0	100.0	100.0

Source: Central Statistics Office, Dublin.

Agricultural exports are also very important to Ireland, being 65 per cent of agricultural output in 1988. Exports of primary food and closely linked food processing industries accounted for 20 per cent of the value of total exports in 1988. However, Riordan (1989) estimates that they accounted for 42 per cent of foreign exchange earnings because of their low import content and low outflows of profits and capital service charges.

Composition of agricultural output

Crops make up a small share of agricultural output, as shown in Table 3.1. In 1988 they contributed only 12 per cent of gross agricultural output and occupied only 8 per cent of agricultural land. Pigs, poultry and eggs accounted for only 8 per cent of output in 1988, so that grazing livestock and their produce accounted for 80 per cent of gross output in 1988. While grazing livestock have been increasing their dominance, they already accounted for over 60 per cent of the value of output in 1972. The contribution of sheep (4 per cent) and horses (2 per cent) is small, so that cattle and milk (from cows) are the main outputs and accounted for 40 per cent and 34 per cent respectively in 1988.

Agricultural policy before EC membership

Market context

Given the high proportion of agricultural production which is exported, export prices have a big impact on to the contribution of agriculture to the domestic economy and to the balance of trade. Before EC membership the main destination for exports was the United Kingdom, so the value of exports were dependent on UK market prices. The UK policy was to import at world prices and to support their farmers' returns by supplementary payments — known as 'deficiency payments.' Hence UK market prices were at the same level as unprotected world market prices and therefore Irish exports were sold at world prices, mainly in the United Kingdom, except in so far as special arrangements were negotiated with the UK Government to give privileged terms of access.

Policy objectives

It is instructive to examine Ireland's policy objectives in the mid- to late 1960s. This period is chosen for comparison as policies were being modified at the beginning of the 1970s, in anticipation of EC membership. An official government document (Department of Agriculture, 1964, p. 188) sets out agricultural policy in 1964. The aims of the policy were:

first to ensure the most intensive use of land within the limits set by market possibilities so that the maximum number of people can be attained in agriculture consistent with social and economic progress; second to create viable family units in small farm areas with minimum disturbance of the population; and third, to ensure as far as is practicable, that those who leave agriculture have adequate employment opportunities in other sectors of the economy.

The aim was to intensify production and maximize the number of family farms which could participate in economic and social progress.

Policy orientation

Agricultural policy is part of a wider policy framework for promoting economic development. In 1958 the first programme for economic expansion changed the orientation of economic development policy from one of protecting domestic manufacturing industry to export-led growth strategy. The basic thrust of policy was to reduce protective tariffs on imports and put emphasis on expanding exports. Industrial expansion was promoted by subsidizing the establishment of foreign firms and giving them tax relief on exports (see Chapters 2 and 7). In the case of agriculture practically all additional production would contribute to exports. Hence agricultural policy was to maintain its orientation towards expansion of production and the promotion of exports. This policy was to be invigorated by increasing subsidies on farm inputs such as fertilizers and farm buildings and equipment, to stimulate in particular production from grassland, and also by improving the promotion of agricultural exports.

Agricultural policy instruments

The operation of agricultural policy is best illustrated by the dairy sector, which was the focus of agricultural development from the 1960s until milk quotas were introduced in 1984. In 1961 the Irish Dairy Board (*An Bórd Bainne*) was established to improve the marketing of milk products outside the state. This Board was eligible for government support to meet up to two-thirds of the losses it incurred in its exports. The milk processing industry also underwent dramatic reorganization in the late 1960s and 1970s, with amalgamation of dairy co-operatives and publicly assisted investment in milk processing equipment.

Farm investment grants were available to give financial aid to expansion of farm production. Price support policies were also in place and milk price support was the major item of expenditure on price support. Price support was seen as both a stimulus to production and a support to farmers' incomes. Farming, like other sectors where the work-force is declining, has a problem of low incomes for many in the sector. In the 1960s it was argued that support should be directed more towards smaller farms, as larger ones were less in need of income support. In the less-favoured areas of the West of Ireland, where poor land quality and small farm size inhibited expansion of farm output, intensive farm advice was implemented in certain pilot areas in 1964. A scheme introduced in 1968 gave cash bonuses to small-scale farmers who achieved agreed expansion targets. In response to the growing budgetary costs of milk price support payments, a tiered milk price was introduced in 1969, with support payments being reduced for supplies in excess of 31,500 litres. This multi-tiered price system was discontinued in 1972, when EC membership became imminent. A government committee reviewing state expenditure on agriculture reported at the beginning of the 1970s and concluded that one-third of farms were non-viable and outside the realm of commercial agriculture; future policy should be focused on a comprehensive farm development scheme aimed at viable and potentially viable farms, with a view to achieving growth in agricultural output.

Agricultural trade and the CAP

Agricultural trade has always been important to Ireland because of its level of agricultural exports. The importance of agriculture was reflected in the first report on economic development (Department of Finance, 1958), in which 82 of its 200 pages were devoted to agriculture (compared with 7 pages devoted to tourism). As regards agricultural development this report concluded that 'the overriding necessity of Irish agriculture is to produce in quantity at prices competitive in world markets' (p. 211). In the second programme for economic expansion (Government of Ireland, 1963) the objective remained 'an expanding and efficient agriculture' (p. 22) but difficulties in export markets gave this aspect a greater emphasis. One of the main thrusts of policy was 'to seek, through trade agreements with other countries, particularly Britain, and through eventual participation in the EEC, improved and stable access on reasonable terms to exports markets' (p. 24). EC membership can be seen as the culmination of a trade policy seeking favourable terms for Ireland's agricultural exports. This evolution is neatly summarized by Kennedy *et al.*, 1988:

In the post-war period, various trade agreements, culminating in the Anglo-Irish Free Trade Area Agreement of 1965, progressively improved the scope and terms of access to the British market. Finally, the most dramatic improvement in the marketing environment for Irish farmers — entry to the EEC in 1973 — was also the outcome of official trade policy. (p. 216)

In 1974, after entry to the EC, agricultural policy is dealt with under the heading 'European Economic Community' in the government's national policy document (Government of Ireland, 1974). Agricultural policy is now the Community's CAP, with agricultural concern focused on the level at which the Community supports its agricultural prices. The CAP applies import levies and export subsidies, and also intervenes by public purchasing, to support its internal price at a level above external market prices. The higher EC price is supported by EC consumers who pay the higher prices and by central Community funds. As a net exporter Ireland had an interest in higher EC prices.

Agricultural policy under CAP

EC membership for Ireland and the United Kingdom in 1973 meant that agricultural prices would rise, over a transition period, to the level of EC prices, which were held above world market prices under the CAP. This provided a very favourable context for Ireland's agricultural policy of increased production and exports. Higher prices, supported by the CAP's import levies, intervention buying and export subsidies, meant that the established policy objectives could be more easily pursued. The size of transfers to large-scale milk producers ceased to be a concern, as it was now a charge on EC consumers and on CAP's EAGGF (European Agricultural Guidance and Guarantee Fund). The policy of maximizing the value of agricultural exports now translated into a policy of maximizing the politically determined CAP prices for agricultural products. Other issues — such as emerging surpluses of production over consumption, the waste in intervention storage, the subsidization of EC exports, the pattern of large transfers to large-scale producers and small transfers to small-scale producers and high prices to consumers — did not carry any weight in the formulation of Ireland's agricultural policy. Agricultural policy was now very simple: higher agricultural prices under the CAP.

The change in the institutional framework for policy formation and implementation altered the process of domestic policy formation within Ireland. Before EC membership the Minister for Agriculture had a difficult task in negotiating with farmers' organizations and with cabinet colleagues. Demands from the farm lobby had to be addressed in the context of competing demands from other sectors and interests, and within the constraints of the national budget. Consequently the relationship between the Minister for Agriculture and farming organizations was often confrontational, as the minister had to defend the position adopted by the government as a whole. Under the CAP it was a case of ask for anything you can get in terms of price rises, as it will not cost the national exchequer and will benefit the economy. Hence Ireland's Minister for Agriculture could be in full accord with the farm lobby seeking to maximize CAP price support.

The distribution of benefits from price support, among farmers, remained a non-issue until the amount of milk production, which would be supported by the CAP, was limited by quota in 1984. The relatively high returns to dairying made it the main enterprise for farm development and the one which gave reasonable income prospects to those on smaller farms. The establishment of national quotas for member-states and the high value of these quotas focused attention on the distribution of support among dairy farmers.

A 'farm modernization scheme', as recommended in a 1970 policy review (see above), was introduced in 1974 under EEC Directive 159/72. It provided grants to aid farm development, with somewhat higher rates of aid for farmers who, through farm development, could bring their incomes up to average industrial earnings in their region. This scheme has been replaced by the 'farm improvement scheme' under EEC Regulation 797/85. The western part of Ireland has benefited from the EC's special measures for less-favoured areas, under Directive 268/75. These involved higher rates of grant-aid for farm investment and additional payments related to livestock numbers. There was also a special EC programme to accelerate land drainage in the West of Ireland under Directive 628/78 and a 'programme for western development' (Regulation EC 1820/80). This programme grant aids not only conventional farm development, but also development of farm infrastructure and forestry and has stimulated private forestry development. The programme has recently been extended to all less-favoured areas.

Within the EC framework of the combined (agricultural, regional and social) structural funds a new approach to development involves an integrated multi-sectoral programme for economic development and Ireland already has agreement on its programme. The CAP is also reorienting towards 'integrated rural development', as an approach to tackling the problems of less-developed rural areas. Ireland has set up eleven pilot areas in which to develop its approach to integrated rural development.

Compatibility of the CAP and Ireland's agricultural policy

Between 1973 and 1984, the CAP facilitated Ireland in implementing the agricultural policies which it had been striving to pursue before membership, by supporting the price of agricultural products and exports. It also contributed to investment aid on farms, with special measures for less-favoured areas which included the West of Ireland. Because Ireland exports a large proportion of its production, it has been highly dependent on intervention to dispose of its output. This has weakened the development of its marketing capacity.

More recent developments in the CAP have restricted expansion in dairying and are weakening the role of intervention buying and price support generally. EC policy, under pressure from expanded production, is moving towards an export orientation and more market-determined prices. It is also under pressure, from EC budget restrictions and from its GATT trading partners, to reduce producer subsidies. While an export orientation would be in accordance with Ireland's policy, there is concern about the potential loss of transfers through higher farm prices. If transfers to producers via price support are to be reduced, the issue of limiting the size of transfers to individual producers, which faced domestic policy in the 1960s, may become a key issue for EC policy in the 1990s. However, in an EC context, Ireland has a relatively small size structure of farm businesses so that limiting support per farm across the Community would not be particularly severe on it.

Development trends in agriculture

Introduction

As discussed above, membership of the Community would, under the CAP, ensure higher prices for agricultural products. Even if there was no change in the levels of agricultural output its value would increase.

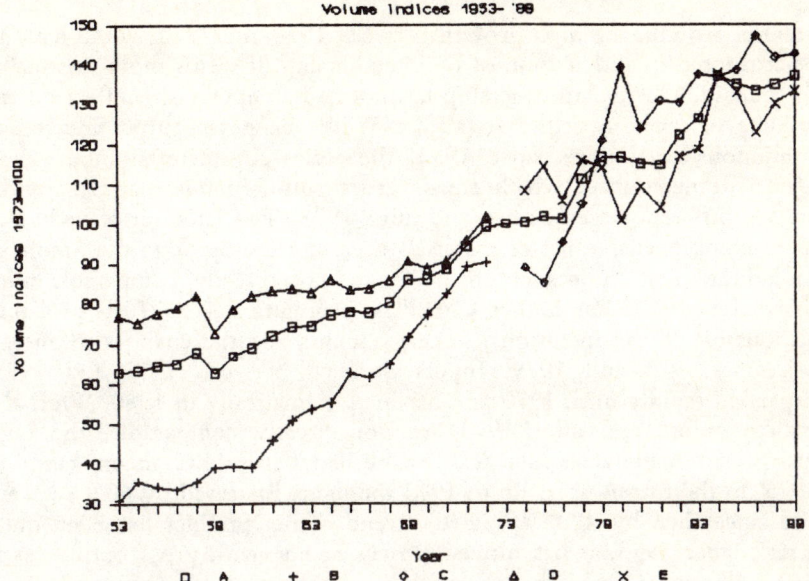

Legend: A — Gross output; B — Material inputs 1953–72; C — Material inputs 1974–88; D — Net output 1953–72; E — Net output 1974–88.

Figure 3.1 *Volume indices of agricultural output and material inputs*
Source: Central Statistics Office, Dublin.

A point of interest is whether, under a higher EC price regime, the volume of agricultural output would increase faster than it had before EC membership. For some products the volume might increase faster or decline slower, while for others it might increase slower or decline faster. An aggregate index of volume is constructed by valuing products at prices prevailing in some particular year (called the base year) and this index shows how the aggregate volume has changed.

Aggregate trends

Figure 3.1 shows the trend in the volume of agricultural output and material inputs over the period 1953–88. The index for gross output increased by 37.1 per cent between 1973 and 1988 and by exactly the same amount in the fifteen years 1958 to 1973. However, since the trend in volume of gross output is quite variable, care is needed in making comparisons over different periods. The volume of output was particularly low in 1958 and the volume for 1988 has only just recovered to its 1984 level. The relatively high rate of growth between 1973 and 1984 was equalled between 1966 and 1973. The relatively high growth trend, evident since the mid-1960s, was sustained into the mid-1980s by EC membership. In order to conclude that EC membership stimulated volume growth, the high growth between 1970 and 1972 would have to be attributed to anticipation of EC membership. It seems more reasonable to conclude that EC membership has not had an appreciable effect on the volume of gross agricultural output. While the gross output index is a continuous data series since 1953, the series for material inputs (and hence for net output which equals gross output minus material inputs) are on different bases before and after 1973. The later series include a more comprehensive list of materials used and the break in the graphs is to indicate that indices before 1973 are not directly comparable with those after 1973. The higher variability in inputs since 1973 is probably attributable to the inclusion of energy inputs and the changes in energy prices in 1973 and 1979. Inputs declined between 1973 and 1975, expanded rapidly until 1979 and declined dramatically in 1980. While the indices before and after 1973 are not directly comparable, the high growth in material inputs was established before EC membership in 1973. In the fifteen years up to 1973 the index increased by 60.9 per cent and since then by 42.6. While the trend of net product has been quite erratic since 1973, it has moved closely in line with gross output, as it had done since 1965. As the variability in material inputs since 1973 is not attributed to EC membership, it is concluded that membership has not had any obvious impact on the volume of agricultural output or material inputs.

Trends in sub-sectors

While aggregate trends have been unaffected by EC membership, there was a definite impact on specific sub-sectors. Figure 3.2 shows how the volume of livestock, livestock products and crops changed since 1968. The growth in crop output has been less than that for livestock output. The most dramatic increase was in livestock products, up to 1985. Growth in livestock products is examined in more detail in Figure 3.3 below, along with its main components — milk and eggs. The high growth in livestock products is due to growth in milk output, as both track closely.

Figure 3.3 shows a high rate of expansion in milk output from 1972 to 1985. The domestic multi-tier price system was abandoned in 1972, when EC membership was anticipated. Thus the CAP facilitated expansion in milk until the milk quota restricted milk output in 1985 and required subsequent reductions in output. The pattern of expansion, and latterly contraction, in milk production is attributable to EC membership. Outside of the EC, even if the tiered milk price arrangement had not persisted, milk prices would have been supported at a much lower level. The CAP, by ensuring a higher relative price for milk, led to milk production accounting for a bigger share of the growth in agricultural output.

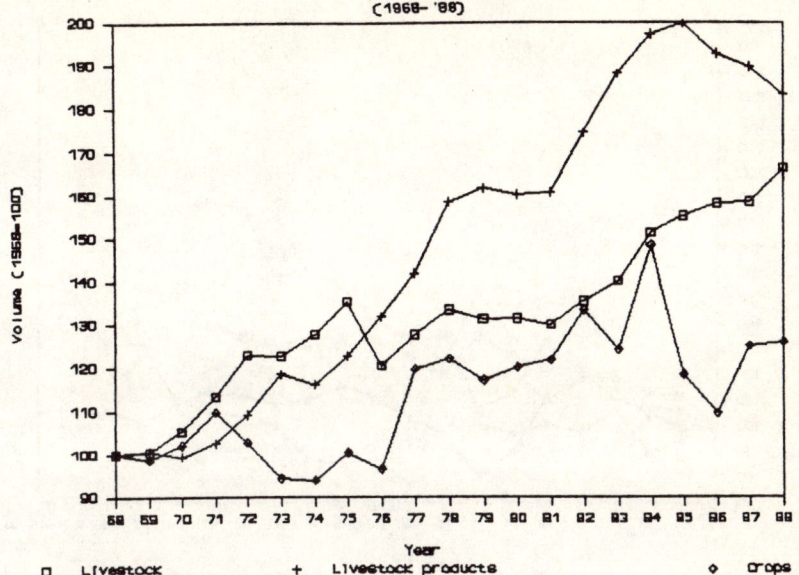

Figure 3.2 *Volume index for main sub-sectors*
Source: Central Statistics Office, Dublin.

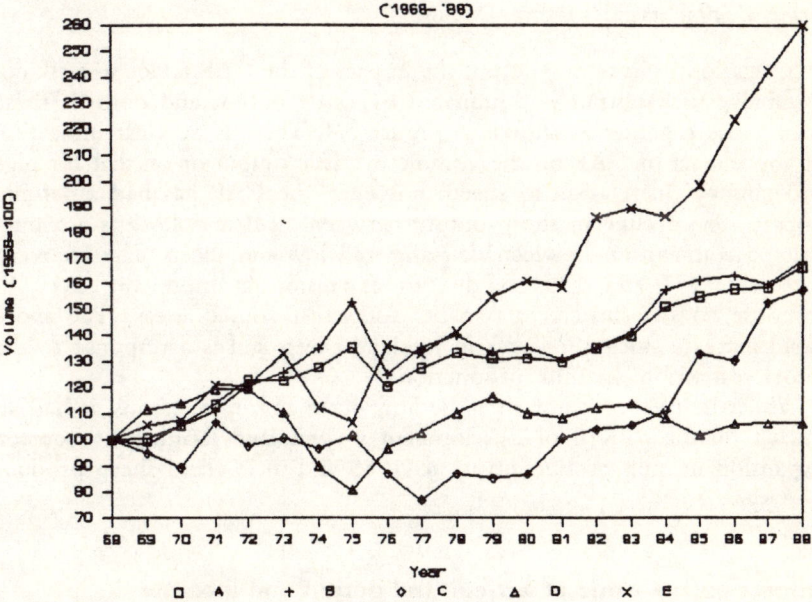

Figure 3.3 *Volume index for livestock products*
Source: Central Statistics Office, Dublin.

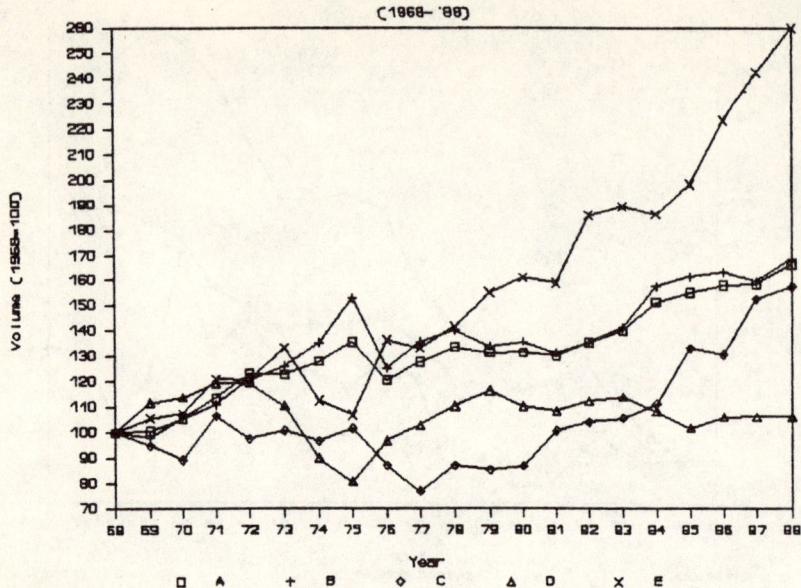

Legend: A — Total; B — Cattle; C — Sheep; D — Pigs; E — Poultry.

Figure 3.4 *Volume index for livestock*
Source: Central Statistics Office, Dublin.

In relation to livestock output the impact of the CAP is not so striking. Total livestock output is dominated by cattle output and both of these track close together as shown in Figure 3.4. There is no clear indication of any impact of CAP on the volume of cattle output or on that for pigs and poultry. In relation to sheep, however, the CAP has had a definite impact. The decline in sheep output between 1971 and 1977 is attributable to competition between dairying and lowland sheep. The recovery between 1977 and 1984 is due to expansion in mountain sheep in response to the headage payments for less-favoured areas. The more rapid increase since 1984 was in lowland sheep and is a response to the quota restriction on milk production.

While the CAP did not alter the long-term aggregate trends, it had an impact on the pattern of development in grassland farming. It boosted expansion in milk production up to 1985 and in lowland sheep production since then.

Impact on the value of agricultural output and incomes

Impact on prices

The price supports of the CAP were a key factor influencing Ireland's interest in EC membership. It meant that over a transition period, 1973—8,

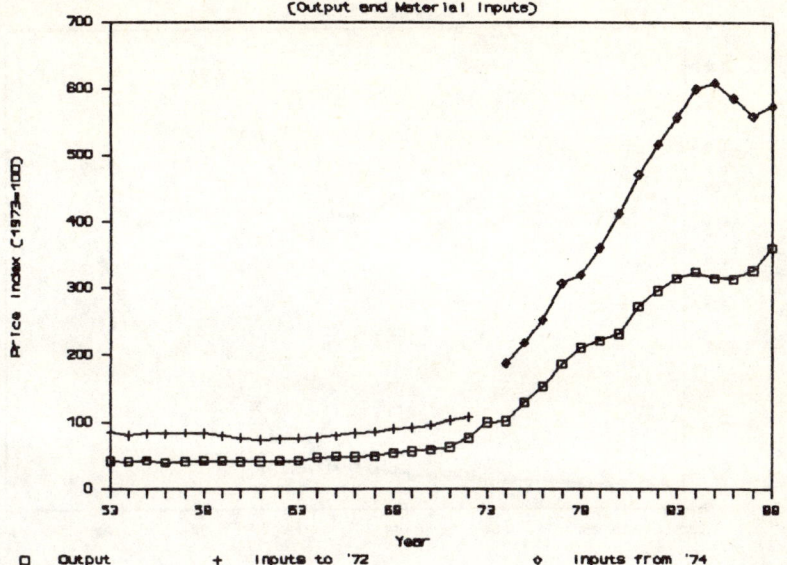

Figure 3.5 *Price indices for output and material inputs*
Source: Central Statistics Office, Dublin.

the price of agricultural output would move from UK market prices to the much higher levels obtaining in the EC.

As it transpired, the price increases (see Figure 3.5) were much greater than had been anticipated. Between 1971 and 1973 the output price index rose by 37 points, due to the boom in world cattle prices associated with a trough in the cattle supply cycle. This was followed by a dramatic decline in cattle prices in 1974. An unanticipated factor was the abandonment of fixed exchange rates in the mid-1970s, so that weaker currency areas found their prices rising more rapidly in terms of domestic currency. Until Ireland joined the EMS, the Irish pound was linked to sterling, whose exchange value declined. Under the influence of market transition and currency devaluation Ireland experienced a dramatic rise in output prices. This amounted to 223 index points between 1974 and 1984.

Since 1973, the price index for material inputs increased even more than for outputs. This contrasts with the period before 1973, when input and output prices moved fairly well in line. The input price rises after 1973 were influenced by steep rises in the cost of fuels and chemical derivatives from fossil fuels.

While the more rapid growth in agricultural input prices eroded some of the gains from increasing output prices, the level of income arising increased dramatically in current value terms (Figure 3.6). The increase between 1973 and 1978 was 350 per cent. The upward trend in current income suffered two serious declines, one in 1978–80 and another in 1984–6. When income arising is adjusted for inflation, using the

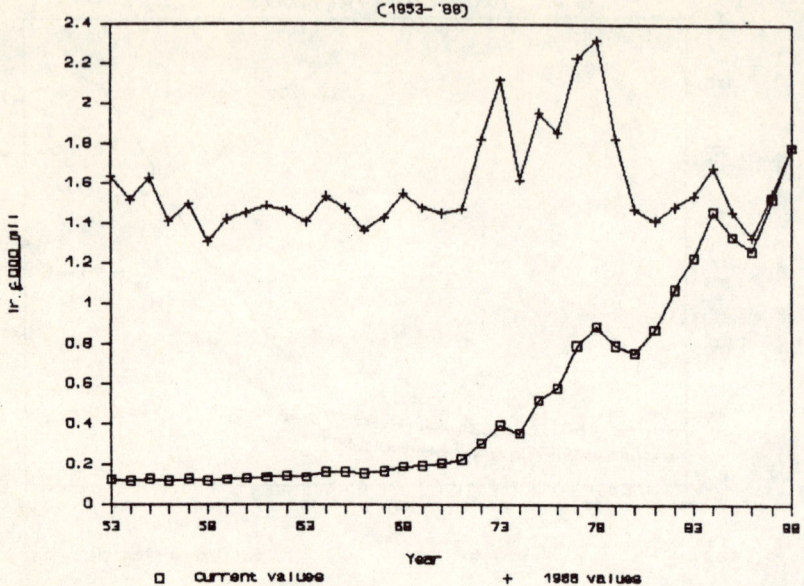

Figure 3.6 *Income arising in agriculture*
Source: Central Statistics Office, Dublin.

consumer price index, the outcome is much different. At 1988 prices, real income arising is around IR£1,500 million in the 1980s, as it was in the period 1953 to 1971.

There was a dramatic increase in real income arising in agriculture between 1972 and 1979. This stimulated invested by farmers developing their farm businesses and had the effect of inflating the prices of land and dairy cows in particular. Banks made credit more easily available to farmers, as their land had higher value as collateral and their improved incomes enhanced their ability to repay loans. There was an increase in farm indebtedness, which also contributed to the inflation of land and livestock prices. From 1978 until 1983 the price of farm material inputs increased at a much higher rate than farm output prices (see Figure 3.5). The price squeeze was also accompanied by increasing interest charges on borrowing and high domestic price inflation. Thus, in the mid-1980s, Irish agriculture was facing difficult economic circumstances and the CAP reform was indicating new limits to price support.

The higher prices under the CAP over the period since 1973, while not giving a sustained increase in income arising, did provide a short-term increase in income arising. This facilitated development, particularly of farm facilities for livestock and of farm dwellings. It also compensated for the high level of inflation experienced since 1973. The higher volatility of income since 1973 is not attributable to the CAP, but to international factors, such as fossil fuel costs, currency fluctuations and increased difficulties of economic management under such circumstances.

The food industry

The areas of major development in the food industry were milk and meat processing. In the case of milk the structure of assembly and processing plants was already changing rapidly before EC membership, but it is likely that anticipated membership had influenced these developments. EC membership was expected to induce expansion in milk production, so the expansion of processing capacity, in the late 1960s and early 1970s, provided the opportunity for restructuring. The limitation on milk production since 1985 and excess capacity, based on the expectation of further expansion, has ushered in another wave of restructuring in the dairy industry.

There has been continuous development in cattle processing facilities to cope with the expanding output (see Figure 3.4), which has increased steadily except for a slump in 1975—6. There has recently been a move towards specialized slaughtering facilities for different animals.

Because milk and meat production are based on grass production, supplies have a strong seasonal pattern. This has favoured the production of commodity-type products rather than higher-value-added products involving further processing. This tendency towards commodity products is to be expected, as investment for further processing is particularly expensive where under-utilization of processing capacity would result from seasonal supplies. The tendency towards commodity products has been reinforced by the CAP's intervention in the market for commodity products, such as butter and skim milk powder in the case of milk and carcases in the case of beef. As Ireland has a high rate of net exports of animal products, it has had a high level of market intervention activity under the CAP. This has led in the past to development of facilities for intervention beef and dairy produce.

Recent developments in food processing reflect a new emphasis on food processing in Ireland's industrial development strategy. Pig processing facilities, for example, have been modernized in recent years, with capacity to double pig throughput. This is part of the industrial development plan which, if realized, would be a departure from past trends (see Figure 3.4). The fact that the development of food processing facilities is eligible for EC aid is not an insignificant factor influencing these developments.

The benefits of the CAP

We now turn from the impacts on agriculture to the question of how Ireland's economy as a whole has benefited from the CAP. Answers to this kind of question have to be somewhat speculative, as they have to be sought by assuming some alternative agricultural policy or arrangement other than EC membership. Matthews has made estimates under two alternatives:

1. The CAP remains in place but is funded nationally rather than by the Community; supply, demand and prices remain the same, so one calculates 'the value of CAP transfers'.
2. The present price support regime is abandoned in favour of free trade, so that supply, demand and prices adjust to free trade conditions; the 'gain from the CAP' is estimated relative to what would happen under free trade.

The value of CAP transfers

Explicit budgetary transfers arise under the EAGGF. These include, under the Guarantee Fund, payments such as export refunds on exports to third countries and compensation for losses arising from intervention storage, and net payments of MCAs (monetary compensatory amounts) on trade with other member-states. Payments under the guidance fund include headage payments on livestock and aids to investment and structural improvements. In order to arrive at the net value of EAGGF transfers, allowance has to be made for Ireland's contribution to the costs of the CAP, such as costs incurred in storing intervention products and in paying co-responsibility levies.

Transfers also arise from net exports to other member-states, as the CAP keeps the price of such exports above world market prices. Applying the difference between world market prices and EC prices to net exports gives the value of 'trade transfer'. Matthews used the level of export refunds as a measure of the EC/world price gap (his estimate of net CAP transfers is given in Table 3.2); they have ranged between 5 per cent and 10 per cent of GNP, so that net transfers have been quite significant.

The gain from the CAP

The net value of CAP transfers, given above, measures the benefit to Ireland from Community financing rather than national financing of the CAP agricultural support policy. The benefits from the CAP policy itself are to be judged in relation to a situation where instead of the CAP we had an alternative agricultural policy. The alternative which Matthews considered was a free trade policy. This is probably a relevant alternative today, as CAP reform moves more towards market-determined prices and the GATT negotiations generate pressure to move towards free trade in agriculture.

If the Community changed its policy to one of free trade, EC consumption would increase and production decrease (or increase at a

Table 3.2 *Net CAP transfers to Ireland*

Source	1979	1980	1981	1982	1983	1984	1985	1986
				(Ir£ m)				
EAGGF	289.6	306.4	253.3	290.1	337.9	490.5	636.2	629.7
Trade	400.6	346.3	250.8	252.0	275.2	420.4	467.1	473.8
Total	690.2	652.7	504.1	542.1	613.1	910.9	1103.3	1103.5
				(% GNP)				
Total	9.7	8.0	5.2	5.0	5.2	7.0	8.0	7.6

Source: Matthews, 1988, table 5.

Table 3.3 *Estimates of Ireland's gain from the CAP, 1979–86*

Free trade zone	1979	1980	1981	1982	1983	1984	1985	1986
EC only:								
— (IR£ m)	450	342	189	212	244	469	648	668
— (% GNP)	6.4	4.2	2.0	2.0	2.1	3.7	4.7	4.6
Global:								
— (IR£ m)	410	274	135	152	196	359	554	611
— (% GNP)	5.8	3.4	1.4	1.4	1.7	2.8	4.0	4.2

Source: Matthews, 1988, table 8.

slower rate) in response to lower prices. As this would lead to higher demand and lower supplies on the world market, we would expect world prices to be higher than they are under the present CAP regime. Hence a lower level of transfers to Ireland would be necessary to give the same level of agricultural price support; these lower levels of support are the benefit to Ireland of having the CAP rather than a free trade policy.

Table 3.3 sets out estimates of Ireland's gain from the CAP over what it would get under free trade agricultural policy in the EC alone and also under global free trade. The latter would give higher world prices than if only the EC adopted a free trade policy; hence Ireland's gains from the CAP are less when compared with global free trade then when compared with the EC only adopting a free trade policy. The gains from the CAP (see Table 3.3) are much less than the net CAP transfers (see Table 3.2). The latter ranged from 5 per cent to 9.7 per cent of GNP over the years 1979–86. Under global free trade gains from the CAP (1.4 per cent to 5.8 per cent GNP) are about 4 per cent points lower than net transfers, while under the EC only, free trade gains (2 per cent to 6.4 per cent GNP) are about 3 percentage points lower.

Summary

Agriculture is relatively important in Ireland and particularly agricultural exports, which are estimated to account for 42 per cent of foreign exchange earnings. Ireland's policy has been to expand agricultural production and exports. Agricultural trade has been an important policy issue, with initial progress in improving access to the UK market and ultimately membership of the EC in 1973. Under the EC's Common Agricultural Policy (CAP) Ireland could more readily pursue its policy, as the CAP supported the price of agricultural products, including exports. Since the 1980s however, price support is weakening due to internal budget constraints on price support expenditure and also there is increasing pressure from GATT negotiations to reduce price support within the EC.

EC membership has not resulted in any notable increase in the rate of growth of aggregate agricultural output or of material inputs to agriculture. However, there was a rapid increase in milk output under the CAP until the milk quota restricted output in 1985 and subsequently reduced milk output. Sheep production has also been affected by the CAP. Lowland sheep were declining under competition from dairy cattle until the milk quota restriction introduced in 1984 and since then lowland sheep have expanded rapidly. Mountain sheep had expanded in the late 1970s, under the stimulus of headage payments. The CAP has definitely influenced the rate of expansion of sub-sectors within agriculture.

Agricultural prices in Ireland rose dramatically over the first decade of membership. As well as the transition to the higher Community price level, price increases were augmented by currency devaluations. While input prices increased more rapidly than output prices, real income arising in agriculture increased up to 1978 but subsequently declined to its historic level.

Milk and meat production are based on grass and hence have a very seasonal pattern of supply. This seasonal supply pattern favours commodity-type products in food processing and CAP's intervention buying of such products has also facilitated this pattern in food processing.

Ireland's gains from the CAP depend on what alternative to the CAP is considered. If the alternative was for the CAP to remain in place but to be funded nationally rather than by the Community, Ireland's gain from Community funding is estimated to have ranged between 5 and 9.7 per cent of GNP in the period 1979 to 1986. If the alternative was free trade then the gain to Ireland ranged between 2 and 6.4 per cent of GNP, over the same period. As a net exporter of food Ireland has gained from the CAP.

Bibliography

Department of Agriculture (1964), *Agriculture in the Second Programme for Economic Expansion*, Dublin: The Stationery Office.

Department of Finance (1958), *Economic Development*, Dublin: The Stationery Office.

Government of Ireland (1963), *Second Programme for Economic Expansion*, Dublin: The Stationery Office.

Government of Ireland (1974), *A National Partnership*, Dublin: The Stationery Office.

Kennedy, K.A., Giblin, T. and McHugh, D. (1988), *The Economic Development of Ireland in the Twentieth Century*, London: Routledge.

Matthews, A. (1988), *Common Agricultural Policy Reform and National Compensation Strategies*, Paper to the Statistical and Social Inquiry Society of Ireland, Dublin.

Riordan, E.B. (1989), 'The net contribution of the agri-food sector to earnings of foreign exchange', *Situation and Outlook Bulletin*, no. 20, Dublin: TEAGASC.

Chapter 4

Regional policy

Rory O'Donnell

Introduction

The regional effects of the EC arise from a number of aspects of its policies and institutions. The most obvious of these, but perhaps not the most significant, is the Community's own regional policy, which has been in existence since 1975. Second, The Community pursues other structural policies — social and agricultural — which have distinct regional effects. Third, other Community policies have a differential impact on different regions. Important examples are the creation of a common internal market, the Common Agricultural Policy, and moves towards economic and monetary union. Finally, the Single European Act has revised the Community's treaties in three ways which may alter the overall regional impact of Community policies. It has placed the existing regional policy on a firmer treaty basis; it has strengthened the Community's commitment to reducing disparities between regions; and it introduced new policies — for research, technological development and the environment — which are likely to have regional effects.

Much of Part I of this volume is devoted to an assessment of the impact of Community policies on a single region, Ireland. Chapters 2, 3 and 5 can be seen as an attempt to identify the impact of three Community policies on this region: the policy of free internal trade, the Common Agricultural Policy and monetary policy. This chapter deals with those Community policies which are *explicitly* intended to address regional problems. The first section identifies Ireland's regional objectives and policy. These are then compared with Community objectives and policy. Next we consider the operation of EC regional policy in Ireland since 1975. This leads us to an assessment of Ireland's gains and losses from Community regional policy. In the final two sections we consider some of the regional policy issues which arise for Ireland and the Community as European integration proceeds. A substantial reduction in regional disparities will require both an extension of the scope of the Community's policies and changes in content of regional policy.

Ireland's objectives and policy

Background

We have noted on a number of occasions in this volume that the objective of Irish economic policy has been the industrialization of the country (see the introductory chapter to Part I and the chapter on the internal market). The achievement of a satisfactory level of economic development was considered to require industrialization. For this reason regional policy in Ireland has to a large extent been viewed as an extension of industrial policy (Boylan and Cuddy, 1985).

The pursuit of regional objectives through industrial and other developmental policies has gone through a number of phases. The Underdeveloped Areas Act of 1952 introduced the first post-war set of regionally differentiated grants and incentives. This can be read as a fundamental commitment to rectify the long-standing problem of regional imbalance within the Irish economy. In the late 1950s and early 1960s Ireland switched from a protectionist trade policy to the pursuit of industrialization by means of export growth, supported by an active industrial policy (see Chapter 7). This switch coincided with a reduced emphasis on regional inequalities; regional policy became subservient to the pursuit of national economic growth. Indeed, during the later 1960s and early 1970s it was argued by significant public bodies and international consultants that the widespread regional dispersal of industry would represent a constraint on rapid industrial growth. A considerable debate ensued between those who considered that regional and national objectives were best pursued by the development of a small number of 'growth poles' and those who favoured wide dispersal of industrial projects (see Buchanan, 1968; O'Farrell, 1974). This debate was largely settled by the publication, in 1973, of the Industrial Development Authority's (IDA) *regional development plan*. This effectively rejected the concept of growth poles in favour of a strategy of wide dispersal of manufacturing plants. However, by and large, this dispersal of new, and largely foreign-owned, plants was to be directed by the *national* industrial policy agency which had considerable discretion in offering different levels of grant aid and in bringing foreign industrialists to specific locations.

Regional policy at accession

Thus by the time of her accession to the EC Ireland had a regional policy with the following characteristics. The objective of policy was the maintenance of a widely dispersed population through the creation of employment in manufacturing industry. This regional policy objective was pursued primarily through an industrial policy, which provided substantial capital grants and ensured that profits earned from the export of manufactures were free from corporation tax. Although the policy favoured very wide dispersal of industrial plants it was conducted by a number of *national* policy agencies. Another important element of Irish developmental policy was the provision of infrastructure through the public capital programme.

It will be seen below that, in its early years, Community regional policy consisted largely of an element of EC support for the national regional policies of the member-states. At the foundation of Community regional policy, in 1975, it was decided that the whole of Ireland was to be treated as a single region for EC regional policy purposes. These two facts meant that Community regional policy was part of national development policy and that, in Ireland, central government had control of the use of funds received from the ERDF (European regional development fund), so long as they were spent in line with the eligibility criteria.

Community objectives and policy

Background

Although the Treaty of Rome makes no provision for a Community regional policy the Preamble to the Treaty included a declaration that the contracting parities were:

anxious to strengthen the unity of their economies and to ensure their harmonious development by reducing the differences existing between the various regions and the backwardness of the less favoured regions.

Article 92, relating to state aids, suggested that the original role of the Community in the area of regional policy was to be largely negative, i.e. the Commission would monitor and vet national aids to industry, but would not be involved in giving them. But, as Swann says, even in the early days there were three Community institutions which were intended to have some impact on the regional problem (Swann, 1988). These were the European Investment Bank, the European Social Fund and the EAGGF (for further information on the latter two see Chapters 24 and 3 respectively). Thus there was, at the formation of the EC, a limited recognition that existing regional disparities, or the effect of integration in creating new ones, could threaten the achievement of Community goals.

The origin of the regional fund

The enlargement of the Community in 1973 to include the United Kingdom, the Republic of Ireland and Denmark provided an important stimulus to the development of a Community regional policy. After difficult and protracted negotiations, a Community regional policy came into being with the establishment of the ERDF in 1975. The Community's regional policies have developed along three main lines: first, the co-ordination of the national regional policies of member-states to ensure their conformity with the treaties; second, an attempt to make other Community policies and financing instruments more sensitive to regional disparities; third, the establishment of specific Community regional policy instruments (see Mawson *et al.*, 1985). The content of the policy agreed under these three headings in 1975 was the outcome of a negotiation process and, given that this process has continued, there has been considerable development in the policy since then.

The main features of Community regional policy at its inception were the following:

1. The small scale of the ERDF relative to the total Community budget or Community GDP.
2. The distribution of the ERDF money on the basis of fixed national quotas which ensured that all member-states received some support whatever the level of national prosperity.
3. Reliance on *national* determination of regions eligible for support and design of approaches to regional problems.

These aspects of the policy meant that its effectiveness in removing regional disparities was severely limited (Armstrong, 1983). These limitations were apparent from the outset and as a result there has been consistent and partially successful pressure for a change.

Both the Commission and the European Parliament identified the following drawbacks in early Community regional policy:

1. The total ERDF was too small in relation both to the scale of regional problems and to the level of regional expenditures by member-states.
2. The system of national quotas meant that the funds were spread over too many Community regions.
3. The three structural funds were not adequately co-ordinated and, in general, other Community policies had substantial regional effects which needed to be checked for consistency with the Community's regional policy objectives.
4. The ERDF could respond only to *national* initiatives in regional policy, and payment of funds to member-*states* meant that direction of policy was too centralized.
5. One of the effects of this system of payments was that it was difficult to ensure that Community funds were truly *additional* to national regional aid (see Armstrong, 1978; Mawson *et al.*, 1985; Robson, 1987).

To overcome these problems, the Commission has, since 1975, put forward many proposals for reform of the ERDF. These proposals are worth stating since they have set the direction, if not the exact path, in which Community regional policy has moved in a series of reforms — the latest of which has only just been completed. The changes proposed by the Commission included the following:

1. The Commission should have a more active role in regional policy.
2. The role of set national quotas should be reduced and more of the ERDF should be distributed according to Community rather than national priorities.
3. Funds should be allocated to development *programmes* rather than *projects*.
4. The regional impact of other Community policies should be monitored and taken into account.
5. Regional development programmes should be 'integrated' — by which it meant that the various Community structural and financial instruments, together with national and sub-national resources, be used in a co-ordinated way.

The Single European Act and after

The most significant reform of Community regional policy was that which followed the revision of the Treaty in the Single European Act (1987). This Act not only provided mechanisms to ensure the completion of the internal market but also made provisions to address some of the regional tensions which could arise from more intense competition and greater mobility of labour and capital.

The Act strengthened the Community's objective (previously in the Preamble to the Treaty of Rome) of reducing disparities between regions (Article 130A). It specified the ERDF as an instrument designated to this task (up to then the Regional Fund did not have explicit status in the Treaty). The Single Act also called on the Commission to submit a comprehensive proposal to the Council concerning amendments to the structural funds which would clarify their tasks and increase their effectiveness in reducing disparities (Article 130D).

In August 1987, the Commission presented the Council with its view on how the structural funds could be made more effective; it proposed that they should be doubled by 1993. It argued that the resources should be concentrated on a set of five specified objectives, which would focus the funds on areas most in need of support. It envisaged a more active role for the Commission in the design and implementation of structural policies. Regional development *plans* and programmes, rather than individual projects, were specified as the main measures to be submitted to and funded by the Commission. Finally, the Commission advocated that the different levels of government should all be involved in the preparation, financing, monitoring and assessment of development programmes.

Table 4.1 *Range of ERDF assistance, percentages of total funds*

Member state	1975–8	1978–80	1981–4	1984–5	1986
Belgium	1.5	1.39	1.11	0.9 – 1.2	0.6 – 0.8
Denmark	1.3	1.20	1.06	0.5 – 0.7	0.3 – 0.5
France	15.0	16.86	13.64	11.1 – 14.7	7.5 – 10.0
Germany	6.4	6.00	4.65	3.7 – 4.8	2.6 – 3.4
Greece	—	—	13.00	12.4 – 15.7	8.4 – 10.6
Ireland	6.0	6.46	5.94	5.6 – 6.8	3.8 – 4.6
Italy	40.0	39.39	35.49	31.9 – 42.6	21.6 – 28.7
Luxembourg	0.1	0.09	0.07	0.06 – 0.08	0.04 – 0.06
Netherlands	1.7	1.58	1.24	1.0 – 1.3	0.7 – 0.9
Portugal	—	—	—	—	10.7 – 14.2
Spain	—	—	—	—	18.0 – 23.9
United Kingdom	28.0	27.03	23.80	21.4 – 28.6	14.5 – 19.3

Source: Commission of the European Communities.

It will be recognized immediately that these proposals were not new. They reflected the Commission's long-standing views about reform of Community regional policy. Once again, these proposals proved controversial in the Council of Ministers and once again the outcome was a compromise between the Commission, member-states supporting most of its proposals and member-states who, at least at present, see a minor role for Community structural policy in reducing regional disparities in Europe.

Community regional policy in Ireland

Financial assistance to Ireland

The Community's regional policy differed from its other structural policies in that it was initially agreed that receipts from the ERDF be allocated on the basis of fixed *national quotas*. After 1984 these quotas were replaced by indicative *quota ranges*. Table 4.1 sets out these national quotas and quota ranges for selected periods. The Table reveals that Ireland has been allocated a sizeable portion of the ERDF. The decline in Ireland's share reflects the accession of Greece, Spain and Portugal. The decline in the share of richer member-states, like Germany and France, reflects the accession of these newer states and the tendency towards a somewhat greater concentration of ERDF spending on the least prosperous regions in the Community.

However, the very small scale of the ERDF should not be forgotten.

Table 4.2 *Structural fund assistance to Ireland 1989–93*

1989	616m ECUs	IR£474m
1990	665m ECUs	IR£512m
1991	723m ECUs	IR£557m
1992	784m ECUs	IR£604m
1993	884m ECUs	IR£681m
Total	3672m ECUs	IR£2828m

Outlays built up rapidly from very small amounts in the early years; but Ireland's receipt of IR£ 87.4 million in 1987 still represented less than a half of 1 per cent of gross national product. By contrast, receipts from the Community's agricultural fund were almost 5 per cent of GNP in the same year.

The recent reform of the structural funds means that Ireland's receipts from the ERDF, the ESF (European social fund) and the EAGGF during the period 1989 to 1993 will be considerably higher than in the past. The recently finalized 'Community support framework' indicates that assistance under all three funds will increase gradually over the five years (see Table 4.2). The significance of these figures can be judged from the fact that Irish GDP in 1988 was IR£ 21,326 million while GNP was IR£ 18,784 million. Of the total of 3672 million ECUs allocated to Ireland, 45 per cent will come from the regional fund, 37 per cent from the social fund and 18 per cent from the structural side of the agricultural fund.

Usage of ERDF receipts in Ireland

We have noted above that in its early years Community regional policy consisted largely of an element of EC support for the national regional policies of the member-states. At the foundation of the policy it was decided that the whole of Ireland was to be treated as a single region for EC regional policy purposes. These two facts meant that Community regional policy was part of national development policy and that, in Ireland, central government had control of the use of funds received from the ERDF, so long as they were spent in line with the eligibility criteria.

Industrial development

Given that the ERDF was defined, at Community level, as primarily a source of capital grants it meshed easily with the development policies of successive Irish governments (Yuill and Allen, 1983). A major part of

Table 4.3 *Breakdown of ERDF grants to industry services and infrastructure projects in Ireland (% of total ERDF receipts)*

	Industry/service	Infrastructure
1975	73.3	26.7
1976	36.7	63.3
1977	42.3	57.7
1978	42.9	57.1
1979	32.9	67.1
1980	13.1	86.9
1981	18.2	81.8
1982	26.3	73.7
1983	12.6	87.4
1984	31.0	69.0
1985	38.9	61.1
1986	25.0	75.0
1987	17.4	82.6
1988	17.7	82.3

Source: Department of Finance.

Irish development policy has been the provision of capital grants for the establishment of manufacturing industries dispersed widely throughout the country. Consequently, a substantial proportion of Ireland's receipts from the ERDF were used to provide grants for the establishment of new manufacturing projects (Hart, 1985).

Infrastructure

Another important element of Irish development policy has been the provision of infrastructure through the public capital programme. The regulations governing the ERDF defined infrastructure projects as eligible, and a significant proportion of Ireland's grants have been used to fund such projects.

Table 4.3 gives a summary of how the Irish Government has used receipts from the ERDF. This shows that infrastructure projects have taken an increasing share of Ireland's ERDF grants. When account is taken of the fact that ERDF grants to Ireland were much larger in later years, when a high proportion was used for infrastructural projects, then it can be appreciated that, taking the period since 1975 as a whole, infrastructure has absorbed much more ERDF funds than industrial or service sector projects. However, the predominance of infrastructural projects in ERDF allocations is even higher in some other member-states.

The overall significance of Community regional policy, and the ERDF, can be judged from the fact that ERDF receipts have risen from 0.37 per cent of the Irish public capital programme in 1975, to 5.6 per cent in 1987. Indeed, much of the increase in this percentage in recent years has arisen due to contraction of the public capital programme rather than increases in ERDF grants. This small scale should be kept in mind when considering decisions concerning the design and administration of Ireland's regional development plans and programmes.

Assessment

Approach to assessment

In making an assessment of the gains and losses of Community membership under this heading we could adopt a number of different approaches. Confining our attention to regional policy *per se* we might ask whether Ireland gains or loses from the existence of a Community regional policy. Likewise we might ask how Community regional policy relates to national regional policy. These questions are relatively easy to answer, but the answers are not very informative. Ireland clearly gains from the existence of Community regional policy, when compared with no Community policy or with non-membership of the EC. Likewise, Community regional policy strongly complements national regional policy — if for no other reason than that Community regional policy has, to a large extent, consisted of Community support for the national regional policies of member-states and, furthermore, Irish regional policy has consisted of little more than regionally differentiated industrial grants and infrastructural investment.

A more fruitful approach to assessing Ireland's gains and losses may be to ask the following questions: How effective has Community regional policy been in achieving its stated objective of reducing regional disparities within the EC? What are the regional effects of the full range of Community policies? And, looking to the future, what set of Community policies will be necessary to achieve economic convergence in the context of economic and monetary union? It is these more interesting, but more difficult, questions which will be discussed in the remaining section.

Limited regional convergence since 1975

One way to assess the achievements of Community regional policy is to measure the degree to which it has achieved a reduction in national and regional economic disparities. Although there are conceptual and methodological difficulties in making international and inter-regional income comparisons (Kravis, 1987) the European Commission regularly calculates the level of real gross domestic product per head in the member-states and regions. In studying the evolution of income levels in the member-states from 1960 to 1989 the Commission has identified two phases. Up until around 1973—4 there was an unmistakable process of convergence; since the mid-1970s there has been a reversal. The disparity between income levels of the Twelve fell considerably till 1973—4. Much of this was the result of very strong growth in Spain, Portugal and Greece between 1960 and 1970 — though these countries were not members of the Community during that period. By and large, disparities between *regional* income levels followed a similar pattern — though the narrowing of disparities in the early period was fairly limited. The turnaround from convergence to divergence was even more marked when unemployment rates are considered.

From an Irish point of view, however, it is of interest that the Commission cites Ireland as an exception to this general trend. Specifically, it notes that

Ireland did not participate in the convergence process during the first period (1960—73). However, it managed to speed up its growth rate after the first oil shock and its accession to the Community and, in so doing, to start catching up belatedly in a process that lasted until the 1980s before it came to a virtual halt. (*Third Periodic Report*)

Other studies have measured not only regional income and unemployment levels but also regional economic *structures* as revealed by the pattern of industry, agriculture, services and demography. One such study, by Keeble, Owens and Thompson (1982), revealed significant *and widening* differences between the economic structure of central and peripheral regions in Europe in the period 1965 to 1979. A later study showed some convergence in industrial structures in the 1980s. Both these studies suggest that, in comparison with the southern European periphery, Ireland's industrial structure has been considerably 'modernized', and the authors consider that this reflects the success of Irish industrial policy — which is, of course, closely related to Community regional policy. But the 'success' of industrial/regional policy has largely been in attracting foreign-owned firms producing relatively high technology products for export. For a number of reasons Ireland's success in this activity has not provided a basis for deeply rooted industrialization and, consequently, has not facilitated convergence towards average EC national or regional income and unemployment levels (see Chapter 2, on the internal market, and Chapter 7, on industrial policy).

Explaining the failure of Community regional policy

Regional income and unemployment disparities widened after 1975 — the very period in which the Community had an expanding regional policy.

A number of related factors can be cited to explain this. First, there are a formidable set of reasons why advanced economic activity will tend to concentrate on certain regions. Second, the process of economic integration is likely to reflect and reinforce existing regional advantages and disadvantages (see Chapter 2). Both these factors are fully explained in the recent report, *Ireland in the European Community* (NESC, 1989). Third, from as early as 1977, attention was drawn to the marked regional impact of certain Community policies which were not explicitly concerned with regional matters. In particular, it was demonstrated that, in general, the CAP *increased* rather than decreased regional disparities within the Community (Cuddy, 1982). A fourth factor which helps explain the lack of regional convergence has been what Padoa-Schioppa has called 'tokenism' in the scale of intervention in the Community's regional and social policies (Padoa-Schioppa, 1987). Fifth, it is likely that the nature and execution of regional policy, at both Community and national level, made it less effective than it might have been. In particular, the emphasis on infrastructural investments, and the attraction of mobile projects with generous incentives, may not have addressed the true constraints on the development of the regions. These five factors are related; if the first three were significant then they will have reinforced the need for a more substantial and effective regional policy, and increased the penalty to be paid for not having this.

Policy issues arising for Ireland and the Community

Introduction

In this final section we look forward and consider what issues arise as the Community moves to the completion of the internal market by 1992 and to economic and monetary union some time in the 1990s. We begin by considering the general pattern of regional and structural policy in the Community and proceed to a number of specific issues.

We can identify four kinds of Community policy which may assist convergence and cohesion.

1. Structural policies.
2. Macroeconomic co-ordination.
3. Budgetary or fiscal transfers.
4. Differential application of other Community policies, such as agricultural policy or internal market policy.

It is important that both member-states and the Community take a broad and realistic view of what can be, and is likely to be, achieved by each of these types of policies in the attempt to pursue economic and social cohesion.

Community structural policy

Despite the objective in the Preamble to the Rome Treaty, and despite the special Protocol concerning Ireland included in the Treaty of Accession, the structural funds did not succeed, between 1975 and 1986, in narrowing the disparities between regional incomes in the Community. The recent reforms certainly create the possibility that these Community policies could have greater impact than they did during the period 1975 to 1986.

However, even after their recent doubling the structural funds will still represent less than one-half of 1 per cent of Community GDP. It has been argued recently that the benefits and costs of the completion of the internal market are likely to be distributed unevenly and to exacerbate regional inequalities (NESC, 1989). Taking all these factors into account, it seems necessary to conclude that the structural funds as currently constituted will not be sufficient to create convergence, let alone establish equality in regional economic structures and income.

It is important to note that this conclusion does not arise only because of the size of the funds. Knowledge of the nature and processes of regional development has not yet reached the stage where plans capable of really reversing regional decline, or initiating regional growth, are available to member-states or the Commission.[1] This implies that a major task facing the Community is to develop the knowledge on which to build more effective regional development plans. When such plans have been developed then significantly larger structural funds are likely to be necessary to implement them.

Macroeconomic co-ordination

It is sometimes argued that the key to regional convergence is the pursuit of sound macroeconomic policies by less developed member-states. While sound macroeconomic policies are warranted to avoid inflationary, balance-of-payments and fiscal problems there is no validity in the notion that the independent pursuit of low inflation, current account balance and fiscal balance by member-states will reduce regional disparities. Indeed, *independent* pursuit of these objectives is likely to lend a deflationary bias to overall macroeconomic management in Europe — and this tends to make reduction of regional disparities more difficult.

Budgetary transfers

The limited ability of either structural policies or co-ordinated macroeconomic policy to achieve convergence naturally focuses attention on the possibility of regional redistribution by means of Community taxes and expenditures. Examination of this subject reveals two striking facts. First, there are very strong arguments, in the principles of public finance, for development of the Community budget and re-assignment of policy functions between the tiers of Community government. Second, in existing economic and monetary unions, normal budgetary contributions and expenditures constitute much the most significant redistributive mechanism between persons, regions and member-states. Consequently, there are very strong arguments, on integration, macroeconomic policy, public finance and equity grounds for considerable and early development of the Community budget. This is one of the central conclusions of an important recent analysis of Ireland's role in the long-run development of the European Community (see NESC, 1989). That analysis shows that the limited scale and ambition of Community policies is likely to frustrate the achievement of its major objectives. Consequently, the extension of Community policy, and the development of the common budget which is the necessary corollary of this, constitutes the major challenge facing European integration. It is for this reason that it figures so prominently in the strategic approach to integration advocated by Ireland's National Economic and Social Council.

Differential application of other Community policies

The CAP, the common market programme, and other Community measures have distinct regional effects. To date, only limited progress has been made in having the regressive regional impact of other Community policies, taken into account. However, Article 130B of the Treaty states the following:

Member States shall conduct their economic policies, and shall co-ordinate them, in such a way as, in addition, to attain the objectives set out in Article 130A. The implementation of the common policies and of the internal market shall take into account the objectives set out in Article 130A and Article 130C and shall contribute to their achievement.

This raises the possibility of Community policies being formulated and applied in a *differential* fashion in order to assist cohesion and convergence. To date, this has occurred to a quite insufficient degree.

There are a number of policy areas where it is possible, and extremely desirable, that the cohesion objective be taken into account by means of differential implementation of Community policy. Examples are the allocation of agricultural quotas, the implementation of transport regulation and deregulation, the implementation of competition policy (especially the monitoring of regional aid), and the allocation of resources for technological research and development.

However, the author is of the belief that there is a definite but *finite* number of policy areas where it is feasible or advantageous to seek differential application of Community policy under Article 130B. In particular, the major elements of the internal market programmes cannot be applied in a differential fashion without frustrating the Community's basic aims. Furthermore, a widespread application of this or other policies on a differential basis would ultimately amount to a 'two-speed' or 'variable-geometry' Europe and neither of these is in Ireland's interest.

Conclusion on policy approaches to achieve convergence

All four policy approaches — structural policy, macroeconomic policy, public finance policy and differential implementation — should be pressed for by Ireland. Ireland should be aware, however, that the greatest direct contribution to convergence is likely to arise from the development of the Community budget.

It must also be noted that if Ireland is to argue that regional convergence is a shared Community objective and responsibility, and to advocate that Community policies to achieve it be adopted on a realistic scale, then Ireland must be capable of making a leading contribution to the formulation of those policies. Both the objective, and the policies to achieve it, must be advocated by argument of the highest quality.

Future development of Community regional policy

The recent reforms have determined the size and nature of the Community's regional policy for the next few years. However, as in the past, debate on the nature of regional and social policy, and on the resources to be devoted to them, will undoubtedly continue. What position should Ireland adopt in this debate?

It can be argued that the broad thrust of the Commission's proposals for regional policy — which enhance the role of the Community institutions *vis-à-vis* the member-states — is in the long-term interest of Ireland and other peripheral regions. We are thinking, for example, of the abolition of the national quotas, the development of European level responsibility for regional policy aimed at convergence, much stronger control of the national regional supports adopted by wealthier member-states, serious consideration of the regional impact of the CAP and of other common policies, and intense Community study of the nature of regional problems and design of the policy instruments which might solve them. Ireland has an unambiguous interest in progress along these lines.

The content of regional policy

Much of our comments so far have been on the *scale* of structural policy in the Community. However, it should be clear that the *content* of regional policy is at least as important as the amount of money spent. Some very significant issues arise for Ireland concerning the content of policies designed to encourage economic development. These issues are, first, the balance between industrial and infrastructural projects, and second, the nature of both industrial policy and infrastructural policy. These issues cannot be considered here (see NESC, 1989).

Assessment

In making an assessment of the gains and losses of Community membership under this heading we have adopted a number of different approaches. Confining our attention to regional policy *per se* we asked whether Ireland gains or loses from the existence of a Community regional policy. Likewise we might ask how Community regional policy relates to national regional policy. These questions are relatively easy to answer, but the answers are not very informative. Ireland clearly gains from the existence of Community regional policy, when compared with no Community policy or with non-membership of the EC. Likewise, Community regional policy strongly complements national regional policy — if for no other reason than that Community regional policy has, to a large extent, consisted of Community support for the national regional policies of members-states and, furthermore, Irish regional policy has consisted of little more than regionally differentiated industrial grants and infrastructural investment.

A more fruitful approach to assessing Ireland's gains and losses was to ask the following questions: How effective has Community regional policy been in achieving its stated objective of reducing regional disparities within the EC? What are the regional effects of the full range of Community policies? And, looking to the future, what set of Community policies will be necessary to achieve economic convergence in the context of economic and monetary union? We have attempted to answer some of these more difficult questions. We found that Community regional policy has achieved little convergence of economic conditions and several aspects of Community policy — the CAP and, possibly, the internal market — tend to widen regional disparities and reinforce existing regional advantages and disadvantages. Looking forward, we argued that reduction of regional disparities in the Community will require four policy approaches: structural policies, macroeconomic co-ordination, budgetary or fiscal transfers and some differential application of other Community policies. While this may seem like a demanding programme for the EC at a time when its agenda is very full it can, in fact, be argued (see NESC, 1989) that these policies, and especially the development of the Community's system of public finance, will complement and facilitate the achievement of a genuine common market and creation of a European economic and monetary union.

Note

1. There is, however, much evidence that in many European countries assisted areas would have been considerably worse off without regional policy (Ashcroft, 1982).

Bibliography

Armstrong, H.W. (1978), 'Community regional policy: a survey and critique', *Regional Studies*, vol. 12, pp. 511—28.
Armstrong, H.W. (1983), 'The assignment of regional policy powers within the EC', in *Britain within the European Community: The Way Forward*, ed. A.M. El-Agraa, pp. 271—99. London: Macmillan Press.
Ashcroft, B.K. (1982), 'The measurement of the impact of regional policies in Europe', *Regional Studies*, vol. 16, no. 4, pp. 287—307.
Boylan, T.A. and Cuddy, M.P. (1985), 'Regional industrial policy: performance and challenge', *Administration*, vol. 32, no. 3, pp. 255—70. Dublin: IPA.
Buchanan, C. et al. (1968), *Regional Studies in Ireland*, Dublin: An Foras Forbatha.
Cuddy, M. (1982), 'European agricultural policy: the regional dimension', *Built Environment*, vol. 7, no. 3, pp. 200—11.
Hart, J. (1985), 'The European regional development fund and the Republic of Ireland', in *Regions in the European Community*, eds. M. Keating and B. Jones, pp. 204—34. London: Macmillan.
Keeble, D., Owens, P.L. and Thompson, C. (1982b), 'Regional accessability and economic potential in the European Community', *Regional Studies*, vol. 16, no. 6, pp. 419—33.
Kravis, I. (1987), 'International comparison of income', in *The New Palgrave – A Dictionary of Economics*, eds. J. Eatwell, M. Milgate and P. Newman, pp. 906—9. London: Macmillan Press.
Mawson, J., Martins, M.R. and Gibney, J.T. (1985), 'The development of the European Community regional policy', in *Regions in the European Community*, eds. M. Keating and B. Jones, pp. 20—60. Oxford: Clarendon Press.
NESC (1989), *Ireland in the European Community: Performance, Prospects and Strategy*, Dublin: National Economic and Social Council.
O'Farrell, P.N. (1974), 'Regional planning in Ireland: the case for concentration — a reappraisal', *Economic and Social Review*, vol. 5, no. 4, pp. 499—514.
Padoa-Schioppa, F. (1987), *Efficiency, Stability and Equity: A Strategy for the Evolution of the Economic System of the European Community*, Oxford: OUP.
Robson, P. (1987), *The Economics of International Integration*, third edition, London: Allen and Unwin.
Swann, D. (1988), *The Economics of the Common Market*, London: Pelican.
Yuill, D. and Allen, K. (1983), *European Regional Incentives*, University of Strathclyde: Centre for the Study of Public Policy.

Chapter 5

Monetary policy

Rory O'Donnell

Introduction

This section discusses the implications of EC monetary policy for Ireland. While it is undoubtedly the case that concrete measures of Community monetary policy are part of a longer-run movement to economic and monetary union this chapter will focus on the European Monetary System (EMS), in existence since 1979, rather than on the much less significant 'Snake' arrangement (1972–9) or the more hypothetical issue of full monetary union. In the next section Ireland's monetary objectives and policy are identified. This is followed by a brief account of the Community's objectives as embodied in the EMS. Some general characteristics of the EMS, as it actually works, are considered, before giving a factual account of Ireland's experience since 1979. The final section provides an assessment of the gains and losses from participation in the system.

Ireland's objectives and policy

Background

The Irish currency had been placed in a one-to-one parity with the pound sterling since 1826. At the achievement of political independence in 1922 there was little serious questioning of the assumption that the British currency should continue to be the legal tender of Ireland. Although many measures of industrial protection were introduced in the early 1930s, it was considered desirable to maintain the link with sterling. Nor did Ireland's departure from the British Commonwealth and declaration of a Republic in 1948 lead to any change in currency arrangements. At the breakdown of the Bretton Woods System in 1971 the Irish pound, known by its Gaelic name 'punt', floated in unison with sterling (Walsh, 1983).

It was not until the mid-1970s that there was systematic discussion of the possibility of breaking the link with sterling. The 1970s saw both an increase in the rate of inflation in Ireland and a change in the way in which most economists explained inflation. Observers were struck by the fact that inflation in the United Kingdom and Ireland was so much higher than that in Germany, and seemed destined to continue so. At the same time many economists abandoned the view that inflation was generated by cost—push factors, such as wages, and adopted the theory that inflation was a purely monetary phenomenon, caused by excess growth of the money supply. In the context of a fixed one-to-one parity with sterling the relevant money supply was that of the United Kingdom plus Ireland together. Indeed, the 'small open economy' theory of inflation states that a small open economy with a fixed exchange rate must experience the same inflation rate as the larger country with which it maintains the parity link. This view became increasingly influential such that, by the mid- to late 1970s many economists advocated that Ireland could achieve much lower inflation by abandoning the link with sterling.

Decision to join EMS

In December 1978 the European summit meeting at Brussels took the decision to launch the European Monetary System (EMS). Two general aspects of the decision which faced Irish policy-makers should be noted. First, it seemed likely that the United Kingdom would not join the exchange rate mechanism (ERM) of the EMS. Consequently, Ireland was faced with the option of breaking a very long-standing currency link and, more significantly, switching its currency link from the country with which about half its trade was conducted, to a group of countries which accounted for less than a quarter of its trade.

Second, Ireland was strongly predisposed towards participating fully in the new initiative because of its consistently *communautaire* stance (see the Government White Paper, *The European Monetary System*).

Ireland's decision to join the EMS was explained by the governor of the Central Bank in the bank's 1979 *Annual Report*. He argued that exchange rate policy should be seen as an instrument to deal with *inflation* rather than any other policy objective. The one-to-one parity with sterling meant that Ireland, as a very small and very open economy, would inevitably acquire the UK rate of inflation. Surveying the options open to Ireland he judged that a freely floating exchange rate was not a viable option, while indefinite adherence to the sterling link had considerable drawbacks. Adherence to a harder currency regime than the sterling link could be a powerful weapon against inflation. While no one could predict how the EMS currencies and sterling would move relative to one another, the governor was quite clear that 'it would be prudent for us to proceed on the assumption that, in the longer term at any rate, membership involves a harder currency regime than non-membership' (Murray, 1979). A final factor which influenced the decision to join was the existence of Community support in the form of transitional resource transfers to weaker countries.

Professional expectations

The governor of the Central Bank left it to a senior economist at the bank to spell out the analytical arguments and to identify what should be expected from EMS membership. Having set out the analytical and empirical case that external sources were the main determinants of Irish inflation under the link with sterling, McCarthy asked how the macroeconomic policy environment was altered by joining the EMS. His answer was

Not very much, since we still have a pegged exchange rate. We are pegged with different currencies now ... our new policy does not represent a major departure from the polar, no-margins peg we used to have. (McCarthy, 1979)

What had changed was Ireland's *policy stance*: 'we have decided to opt for a hard currency policy, or a more anti-inflationary policy, which amounts to the same thing.'

What then would be the macroeconomic effects of a harder currency option? These depend on the macroeconomic effects of currency depreciation or appreciation. The analytical framework which prevailed at the time, and which underlay the decision to join the EMS, known as the 'monetary approach to the balance of payments', provided the answers to these questions. The theory said that the level of output and employment in an open economy is determined purely by real forces such as labour supply, the capital stock, and the levels of taxes and transfers; indeed, the theory proposes that the level of output and employment have a strong tendency to gravitate to their full employment levels. It follows, of course, that changes in the exchange rate can have no lasting effect on output or employment. For example, a devaluation of the currency, which initially makes exports cheaper and imports dearer, and therefore expands aggregate demand, *will not increase output and employment* because it will soon be followed by an increase in domestic wages and prices, such that the *real* exchange rate will return to its original level. Consistent with this analytical framework McCarthy's conclusion was that 'devaluation does not confer any permanent competitive advantage just as Germany's revaluationary policy has not created a permanent competitive handicap' (McCarthy, 1979).

Turning to interest rates, it was predicted that if EMS exchange rate commitments are seen as durable then interest rates on EMS currencies would tend to converge — since interest rate differentials reflect expectations of currency movements. It was argued that government foreign borrowing to finance current budget deficits would simply increase the balance-of-payments deficit — again a reflection of the idea that the level of domestic output and employment is given.

Concern was expressed about the prevailing high level of wage settlements in Ireland. The fear was not that they could generate *inflation*, but that until the rate of increase of *wages* came down to a level consistent with the rate of interest *in prices* available to producers of internationally traded goods (i.e. the rate of price increase determined by the EMS inflation rate) then Irish firms would experience a *profits squeeze*. In McCarthy's words: 'such high settlements do not recommend themselves to a situation where price inflation seems likely to decelerate well into single figures fairly quickly' (McCarthy, 1979). This reflected a fairly widespread belief, at least among economists who adhered to the monetary approach to the balance of payments, that the adjustment of Irish inflation and interest rates to German levels would be a *rapid* process.

Community objectives and policy

A Community initiative for the creation of economic and monetary union was abandoned in the early 1970s in the face of international currency crises and internal unwillingness to seriously co-ordinate economic policies (see Swann, 1988). A much more modest attempt to limit exchange rate volatility, the 'Snake', had only very limited success between 1972 and 1979. Nevertheless, there was a general dissatisfaction with the floating exchange system which had replaced the fixed rates of the Bretton Woods era. Exchange rate movements disrupted production and trade and seemed to reflect speculative whims more than underlying economic conditions. This was the context in which the EMS was devised in 1978 and introduced in early 1979.

The European Monetary System

The purpose of the EMS was to minimize fluctuations between currencies thereby creating a 'zone of monetary stability'. A central feature of the system is the European Currency Unit (ECU). This is a composite currency made up of specified amounts of all member-state currencies. At any point in time each currency participating in the EMS has a given value — called a 'central rate' — in relation to the ECU. These values, once fixed collectively, have to persist until a decision is made by the participating states to alter them. The central rates, expressed in terms of the ECU, are then used to establish a grid of exchange rates between each pair of currencies in the system. The key obligation on a country participating in the system is to prevent its currency diverging more than

2.25 per cent above or below these central rates.[1] The general means for achieving this is the conduct of national fiscal and monetary policy in such a way as to ensure that the currency's market value does not rise or fall out of this narrow band. However, should this occur, the countries concerned are obliged to intervene in the foreign exchange markets or to undertake other measures, such as changes in interest rates or fiscal policy. In order to facilitate these interventions the EMS has some shared foreign exchange reserves and has facilities to provide credit to countries having to undertake balance-of-payments financing. At the formation of the EMS it was agreed that there be a limited transfer of resources to weaker countries in the form of interest rate subsidies on additional loans from the European Investment Bank.

Although all member-states' currencies are represented in the ECU, only eight countries — West Germany, France, Belgium, Luxembourg, the Netherlands, Denmark, Ireland and Italy — initially participated in the exchange rate mechanism of the EMS. It was only these countries that took part in the periodic negotiations to reset the central exchange rates. There have been eleven realignments to date; in recent years these have reduced in both frequency and size (Swann, 1988).

General characteristics of EMS

Although Ireland's position within the EMS has had some unique characteristics, as will be seen below, it is important, in assessing Ireland's experience of EMS, to be aware of the general characteristics of the system. These will be briefly listed before Ireland's particular experience is considered.

A fixed but adjustable regime

The system has definitely been more of a fixed *but adjustment* peg regime than a *fixed* parity system. Weaker countries have used realignments to avoid the full effects of their higher inflation. However, in general such realignments were less than fully accommodating, and this has led to real appreciation of the weaker currencies against the Deutschmark.

EMS and disinflation

Contrary to expectations, inflation rates in some EMS countries declined quite slowly and, most significantly, no faster and no more than in European economies outside the system. However, as will be discussed below, this does not imply that the EMS played no role in reducing inflation in several member-countries, including Ireland.

Exchange rate volatility

One of the principal objectives of the EMS was to establish a 'zone of monetary stability'. Many studies confirm that the EMS has indeed reduced the volatility of both nominal and real exchange rates between EMS currencies (Artis and Taylor, 1989).

Exchange rate stability and macroeconomic performance

This exchange rate stability seems not have improved the general macroeconomic performance of the member-countries. Indeed, during the 1980s growth of output has been slower, and the increase in unemployment greater, in EMS countries than in non-EMS ones (Dornbusch, 1989). Opinions differ as to whether the EMS itself has a *deflationary bias* arising from the low level of co-ordination of national fiscal and demand management policy (Tsoukalis, 1989).

The EMS and interest rates

Reduced volatility of exchange rates would be expected to lead to reduced volatility in interest rates and to a narrowing, and perhaps ultimate elimination, of differences between the interest rates in member-countries. The evidence suggests that these expectations have not been met. Not only have interest rate differentials between weaker countries and Germany remained highly variable, but in some instances, they have *increased* during the EMS period.

The role of exchange controls

It has been argued by some economists that the retention of exchange controls by some members has played an important part in the functioning of the EMS. The idea is that exchange controls have helped to make exchange rate targets credible by limiting the possibility of speculative attacks on weaker currencies, so allowing their authorities to maintain more stable domestic interest rates (Giavazzi and Giovannini, 1986; for a contrary view see Gros and Thygesen, 1988; for an evaluation of the two views see De Grauwe, 1990).

An asymmetric system

Many would support the view that the EMS has functioned in distinctly asymmetric fashion (Giavazzi and Giovannini, 1986; Tsoukalis, 1989;

Katseli, 1989). What is usually meant by asymmetry is that Germany has, by and large, retained the ability to set monetary policy independently, and that other countries then peg to the Deutschmark. It can be argued that, in its present state of development, the EMS 'has to be asymmetric'. The alternative to an asymmetric system would be to formulate a common European monetary policy, 'but this would involve a jump to different degrees of political and economic integration' (Gros and Thygesen, 1988; see also De Grauwe, 1990).

Ireland's experience in the EMS

Introduction

In this section we briefly record the main developments since the formation of the EMS. It will be seen that while much of Ireland's experience reflects the general characteristics of the system, as outlined above, Ireland's position does have certain unique features.

Inflation

The reduction of Irish inflation after formation of the EMS was certainly slower than had been expected. Ireland's relative inflation record, both before and after 1979, is summarized in Table 5.1. This shows that, historically, Ireland is a relatively high inflation country. We noted above that in the mid- to late 1970s both Ireland and the United Kingdom had higher inflation than other EC countries. Both European and UK inflation were significantly reduced in the deep recession of the early 1980s. But Irish inflation *continued to rise* through 1980 and 1981 and was, consequently, far higher than the EC average or the UK rate in 1982. In 1983, the Irish rate of inflation began to drop rapidly and, although the average EC rates also continued downward, the gap was quickly narrowed.

Nominal exchange rates

The Irish punt has, in general, maintained a stable nominal value against the basket of EMS currencies. In the first six realignments of EMS currencies Ireland steered a middle course between revaluations of the Deutschmark and devaluations of the franc and the lira. However, in the March 1983 realignment Ireland devalued the punt by 3.5 per cent, and in August 1986 Ireland initiated a unilateral devaluation of 8 per cent. As a result of all these changes the punt now has a nominal value relative to the narrow band EMS currencies which is more than 15 per cent

Table 5.1 *Inflation (deflator of private consumption) annual percentage change*

	1961–73	1974–81	1982	1984	1986	1988**
Ireland	6.0	16.6	15.3	9.4	3.6	2.1
UK	4.3	15.1	8.6	4.8	3.6	4.5
Eur-12	—	10.6	10.4	7.1	3.6	3.5
EMS*	—	—	9.8	6.5	2.4	2.7

* Countries participating in the exchange rate mechanism of the EMS.
** September/October forecasts of the Commission services.

Source: Annual Economic Report 1988–89, European Commission.

lower than in 1979. In 1979 there were 3.80 DM to the Irish punt; in December 1990 the punt can buy only 2.7 DM — a nominal depreciation of 29 per cent. Nevertheless, the EMS has certainly reduced the volatility of the Irish currency relative to EMS currencies.

Not surprisingly, the EMS period saw an increase in the volatility of the punt relative to sterling. The punt fell dramatically against sterling in 1979, 1980 and 1981, as sterling was driven high by Britain's oil revenues and tight monetary policy. Ireland's decision to devalue in March 1983 and August 1986 both occurred when sterling weakened against EMS currencies (including the punt) and put pressure on Irish exporters to the UK market. Since 1986 sterling was generally strong, reflecting a British policy of shadowing the Deutschmark. However, in recent months sterling has weakened considerably and the punt has moved back towards parity with it.

Real exchange rates

We have summarized developments in relative inflation rates and nominal exchange rates since formation of the EMS. From these two together we can calculate the *real exchange rate* — the nominal exchange rate adjusted for the rates of change of prices or earnings in each country. For example, if Ireland had an *inflation* rate of 5 per cent faster than, say, the United Kingdom, and the *nominal* exchange rate of the punt depreciated by just 3 per cent against sterling, then the *real* exchange rate (the price which Britons must pay for Irish goods) would have appreciated by 2 per cent. If, however, the nominal exchange rate had depreciated by a full 5 per cent, then the real exchange rate would be unchanged.

We have seen that the nominal value of the punt has declined somewhat against EMS currencies. In Table 5.1 we saw that for much of the period since 1979 Irish inflation was very much higher than the EMS average. Overall the nominal value of the punt has not depreciated sufficiently to fully accommodate Ireland's relatively high inflation and, consequently, Ireland's real exchange rate against EMS currencies has risen. This real appreciation, or loss of cost competitiveness, has been about 40 per cent since 1979.

We have noted that immediately after the formation of the EMS the punt depreciated against sterling. In fact it depreciated to an extent sufficient to more than offset the faster rate of inflation in Ireland. Consequently, the real exchange rate against sterling declined from 1978 to 1982 — increasing Ireland's competitiveness versus the United Kingdom. Subsequent weakening of sterling on the foreign exchanges wiped out this competitive gain to Ireland. In the later 1980s inflation was somewhat lower in Ireland than in the United Kingdom and, so long as sterling remained strong, this tended to create a real depreciation of the punt.

Interest rates

Contrary to expectations, and the predictions of theory, Irish interest rates did not unambiguously decouple from UK rates and converge on German rates after the formation of the EMS. From 1979 to 1987 Irish rates were on average about 2 percentage points higher than UK rates and more than 6 percentage points higher than German rates. Given Ireland's inflation in the early years, these differentials meant that *real* interest rates were relatively low in Ireland. But in later years high nominal rates in Ireland have denoted relatively high real rates also. In general, the interest differentials between Ireland and Germany has been greater than any actual decline in the punt/Deutschmark exchange rate. By mid-1988 the decoupling from the UK financial markets and the convergence towards German rates seemed, finally, to be at hand. But in late 1989 and early 1990 interest rates in Ireland have again diverged from those in Germany.

Real economic performance

The period since the formation of the EMS was one of extremely poor relative and absolute economic performance in Ireland (see Chapter 2, internal market policy). From 1979 to 1986 Ireland experienced stagnation, and at times contraction, of disposable income per head. The rate of unemployment increased from 7.1 per cent to almost 19 per cent — and has remained above 17 per cent, despite an annual outflow of about 1 per cent of the population in each year since 1985. Total employment declined by almost 6 per cent and employment in manufacturing by 25 per cent. However, since 1987 there has been a resumption of economic growth (over 3 per cent per annum). This has yet to have a large or sustained impact on consumption, employment or unemployment.

Assessment

Introduction

The contrast between expectations and experience raises a number of difficult and related questions concerning Ireland's participation in the EMS. What was the role of the EMS in the reduction of inflation in Ireland? Did non-participation of the United Kingdom force Ireland to compromise its policy objectives? Did participation in the EMS have any role in the appalling performance of the Irish economy through most of the 1980s? And, finally, why did the experience of the EMS differ so much from what was expected, and why does it continue to do so in certain important respects?

The role of EMS in Ireland's disinflation

Convergence of Irish inflation to a level consistent with a fixed parity with the Deutschmark took much longer than was expected by most economists. Likewise, the reduction in inflation in a very wide group of OECD countries — most of them outside the EMS — casts doubts on the notion that EMS membership, in general, provided especially favourable disinflation conditions. However, it does not follow from these facts that membership of EMS did not play a large role in Ireland's achievement of low inflation. It may be the case that several EMS countries *required* EMS to achieve disinflation — despite the fact that *other* countries (with different social and political structures) could achieve it without a firm external anchor. The conduct of economic policy in Ireland throughout the 1970s and much of the 1980s strongly suggests that this argument applies to Ireland. Despite their disagreements about some aspects of Ireland's EMS membership, most authorities would agree that it has aided the achievement and maintenance of low inflation (Dornbusch, 1989; Honohan, 1989; Kremers, 1989). The *delay* in achieving German levels of inflation can be explained by unforeseen circumstances in the early years and by the fact that the process of disinflation generally takes much longer than is expected by those who apply mechanistic economic models in a credulous fashion.

Contradictions in Irish policy objectives

Membership of the EMS implied a commitment to maintain the *nominal* value of the punt in the EMS band. But, given the assumption that prices in Ireland would respond to prices elsewhere, membership of the EMS implicitly involved a *real* exchange rate, or competitiveness, target as well. In the Irish case this real exchange rate target was dominated by an anxiety not to suffer any severe loss of competitiveness *relative to sterling*. As Walsh says, in the early 1980s the strength of sterling allowed Ireland to reconcile this real exchange rate target, versus the United Kingdom, with the nominal exchange rate commitment of EMS (Walsh, 1986). The fall in sterling in 1983 and in 1986 revealed a contradiction in Irish exchange rate policy. Forced to choose between the two objectives the authorities devalued the punt within the EMS.

Opinions differ as to the wisdom of this response to what was, undoubtedly, a difficult dilemma. Supporters would argue that the 1986 devaluation was not eroded by subsequent wage or price increases and that it therefore achieved a lasting improvement in competitiveness against the United Kingdom. Critics would contend that these devaluations created uncertainty about Ireland's exchange rate policy and, consequently, drove Irish interest rates higher than they otherwise would be. In addition, it can be argued that the Irish authorities did not, and could not, avert *all* losses of competitiveness, especially versus EMS currencies, and to respond selectively to exchange rate movements smacks of *ad hoc* decision-making. In recent years a consensus would seem to have emerged that Ireland should maintain the value of the punt in the EMS band, regardless of any loss of competitiveness created by a weakness in sterling. In general, there can be no doubt that the UK absence from the exchange rate mechanism of the EMS has greatly qualified Ireland's management of policy and its gains from membership of the system.

Role of EMS in poor economic performance

In our survey of developments since 1979 we have noted that there was a considerable appreciation of Ireland's real exchange rate against both EMS currencies and those of 'all trading partners', and alternating periods of real depreciation and real appreciation against sterling. Did this loss of competitiveness play a role in the appalling economic performance of the 1980s, and especially in the collapse of employment in indigenous manufacturing industry? Even if agreement could be reached on this question there would remain intense dispute about *why* EMS membership should have had a deflationary effect.

The view that loss of competitiveness probably had *some* role in the poor performance of the real economy has been stated by the National Economic and Social Council (NESC, 1989) and Dornbusch (1989). The NESC has pointed out that not only was there a significant real appreciation between 1979 and 1987, but that this contrasted sharply with the years from 1970 to 1978 — when Ireland experienced a significant *gain* in competitiveness (a real depreciation) as a result of the depreciation of sterling (to which the punt was linked) (NESC, 1989). In his analysis of the Irish case Dornbusch says that the 'triumph of low inflation has ... come about at the cost (perhaps inevitable) of extraordinary high unemployment, massive emigration and a precarious debt overhang' (Dornbusch, 1989). Others would dispute that EMS membership, and the associated real appreciation, depressed growth and increased unemployment — pointing to other factors which were highly unfavourable.

If a consensus were ever to emerge on this issue it is certain that there would be sharp disagreement on *why* EMS membership was more difficult than had been expected. One view, which is undoubtedly the conventional one among Irish economists, is that any problems which arose did so because domestic monetary and fiscal policy from 1979 to, at least, 1982 was incompatible with EMS membership. An alternative view is that, while domestic policy was undoubtedly too expansionary, it should not be inferred from this that had macroeconomic policy been adjusted in 1979 *no* real appreciation or loss of competitiveness would have followed the change in exchange rate regime. Prompt policy adjustment would certainly have lead to much *earlier* achievement of low inflation, but would also have involved a severe deflation of output and employment. All the international evidence suggests that substantial reduction in price inflation, when pursued by means of monetary or exchange rate policy or both (as was the norm in the EMS countries), takes considerable time and impacts severely on the real economy as well as on prices and costs (NESC, 1989; Perry, 1986; Dornbusch, 1989).

Why EMS differed from expectations

We have seen that Ireland's experience of EMS differed from what was predicted by policy-makers and analysts on at least three fronts: inflation, interest rates and the level of output and employment. To these we can add a fourth: despite very large balance-of-payments deficits, fuelled by expansionary deficit spending and foreign borrowing, the punt did not come under pressure in the foreign exchange markets. In the face of these gaps between expectations and out-turn several questions arise and remain to be answered. Was the theory used to analyse Ireland's EMS membership wrong? Was the theory basically correct, but was it applied in too mechanical a fashion? Was the theory correct, but was domestic policy responsible for the difficulties experienced? Was the unexpected strength of sterling in the early 1980s responsible? The conventional view is that Ireland's excessively expansionary fiscal and monetary policy in the early 1980s explains the difficulties experienced, and specific circumstances are cited to explain more recent problems. This explanation is not fully convincing, and there seems little doubt that the theory of inflation and full employment output, which are one and the same theory, was not adequate. Trying to tease out Ireland's experience of EMS from 1979 to 1990 may seem to be an academic exercise, but it could help to achieve what is absolutely crucial: that Ireland's policy-makers, and their economic advisers, now undertake a thorough, realistic and nondogmatic analysis of how economic and monetary union is likely to function.

Note

1. Italy is allowed a margin of 6 per cent variation around the central rates.

Bibliography

Artis, M.J. and Taylor, M.P. (1989), 'The achievements of the European Monetary System', *Economic and Social Review*, vol. 20, no. 2, January, pp. 121–45.

De Grauwe, P. (1990), 'Liberalisation of capital movements in the EMS', in *The Macroeconomics of 1992: Papers from the CEPS Macroeconomic Policy Group*, Brussels: Centre for European Policy Studies.

Dornbusch, R. (1989), 'Credibility, debt and unemployment: Ireland's failed stabilisation', *Economic Policy*, 8 April, pp. 174–209.

Giavazzi, F. and Giovannini, A. (1986), 'The EMS and the dollar', *Economic Policy*, 2 April, pp. 456–85.

Gros, D. and Thygesen, N. (1988), *The EMS: Achievements, current issues and directions for the future*, Brussels: Centre for European Policy Studies.

Honohan, P. (1989), 'Comments on Dornbusch, 1989', *Economic Policy*, 8 April, pp. 202–5.

Irish Government (1978), *White Paper – The European Monetary System*, Dublin: The Stationery Office.

Katseli, L.T. (1989), 'The political economy of macroeconomic policy in Europe', in P. Guerrieri and P.C. Padoan (eds), *The Political Economy of European Integration*, Hemel Hempstead: Harvester Wheatsheaf.

Kremers, J.M. (1989), 'Gaining policy credibility in the EMS: the case of Ireland', International Monetary Fund Working Paper, 89/36, Washington: IMF.

McCarthy, C. (1979), 'The European Monetary System and Irish macroeconomic policy', *Annual Report of the Central Bank of Ireland*, pp. 109–21.

Murray, C.H. (1979), 'The European Monetary System: implications for Ireland', *Annual Report of the Central Bank of Ireland*, pp. 96–108.

NESC Report No. 89 (1989), *Ireland in the European Community: Performance, prospects and strategy*, Dublin: National Economic and Social Council.

Perry, G. (1986), 'Policy lessons from the post-war period', in W. Beckerman (ed.), *Wage Rigidity and Unemployment*, London: Duckworth.

Swann, D. (1988), *The Economics of the Common Market*, 6th edn, London: Penguin.

Tsoukalis, L. (1989), 'The political economy of the European Monetary System', in P. Guerrieri and P.C. Padoan (eds), *The Political Economy of European Integration*, Hemel Hempstead: Harvester Wheatsheaf.

Walsh, B. (1983), 'Ireland in the European Monetary System: the effects of a change in exchange rate regime', in M. de Cecco (ed.), *International Economic*

Adjustment: Small countries and the European Monetary System, Oxford: Basil Blackwell.

Walsh B. (1986), 'Irish exchange rate policy', University College, Dublin: Centre for Economic Research.

Chapter 6
Competition policy
Rory O'Donnell

Introduction

Given the prominence of the common market in the integration programme of the European Community to date, it is not surprising that competition is one of the most developed areas of Community policy. However, when a distinction is drawn between internal market policy and competition policy, and when account is taken of Community regional objectives and the size of the Irish market and Irish firms, then it emerges that Community competition policy is responsible for few of the gains or losses arising from Ireland's membership of the EC. For this reason we deal with this area of policy in a relatively brief entry. In the first section we outline the main elements of Community competition policy, and, where necessary, link these to other areas of policy. Next, Ireland's objectives and policies are identified. Finally, we assess the gains and losses, explaining why Community policy has, to date, had a limited impact on Ireland's economy or Ireland's conduct of its own policy.

Community competition policy

Formally, Community competition policy consists of those measures, deriving from Articles 85 and 86 of the Treaty of Rome, which aim to suppress cartels and the abuse of monopoly power or dominant position. However, from an economic point of view it is sensible to include also Community policy on state-aids, technical standards, public purchasing and state-monopolies.

Cartels and restrictive practices

Community policy in this area derives from Article 85 of the Treaty of Rome. This article prohibits, and declares void, any agreements and concerted practices which restrict and distort competition in the EC and which 'may affect trade between member-states'. However, the Treaty identifies a number of exemptions. Article 85(3) stipulates that the prohibition on restrictive practices may not apply if an agreement between firms 'contributes to improving the production or distribution of goods or to promoting technical progress'. Furthermore, the prohibition does not apply unless there has been an *appreciable* restraint on competition. The Commission has interpreted this to mean that a significant restriction of competition can only exist where the firms participating in an agreement have a market share of more than 5 per cent in a substantial part of the EC and where their aggregate turnover exceeds ECU 50 million.

The Commission has used these articles, and the substantial powers conferred on it, to vigorously attack restrictive agreements between manufacturing firms. Exemptions have allowed continuation of sole distribution agreements and joint research and development projects. Application of EC competition policy to service industries, such as road haulage and air transport, is a much more recent development.

Dominant firms and mergers

Article 86 of the Rome Treaty prohibits abuse of a dominant position which may affect trade between member-states. The content of Community policy derives from the interpretation of this article by the Commission and the Court of Justice. This has successfully removed many practices but, although it has been applied to mergers between dominant firms, it does not constitute an adequate Community policy on mergers. Merger-control regulations are currently being passed into Community law.

State-aids

Articles 92 to 94 of the Treaty are designed to deal with the distortions of competition which arise from state-aids to industry. The basic principle is that aids which affect trade between member-states are prohibited. However, two important exemptions are provided for in the Treaty. Much the more important of these is the provision that regional (and sectoral) aids may be compatible with the common market. Although the Rome Treaty made no provision for a common industrial or regional policy this was an implicit recognition that regional differences within the EC would require interventionist measures — but also a pragmatic recognition that governments would, in fact, provide aids to poorer regions within member-states.

Given these exemptions, Community competition policy on state-aids consists of a review and control of the quantity and type of aids, rather than a prohibition. This limited role was especially significant after the economic crisis of 1974. Community policy on regional aids is discussed in more detail in Chapter 4, on regional policy, and Chapter 7, on industrial policy. Policy on sectoral aids is reviewed in Chapter 7 also.

In recent years the Commission has become more sympathetic towards aids designed to stimulate research and development. This reflects the recognition of the technological superiority of the United States and Japan and the emergence of a Community technology policy (see Chapter 12).

Technical standards

National technical standards, laid down to protect consumers, can constitute a non-tariff barrier to trade between countries. This restricts competition and can prevent the exploitation of economies of scale. The solution is to harmonize standards, and provision for this was made in Articles 100 to 102, on the approximation of laws. Up to 1985 the Community had adopted approximately 180 directives relating to industrial products and approximately 60 concerned with foodstuffs. However, the process of adopting common standards is extremely time-consuming. In defining the project of completion of the internal market the Commission adopted a new approach, based on mutual recognition, where possible, and, since the Single European Act, majority voting where harmonization is really necessary.

Public purchasing

Preferential public purchasing is contrary to the Treaty of Rome and the Council of Ministers has adopted directives on public works contracting and public procurement. These rules would seem to have been widely ignored and, in addition, the purchases of transport, water, energy and telecommunications authorities are not covered by the directives. It is intended that these deficiencies will be addressed in the completion of the internal market.

State-monopolies

A number of member-states have state-monopolies in the alcohol, tobacco and petroleum industries. The Commission has made considerable progress in curbing the restrictive practices of such companies in the original Six.

Irish competition policy

Ireland has a very limited competition policy and little anti-trust legislation. Investigations are undertaken by the Restrictive Practices Commission which can issue orders where it finds anti-competitive practices as defined by the Restrictive Practices Act. To date only ten such orders have been issued. However, legislation is now being prepared to replicate Articles 85 and 86 of the Treaty of Rome in Irish law. This will constitute a major development of Irish competition policy.

Gains and losses to Ireland

An assessment of the effects of Community competition policy on Ireland reveals that competition policy is responsible for few of the gains and losses arising from Ireland's membership of the EC.

Cartels and concentration

We noted that the EC prohibition on cartels and other agreements does not apply unless the firms involved have a market share of more than 5 per cent in a substantial part of the EC and their aggregate turnover exceeds ECU 50 million. Given the small size of the Irish market, and the even smaller size of Irish manufacturing firms, it follows that few Irish firms have fallen foul of, or are likely to fall foul of, Community competition law.

This does not mean that EC competition policy has no economic effects on Ireland. Vigorous suppression of cartels, etc. in other member-states reduces the barriers to entry faced by Irish firms and firms located in Ireland. In this sense EC competition policy is beneficial to Ireland. However, it is noteworthy that for many years EC competition policy was not applied as vigorously to service industries as to manufacturers — reflecting the fact that the common market, such as it was, was a common market for manufactured goods only. In recent years competition policy has begun to be applied more widely and this is an important part of the 1992 internal market project. While the overall effects on Ireland of free trade in services are uncertain (see NESC, 1989, chapter 10) it seems likely that Ireland stands to gain from a more thorough application of EC competition policy to services. An important example of this, in air transport, is discussed in some detail in Chapter 8, on transport and communication policy.

Another important potential effect of EC competition policy arises when we consider price differences between Ireland and other EC countries. Research has confirmed the existence of substantial price differences between member-states — even for manufactured goods. These differences cannot be fully explained by indirect taxes, and a slow response to exchange rate changes, and differential transport costs, are additional causes. However, as FitzGerald (1989) notes, in the Irish case, some of the differences seem to be the result of market differentiation by manufacturers. The important point is that this ability to charge different prices in different markets is sustained by the existence of customs barriers and the related documentation, on the one hand, and by the prevalence of block exemptions from EC competition law, allowing exclusive distribution agreements, on the other. The removal of customs, after 1992, may be sufficient to undermine this market segmentation — if competition law is vigorously enforced to allow Irish retailers to obtain supplies from outside Ireland (i.e. undertake what is known as 'parallel importing'). Thus Irish consumers, at least, would benefit from enforcement of EC competition policy.

Dominant firms and mergers

Very few Irish firms have sufficient scale or scope to qualify as having a dominant position under Community law. However, we noted that Article 86 has been applied to mergers involving dominant firms. It is this which has given rise to the main impact of Community competition policy, narrowly defined, on Ireland. In 1988 the Commission stepped in to restrict the takeover of Irish Distillers by GC and C Brands, on the grounds that this would be anti-competitive. As a result, the rival bid by the French company, Pernod Ricard, was successful. Our concern in this book is to assess the gains and losses arising from Community membership and Community policy. It is not possible to say whether the takeover by Pernod Ricard rather than Grand Metropolitan, is a gain or a loss — though the balance of argument suggest that Grand Metropolitan were better placed to provide access to the distribution networks that the Irish spirits industry requires. It is perhaps more significant to note that the position of the industry by 1987 — requiring takeover by some international drinks business — reflects the abject failure of much of Irish business and of industrial policy. The business failure was the lack of any strategic approach in an industry which was relatively immune from import competition, and yet had a potential export product. The policy failure was the lack of strategic focus on indigenous industry generally, and on firms like Irish Distillers in particular — while at the same time providing public money for capital investments.

State-aids

Most state-aids offered by Ireland have qualified for exemption from the general Treaty prohibition, on the grounds that they are justified for regional purposes. However, as we explain in Chapter 7, on industrial policy, Ireland's preferential tax treatment of profits earned on exports was judged to be discriminatory, and has been replaced by a uniform tax rate on all manufacturing industry. State-aids are discussed in more detail in the chapters on industrial policy and regional policy, Chapters 7 and 4, respectively.

Technical standards

The existence of differences in national technical standards is disadvantageous to Ireland, because Irish standards exclude few foreign products, whereas German or French standards, for example, may exclude Irish products. Consequently, Community harmonization of standards has benefited Ireland. The speeding up of harmonization, which is an important part of the internal market programme, should confer further benefits.

Public purchasing

Promotion of Irish products, over imported ones, by Irish state-agencies has attracted the attention of the Commission and changes in practice have resulted. However, this fairly minor curtailment of Irish policy, and the associated loss to the Irish economy, is by no means the most important economic effect of Community policy on public purchasing. Much the most noteworthy fact is that the prohibition on preferential public purchasing has been ignored by most member-states. Furthermore, this confers a much greater economic advantage on large member-states, whose public authorities can purchase virtually anything domestically, than on small countries like Ireland or Denmark, where many things which public authorities require must, perforce, be imported.

Assessment

Although we have found that EC competition policy has had few direct effects on Irish firms we have identified a number of indirectly beneficial effects for Ireland. Few Irish firms have fallen foul of EC competition law, but they benefit indirectly from its vigorous enforcement in other member-states. Irish consumers have been unable to reap the full benefits of the competition policy because of the way in which customs barriers inhibit parallel importing. Likewise, both Irish consumers and some Irish firms stand to gain when EC competition law is fully enforced in service sectors, such as air transport. Most state-aids offered by Ireland have been considered not to violate the Treaty of Rome because they are justified on regional grounds. A more complete harmonization of technical standards, than has been achieved to date, would be in Ireland's interest, given its inability to use technical standards as non-tariff barriers to imports. Likewise, although Irish state-agencies have been forced to limit their promotion of Irish products over imported ones, Ireland would undoubtedly gain rather than lose from a general and complete enforcement of the EC prohibition of preferential public procurement. In conclusion, Ireland gains more than it loses from EC competition policy, *per se*. However, as will be seen in the next chapter, it is not in Ireland's interest that competition policy is the only well-developed part of the Community's overall intervention in industry.

Bibliography

FitzGerald, J. (1989), '1992: The Distribution Sector', in J. Bradley (ed.), *The Economics of 1992: A Symposium on Sectoral Issues*, Dublin: Economic and Social Research Institute.

NESC (1989), *Ireland in the European Community: Performance, Prospects and Strategy*, Dublin: National Economic and Social Council.

Chapter 7

Industrial policy
Rory O'Donnell

Introduction

Although industrial policy has been one of the central elements of Irish economic policy since well before 1973 it cannot be said that Community industrial policy has generated significant gains or losses for Ireland. This is so because of the size and nature of the Irish economy and the limited scope of Community industrial policy. This note begins with a brief account of the main features of Community industrial policy. We then consider Ireland's objectives and policy and assess the extent and nature of the gains and losses arising.

Community objectives and policy

In considering the emergence of European industrial policy it is important to distinguish between the European Economic Community (EEC) and the European Coal and Steel Community (ECSC). The Treaty of Paris (1951) which founded the ECSC addressed the structure of two very important traditional industries and conferred considerable powers on an executive to determine and enforce policy. It can be argued that both political concerns and attitudes to economic and industrial questions had changed somewhat by the time of the Treaty of Rome (1957) founding the EEC. While many aspects of the Treaty bear on industrial policy the Treaty does not call for a Community industrial policy.

Indeed, most of the industrial policy topics referred to in the Treaty — state-aids, dominant firms, cartels, the right of establishment, the free movement of capital and labour, and dumping — are those subjects where industrial policy intersects with competition policy (Baylis, 1980). The emphasis in the Treaty, and to a large extent in subsequent Community industrial policy, was on the creation of the common market. As will be seen below, much of what might be identified as Community industrial policy consists of measures to remove obstacles to the creation of a European industrial base and an integrated business system.

Four elements of Community industrial policy can be identified (Swann, 1988). The first is concerned with the creation of a European industrial base, or, in other words, a genuine common market. Second, the Community has acted to promote business integration. Third, the Community has policies designed to close the technological gap between the EC and countries such as the United States and Japan. Finally, the EC has sectoral policies to address the problems of industries encountering structural difficulties.

The European industrial base

The Community has made significant progress on this front through the removal of tariffs and quotas and, in recent years, the attack on non-tariff barriers in the 'completion of the internal market'. This aspect of economic policy, and its implications for Ireland, are dealt with in Chapter 2 on the internal market.

Business integration

The Community's concern to facilitate and, indeed, encourage the creation of European firms, and deeper interaction between firms, can be viewed as, in part, an industrial policy. However, there are two reasons why we will not dwell on this here. First, the Community has, until very recently, made very little progress in overcoming the fiscal and legal problems which inhibit cross-frontier mergers and other forms of collaboration. Second, because the issues involved are legal and fiscal they are dealt with in a little more detail in the entries on competition policy and fiscal policy (Chapters 6 and 11).

Science and technology

While policies to narrow the technological gap between the EC and its major rivals are now an important part of Community industrial policy these, and their implications for Ireland, are best considered in Chapter 12, on technology policy.

Sectoral industrial policy

The most active element of Community industrial policy has consisted of measures designed to address the problems of industries which exhibit structural weaknesses. The EC has sectoral policies for textiles, steel, shipbuilding, coal and electronics. The latter two are dealt with in the entries on energy policy and technology policy (Chapters 9 and 12). The Community's interventions in textiles and steel differ, and the main features of each are briefly outlined below.

In general, the Commission's powers of industrial policy are limited to control of state-aids — to ensure that they encourage restructuring — and control of imports, which can give problem industries a breathing space within which to adjust (Swann, 1988). Both these powers have been used in the case of textiles. From as early as 1971 the Commission recognized that textile production within the Community would shrink and that member-states would seek to protect their industries by giving aids. The Commission laid down rules designed to prevent distortions of competition within the EC, and to ensure that aids should reduce capacity and facilitate diversification away from products in which the Community could not, in the long run, compete with newly industrialized countries. Imports into the EC (and other major developed countries) were regulated under a series of Multi-Fibre Arrangements (MFA), the first of which was negotiated in 1973. These arrangements have varied in the extent and the manner in which they have restricted import penetration — reflecting variations in the pace of industrial decline in the Community. By 1985 the Commission was able to report that substantial restructuring of the textile industry had been achieved and the industry was once again competitive.

In the case of iron and steel the Commission's powers extend beyond control of state-aids and imports, to influence over internal competition, price, output and investment. This reflects the fact that policy in this area derives from the more *dirigiste* Paris Treaty. Since the recession of 1974 the Commission has used these powers and, when voluntary restraint on output collapsed in 1980, it imposed mandatory output and sales quotas. These quotas were to remain in place until capacity reductions were agreed and achieved. While that process has proved difficult, quotas should finally be abolished in 1990.

Irish objectives and policy

It was stated in Chapter 1 that industrialization was among the major economic goals of the independent Irish state. It is not surprising, therefore, that industrial policy was, and remains, one of the most important areas of policy in Ireland. Given this central role, the development to Irish industrial policy, and its main elements, featured prominently in our introduction to the economic policy section of this volume (see Chapter 1). Consequently, we now need only a brief outline of Irish industrial policy.

For three decades, 1930 to around 1960, Ireland sought industrialization by means of trade protection. In the late 1950s Irish policy-makers decided that further industrialization and prosperity depended on export-led growth which, in turn, required more active involvement in the international trading system. Modern Irish industrial policy grew out of this decision.

Initially, the policy had two main elements: first, encouragement to foreign firms to locate in Ireland — especially in the least developed, peripheral, regions of the country — and, second, action to re-orient indigenous firms from production mainly for the small domestic market to exporting. These objectives were, and are, pursued by means of both financial and fiscal instruments. The financial instrument consisted of direct grants towards the capital cost of establishment or expansion. The main fiscal instrument was export profits tax relief (EPTR), which involved complete tax exemption for profits earned on exports.

From the start Irish industrial policy achieved far more success in its first objective — attraction of foreign corporations — than its second — reorientation of indigenous manufacturing industry (see Kennedy *et al.*, 1989). The reasons for the difficulties experienced in preparing Irish industry for free trade have been explored in some detail in Chapter 2 on the internal market. The reasons for the remarkable success of the Industrial Development Authority (IDA) in attracting foreign firms have been analysed in the extensive literature on Irish industrial development (see O'Malley, 1981 for a survey and O'Malley, 1989, for a critique). One result of this greater facility to attract foreign firms than to reorient or develop indigenous ones, was that Irish industrial policy came, in practice, to mean job creation in foreign-owned production plants attracted to Ireland by generous capital grants and tax-free profits.

While this remains an extremely important part of Irish policy there have, in the 1980s, been a number of developments. Early in that decade the tripartite National Economic and Social Council undertook a series of studies of industrial policy. These studies, and work by other researchers, revealed important weaknesses in policy design and execution. Capital grants were excessively generous (given the value of tax exemption) and in practice, if not intention, favoured foreign firms over indigenous ones. Foreign firms in Ireland had very few forward or backward linkages with the Irish economy. Policy was executed with an eye to short-term job creation, often in response to temporary and local political pressures, rather than to the development of a number of strong Irish corporations. The incentive package lowered the price of capital relative to labour and may have induced high capital intensity. Public policy in the areas of industrial grants, technology, training, taxation and export promotion influenced business in a myriad of unco-ordinated and sometimes contradictory ways (see Chapters 11, 12 and 25). Finally, the IDA, charged with *execution* of industrial policy, had by default, acquired control of policy *formation* as well. These criticisms have prompted a number of changes in policy, among which the following would seem to be the most noteworthy. Action has been taken to develop greater linkages between the multinationals and the Irish economy. Greater emphasis has been given to the development of indigenous firms and there is some recognition that, in many industries, they need to achieve sufficient *scale* to survive in the international market. Finally, active industrial policy has been extended to internationally traded *service* sectors.

Gains and losses to Ireland

Impact of Community industrial policy

In assessing implications of Community industrial policy for Ireland the essential point is to recognize that the Community has had very little active policy in this area, while Ireland has pursued an extremely active approach. Consequently, the main question is: how has Ireland's pursuit of its industrial policy objectives been affected by Community membership? The answer is that Ireland's approach has been greatly facilitated, but little changed, by her membership of the EC. We now explain why this is so.

In saying that Ireland's approach has been facilitated we have in mind the fact that membership of the EC gave producers located in Ireland tariff-free access to the markets of all member-states. There can be no doubt that this access, and even the prospect of it before 1973, increased the attraction of Ireland as a production location for US, Asian and other multinationals. We are, therefore, talking about the effects of the Community's *internal market policy* on Irish industrial policy. It is likely that this, generally positive, effect has greatly exceeded any, positive or negative, effect of Community *industrial* policy on Ireland.

This latter statement reflects our conclusion that Irish industrial policy was *little changed* by Community membership. There were two reasons for this. First, as we noted above, the Community has not developed a common approach across the range of industrial policy instruments. The second reason is one that we established in Chapter 6, on competition policy. Although state-aids to industry are prohibited by Article 92 of the Treaty of Rome, the treaty allows that provision of *regional* aids may be compatible with the common market. At its accession Ireland declared that its policies for industrialization were essential to its national interest and, since the formation of Community regional policy in 1975, Ireland has been classified as a less-developed region. For these two reasons Irish industrial policy has been altered or curtailed very little as a result of EC membership.

That is not to say that membership has had no impact on Irish industrial policy. Indeed, the tax relief on export sales was found to be discrimination under the Treaty of Rome and has now been replaced by 10 per cent tax rate on all manufacturing firms. State-sponsored promotion of Irish goods, in preference to imported ones, was found to contravene the Treaty and the relevant agency was subsequently privatized. Against these minor curtailments other parts of Ireland's industrial policy have been explicitly sanctioned. The IDA's linkages programme has recently been cleared by the Commission. Indeed, Ireland has officially submitted its industrial development plans, as part of its national development plan, in pursuit of the structural funds. The eligibility of Ireland's proposed measures for Community support implies that they are not considered contrary to the Treaty.

There is one negative aspect of this weak impact of Community membership on national industrial policy. It reflects not only the fact that Irish policy intervention is considered valid, given the country's relative under-development, but also the fact that regional-and sectoral-aids have continued to be offered on a large scale by all other member-states (see Chapter 4 on regional policy and Chapter 6 on competition policy). Indeed, there has been competitive bidding which drives up the level of aids and imposes a heavy burden on precisely those states and regions where aids to industry are genuinely needed. Thus a more vigorous implementation of competition policy and a more developed Community industrial policy would be in Ireland's interest.

Community sectoral policy

We noted that the most active element of Community industrial policy has consisted of policies for sectors such as steel, shipbuilding, coal and textiles. While these have, indeed, been vigorous policies they have had a limited impact on Ireland for a number of reasons. These sectors were all characterized by structural weaknesses in the post-war period and especially since the collapse of the 'golden age' in the early 1970s. These structural weaknesses reflect their historical role in the industrial revolution. But, since Ireland did not experience that industrial revolution in the same way as Britain or the countries of Northern Europe, it was an insignificant producer of these products. As a result, Irish production has attracted less attention from the Commission. While Irish officials had anxious moments in negotiation with the Commission on Irish Steel and the Verolme Cork Dockyard, the strategic significance of these remaining firms to Ireland, and their lack of significance to the wider market, seems to have left Irish policy interventions relatively intact. In the case of textiles the Community policy on synthetic fibres, and especially the restriction on creation of additional capacity, had some impact on Irish policy, which involved the attraction of US or Japanese producers to Ireland. The Community has recently developed an industrial policy for the electronics sector — reflecting the EC's anxiety to close the technological gap with the United States and Japan. This involves various measures to support the advance of the leading EC firms in the electronics and telecommunications industry (see Chapter 12 on technology policy). In some respects this cuts across Ireland's industrial policy, since that policy involves attraction of the leading *non-EC* firms in these sectors. This slight conflict of interest reflects Ireland's anomalous position within the European economy and its unusual pattern of industrial development (O'Donnell, 1989).

Conclusion

The most important effect identified in this chapter has been a positive one — the fact that membership of the internal market (rather than Community industrial policy) facilitated Irish industrial policy by increasing the attractiveness of Ireland as a location for foreign direct investment. In judging this to be a positive effect we mean only that attraction of foreign firms was a major part, indeed *the* major part, of Ireland's declared industrial policy objectives. In assessing the overall gains and losses this effect of the internal market must be weighed against its other effects (see Chapter 1 and the concluding chapter). Focusing on industrial policy itself, we found that Irish industrial policy was little changed by Community membership — a fact which reflects the underdeveloped nature of Community industrial policy and the continuation of regional- and sectoral-aids by all member-states. More recent Community industrial policy, focusing on advanced sectors such as electronics and telecommunications, is likely to have a somewhat negative effect on Ireland — to the extent that Ireland's interest is genuinely served by relying on the attraction of non-EC multinationals.

Bibliography

Bayliss, B.T. (1980), 'Competition and industrial policy', in A.M. El-Agraa (ed.), *The Economics of the European Community*, London: Philip Allan.
Kennedy, K.A., Giblin, T. and McHugh, D. (1988), *The Economic Development of Ireland in the Twentieth Century*, London: Routledge.
O'Malley, E. (1981), *Industrial Policy and Development: A survey of literature from the early 1960s to the present*, Dublin: National Economic and Social Council.
O'Malley, E. (1989), *Industry and Economic Development: The challenge for the latecomer*, Dublin: Gill and Macmillan.
O'Donnell, R. (1989), 'Manufacturing', in J. Bradley (ed.), *The Economics of 1992 - A Symposium on Sectoral Economic Issues*, Dublin: Economic and Social Research Institute.
Swann, D. (1988), *The Economics of the European Community*, London: Penguin.

Chapter 8

Transport policy

Tom Ferris

Introduction

Transport has a significant influence on almost all aspects of commercial and social life. The transport of goods is almost entirely motivated by the fact that they are in one place, but they are wanted in another place. As regards the transport of people, most of the journeys that people make are not made solely for pleasure; they would not be made if there were not some additional objective, namely the desire to be in one place rather than in another place (Ferris, 1987: 52). The potential of people to move around, and the scope of industry and services to trade widely, can be severely limited to the extent that distortions operate in transport markets. The importance of removing such distortions (or potential distortions) was recognized in the Treaty of Rome, which established the European Community. Article 3(e) of the Treaty indicated that the activities of the EC should include the inauguration of a common transport policy (CTP). That Article (and the separate chapter on transport in the Treaty) demonstrated that freedom for goods and persons to move without obstacles and barriers was fundamental to the achievement of a real common market.

Progress in the development of a CTP by the EC has been slow during the past three decades. It must be recognized, however, that the EC institutions have had to contend with a very diverse range of national transport policies, often with quite conflicting objectives. Also the sheer scale of the sector and the different modes within the sector have made it difficult to package transport into a single 'common' policy.

In recent years there is increasing evidence that the regulation of the transport markets of the EC is ceasing to be a matter primarily reserved to national governments. The European Commission's Fourth Progress Report, concerning the implementation of the Commission's White Paper on the completion of the internal market, demonstrated that the balance of power is shifting and increasingly transport, as indeed other sectors, is being controlled by legislation adopted at an overall EC level (Commission, 1989a: 30—64).

The EC Commission has consistently emphasized the vital role to be played by a liberalized transport industry in its attempts to bring about a single EC market. The position of the EC Commission was strengthened considerably when, in 1985, the European Court of Justice in ruling on a case brought against the EC Council of Ministers by the European Parliament, instructed the Council to fulfil its obligations under the Treaty of Rome and adopt measures to ensure the creation of a CTP.

The European Court of Justice ruling, together with the qualified majority voting procedures introduced by the Single European Act, has resulted in increased momentum within the EC in terms of formulating a CTP in the second half of the 1980s. Agreement has been reached over the past four years in a number of significant areas of transport; for example liberalization in maritime transport, air transport and road freight transport. Nevertheless, decisions of particular significance for the creation of a CTP remain to be taken.

In the absence of a comprehensive CTP it is premature to attempt to provide a detailed assessment of how Ireland has been affected by EC transport policies. Yet while the CTP envisaged in the Treaty of Rome has not been established, a number of individual EC regulations and directives in the area of transport have entered into force, which do allow some tentative conclusions to be drawn as far as the impact of aspects of a CTP on Ireland is concerned.

The balance of the review is presented here in nine sections. *Section 2* provides an overview of some of the key features of the Irish transport sector. *Sections 3 and 4* discuss the effects of the CTP on the road haulage and road passenger sectors. *Section 5* deals with investment in Irish roads. *Sections 6, 7 and 8* discuss the impact of the EC on rail, air and sea transport, *Section 9* discusses the question of transport infrastructure. Finally *Section 10* provides a general assessment of the impact of the CTP on Ireland.

Some features of Irish transport

Ireland has a relatively greater dependence on transport than most other EC member-states because of its peripheral and island location, with a consequent heavier reliance on air and sea access transport services. In 1988 merchandise exports of IR£ 12.3 billion represented 58 per cent of GDP (and imports of IR£ 10.2 billion represented 48 per cent of GDP). In tonnage terms, the dominant access mode is sea, accounting for 81 per cent of total merchandise trade. Tonnage crossing the land frontier with Northern Ireland accounts for nearly 19 per cent of trade and freight traffic tonnage by air represents less than 1 per cent of total merchandise trade.

As regards passenger movements to and from Ireland, two-thirds of the passengers now travel by air and only one-third by sea. Air, which accounted for 50 per cent of the passenger market in 1983, increased its share to 66 per cent by 1988, reflecting a very positive market response to the lower air fares regime which emerged during that period. The swing in market shares is reflected by the fact that passenger movements by sea fell by 10 per cent between 1984 and 1988, while air passenger movements grew by 70 per cent over the same period (Ferris, 1990: 5).

As regards inland transport in Ireland, over 90 per cent of all freight tonne-kilometres are carried by road, with only 10 per cent travelling by rail. In the case of inland passenger movements it has been estimated that over 96 per cent of all passenger-kilometres are by road and only 4 per cent by rail. It is generally true to say that, as far as inland transport is concerned, the geographically peripheral member-states of the EC are more dependent on road transport than the central member-states, which tend to rely more heavily on railways. As a result, the former tend to favour deregulation of road transport whereas the latter attach more priority to uniform conditions of competition (Abbati, 1987: 19).

Transport costs are a significant factor affecting the competitiveness of the Irish economy, both at domestic and international levels. The Irish Government's *National Development Plan* of 1989 pointed out how Ireland suffers from major cost disadvantages *vis-à-vis* other EC member-states due to the generally poor quality of the internal transport network and Ireland's peripheral and island location (with a consequent heavier reliance on air and sea access transport services). The small size of the Irish market — less than 1 per cent of the EC total — compounds the problem of Ireland's peripherality, as it makes producers relatively more dependent on exports.

The thrust of the action proposed by the Irish Government for the transport sector over a five-year period is to develop an adequate internal transport structure that will be fully integrated with improved access transport services. In the context of addressing Ireland's peripherality problems the plan highlighted the importance of ensuring the maximum integration of services with the European transport network (Government of Ireland, 1989: 39).

Road haulage

The EC Transport Council is committed to the removal of all quantitative restrictions on road haulage by the end of 1992. The movement of goods by road within the EC is partly restricted at present and there are differences between the national regulations on capacity and tariff control. The EC Transport Council has taken action to facilitate safe (and standardized) movement of vehicles throughout the EC by harmonizing certain standards relating to vehicles and certain social legislation affecting drivers. The EC Transport Council has also taken decisions which have helped to open up the EC (and domestic) road haulage markets. Such developments are particularly relevant to Ireland because of the potential for export earnings in the sector. Indeed, the Irish road haulage sector has to date made good use of its share of the system of EC multilateral authorizations that permit the international carriage of goods by road for hire or reward.

In December 1989, the EC Transport Council decided to allow hauliers registered in one member-state to operate transport services wholly within another member-state ('cabotage' as it is known) on a limited basis and with certain safeguard provisions to avoid excessive penetration of any particular market or geographic zone. Under this transitional arrangement for 'cabotage', Irish hauliers should be able to reduce 'empty-running' on return journeys of their lorries from the United Kingdom and the European mainland. The level of penetration of the Irish market by European operators, except for those from Northern Ireland, is likely to be small. The interim EC 'cabotage' scheme will be in operation from July 1990 to the end of December 1992, as a prelude to complete 'cabotage' (the details of which will have to be agreed prior to implementation on 1 January 1993).

As regards the maximum lorry weights and dimensions, substantial progress has already been made in achieving consensus at an EC level. Ireland's national limits will be in line with most of the limits so far adopted by the Community by 31 December 1998, following the derogations granted to Ireland and the United Kingdom on 5 June 1989. Decisions have still to be taken on harmonization in the area of vehicle-related taxes; accordingly, the impact on Irish road haulage is not yet clear. Overall, however, it would appear that the deregulation of road haulage, together with the benefits of removal of non-tariff barriers should create opportunities for professional haulage firms (and own account transport firms) in Ireland to develop their business to a much greater extent.

Road passenger transport

The EC Commission is seeking to open up the market in the provision of road passenger transport. Yet very little progress has been made in the deregulation of road passenger services to date. To that extent, it is not possible to conclude that the EC's CTP has had a direct impact on the Irish road passenger sector. There are, however, a number of proposals that the EC Commission has put forward, which if implemented would be likely to remove many of the current market restrictions. These concern the freedom for non-resident carriers to operate national road passenger services within a member-state and common rules for the international carriage of passengers by coach and bus. Discussions on these proposals are continuing within the Council of Ministers. These proposals could have major implications for Irish bus operators, in the public and the private sectors, and in both the domestic and international markets. It should be noted that on the domestic front the Irish Government has decided to introduce new legislation to replace the Road Transport Act, 1932, which regulates access to the domestic bus passenger market. The new legislation is likely to contain provisions for greater liberalization of the licensing system.

Road investment

Ireland depends on the roads system to a far greater extent than most other member-states, because of its small size, island status and low-density dispersed population. The network of national roads and the access roads to Ireland's principal ports and airports, which are an important part of the strategic infrastructure, are seriously deficient by Community standards.

Road investment has not kept pace with the growth in vehicle numbers and the changing vehicle composition and, consequently, future investment will have to remove existing backlogs as well as providing for future growth. During 1987 the Irish Department of the Environment carried out a review of road development needs covering an evaluation period of twenty years. This review identified long-term road needs for the entire network of about IR£ 9 billion.

The data on past Irish road investment clearly indicate however, that EC financial assistance has been of major importance to the funding of the national road and major road improvement programme in Ireland. Indeed, without EC funding it would not have been possible to sustain the level of investment. The ERDF grants represent the main source of EC assistance; roads accounted for over IR£ 287 million (or 26 per cent) of the ERDF commitments of IR£ 1,125 million to the Irish Exchequer in the years 1975 through 1989. In addition to the ERDF grants, European Investment Bank (EIB) loans represent a key source of EC assistance for roads. Of the total EIB loans of IR£ 1,084.8 million received by the Irish Exchequer between 1973 and 1987, nearly a quarter (or IR£ 255.9 million) was in the form of loans for roads (Ferris, 1990: 11).

Rail transport

The special nature of the rail transport system of the EC largely precludes competition or free market access in international rail transport services. Tariffs on international routes are negotiated bilaterally and the revenue from international rail traffic is shared between the participating national rail companies (Commission, 1988: 97). What measures have been introduced by the EC to date have had no significant impact on Irish railways *per se*. The EC White Paper on the completion of the international market does not propose measures of liberalization for rail transport.

Air transport

The competition rules of the Treaty of Rome were not applied to the air transport sector until recent years. However, a European Court of Justice judgment in April 1986 (commonly referred to as the *nouvelles frontières* judgment) confirmed that the general rules of the Treaty of Rome, and in particular those on competition, do in fact apply to air transport, in the same way as to the other modes of transport. This paved the way for the first steps to be taken towards a more liberalized regime in civil aviation. Accordingly in December 1987 the EC Transport Council adopted a package of measures covering air fares, capacity, access to routes and the application of the competition rules of the Treaty of Rome to civil aviation. The package was designed to override less liberal provision in bilateral agreements between member-states. This package has already enabled Irish airlines to expand their operations significantly. New routes and new fifth freedom services have already been inaugurated to points in the United Kingdom and mainland Europe. (A 'fifth freedom right', under an air transport agreement relating to scheduled international air services, it the right of the airlines of one country to carry traffic from a second country, with which it has an agreement, to a third country.) Lower fares have been introduced as a result of the new procedures for fares determination. The market has responded to the lower fares with considerable growth.

The move to liberalize the air transport market at the EC level has been accompanied by the introduction of more liberal arrangements between individual member-states through bilateral agreements. For example, an agreement to authorize considerably reduced passenger air fares on the Dublin/London route in early 1986 resulted in considerable increases in air traffic carryings on the main British/Irish air route (Commission, 1988: 98).

The second stage of the measures to bring about the completion of the single market in civil aviation in the EC is now being put in place. In December 1989 the EC Transport Council agreed on the set of principles to be included in the next stage of air transport liberalization. The Irish Government decided that liberalization of European air transport was to be a priority for it during the Irish presidency of the EC in the first half of 1990. The principal objective, in so far as Ireland is concerned, is to move as far as possible towards a fully liberalized system with major emphasis on relaxed capacity controls, lower fares, less restrictions on fifth freedom rights, improved access to new routes and increased capacity and liberalized arrangements governing air freight transport. A third stage leading to the completion of the internal market in civil aviation is to be tabled by the EC Commission in 1992. The EC Commission is at present formulating proposals for the harmonization of the conditions of competition, including flight time limitations for crews, harmonization of personnel licensing arrangements and airworthiness standards. These measures are to be designed to accompany the liberalization process.

Sea transport

The first moves towards a CTP for shipping were made in 1986, with the adoption of four major regulations designed to maintain a competitive shipping sector in the EC. The key regulation liberalizes the EC's international trades and by 1993 will ensure freedom to provide shipping services to, from and between member-states. The other three regulations enable the EC to take concerted action to combat protectionism by non-EC countries, to counter unfair pricing and to establish a competitive regime for shipping in the EC. Given the fairly recent origin of these regulations, and the fact that the significance of Ireland's deep-sea shipping capacity is limited, it is fair to conclude that the EC's common shipping policy has had little, if any, impact on shipping in Ireland.

No further progress has been made by the EC Council on the proposals to allow 'cabotage' services since the adoption in December 1986 of the package of measures guaranteeing the freedom to provide shipping services. Such 'cabotage' proposals could be of interest to Ireland, particularly if opportunities were created for Irish companies to operate commercially within EC shipping markets. In the context of its proposals concerning 'positive measures' of 31 May 1989, the Commission has been taking new initiatives to maintain and develop a competitive and efficient shipping industry and to ensure the supply of competitive shipping services in the interests of Community trade.

Transport infrastructure

The EC Commission had been making efforts for over a decade to establish a specific transport infrastructure fund which would provide financial support for the implementation of transport infrastructure projects of Community interest. In June 1990, the EC Transport Council finally reach agreement in principle on the granting of financial assistance to transport infrastructure projects forming part of a three-year action programme (i.e. financing years 1990, 1991 and 1992). Obviously, given Ireland's dependence on sea and air services for access to European markets, the proceeds of this programme will be of particular interest to

Ireland, especially if it is applied to access transport services and infrastructure. It should be pointed out that, under *ad hoc* arrangements, the EC has been giving a limited amount of financial support, during the past decade, to a number of selected transport infrastructure projects of Community interest, including Irish road infrastructure projects. These *ad hoc* arrangements have been made under Article 580 of the EC Budget. The EC structural funds also provide funds for transport development. During 1989 much discussion and negotiation took place between the Irish Government and the EC Commission on the level of assistance to be provided to Ireland from the increased level of structural funds which the EC had decided should go to the less-developed regions. The base document under consideration was the Irish Government's *National Development Plan* which sets out the structural measures which Ireland proposes to implement over the years 1989 through 1993, in conjunction with the European Community structural funds, with a view to achieving the national and Community aim of greater economic and social cohesion. Considerable emphasis has been placed on transport development in the plan (Government of Ireland, 1989: chapter 3).

The EC adopted the community support framework for Ireland in October 1989 (Commission, 1989b). That framework groups the measures to be assisted under four specific areas of priorities with transport being dealt with under the priority which is described as 'measures to offset the effects of peripherality'. All types of infrastructure which will facilitate communication between Ireland and the rest of the EC are considered under the operational programme on the reduction of the effects of peripherality. The total expenditure on roads and other transport infrastructure under the 'peripherality' programme will amount to IR£ 818 million, of which IR£ 516 million will be provided by the European Regional Development Fund.

Impact on Ireland of the Common Transport Policy

It is only in the past five years that there has been any significant evidence of a CTP being put into place in the EC. To that extent it is premature to attempt to arrive at a 'balance sheet' for Ireland in terms of the impact of the EC's CTP. Nevertheless, as is evident from the foregoing review, there has been some limited evidence of EC policy measures in parts of the transport sector having some impact on Ireland, albeit that the overall impact of the CTP in Ireland would appear to have been limited.

The EC regulations that have come into force have resulted in a partial liberalization of the road haulage sector. To that extent Ireland has, on balance, probably gained net benefit through the greater penetration of the transport markets of other EC member-states. The other area of transport that has provided some net benefit to Ireland is air transport.

This package of liberalization measures agreed as part of the EC's CTP has enabled Irish airlines to expand their operations. However, from the evidence available for the other areas of transport — rail and sea in particular — it is not possible to draw any firm conclusions about the impact of the EC's CTP.

As regards infrastructure investment, Irish transport has benefited from the EC (although the funding has not come directly from the CTP). For example, investment in Irish roads has benefited considerably from ERDF funds and loans from the EIB. As regards future investment in Irish transport systems, the EC has recently adopted a community support framework which provides for further investments in a range of transport-related projects under an operational programme on the reduction of the effects of peripherality.

Looking to the future, there are some minus signs and some plus signs in terms of the likely impact of the evolving CTP (and associated policies) on Ireland. In overall terms the continued liberalization of transport is likely to make most modes of transport more competitive and to allow them to expand their trans-frontier activities (including the opening up of national transport markets to non-resident operators). However, if the EC proposals (which are still at the discussion stage) to apply VAT to both passenger fares and freight rates and to remove duty-free sales are adopted then ironically transport costs could increase. On the other hand, to the extent that the final tax harmonization package includes lower fuel and vehicle taxes, Irish transport will benefit and that, in turn, should enhance the competitive position of Irish exporters generally. It must be recognized, however, that the impact of reduced transport costs on the relative profitability of Irish industry (which is the main determinant of industrial output and a mainstay of the Irish economy) will be limited to the extent to which there is a greater reduction in transport costs in Ireland than in other countries (Economic and Social Research Institute, 1989: 52).

Bibliography

Abbati, Carlo degli (1987), 'Transport and European integration', Luxembourg: Commission of the EC.

Commission of the EC (1988), 'The economics of 1992', *European Economy*, no. 35, Brussels, March.

Commission of the EC (1989a) 'Fourth Progress Report of the Commission to the Council and the European Parliament concerning the implementation of the Commission's White Paper on the Completion of the internal market', Brussels, 20 June, Annex.

Commission of the EC (1989b), 'Community Support Framework for Ireland (1989–1993)', Brussels, 31 October.

Economic and Social Research Institute (1989), 'Medium-term review: 1989–1994', Dublin.

Ferris, Tom (1987), 'Who needs a transport policy?', Dublin: *Seirbhis Phoibli*.
Ferris, Tom (1990), 'Aspects of current Irish transport policy', UCD Conference on Infrastructure, 3—4 April, Dublin.
Government of Ireland (1989), 'National Development Plan: 1989—1993', submitted to the European Commission on 22 March 1989, PL 6342, Dublin.

Chapter 9

Energy policy
Rory O'Donnell

Introduction

Although policies in the energy area were of considerable significance in the development of the European Communities there are a number of reasons why the effects of energy policy are not among the significant gains or losses from Ireland's membership. These reasons relate to the nature of Community energy policy — especially in the period since Ireland joined in 1973 — and the insignificance of Ireland as an energy producer or consumer. In this short entry we report the main features of Community and Irish energy policy and identify the effects of Community membership for Ireland.

Community energy policy

1956 to 1973

Although progress in the field of energy at the Community level has been very limited there can be no doubt that problems in the energy sector were among those which loomed large in the early stages of European integration. In particular, several members of the original Six were confronted with a series of economic and social problems arising from the run down of the coal industry in the face of imported oil. The response of national governments to this was to subsidize coal production and, in some cases, to take action to reduce dependence on imported oil. Not surprisingly then, early action to create a Community energy policy consisted of proposals for a co-ordinated system of state-aids or subsidies — to avoid the most gross distortions of competition — and action to promote the civilian utilization of nuclear energy through the formation of the European Atomic Energy Community (EURATOM).

Although subsidies for coal production generally, and subsidies for coal and coke production for the steel industry, in particular, have been a part of the Community energy scene ever since, these are primarily *national* rather than Community supports and reflect national energy and regional policies (Swann, 1988). In the pursuit of reduced dependence on imported oil, and reduced exposure to fluctuations in oil supplies, the Community made limited progress through EURATOM and, in 1968, adopted directives requiring member-states to hold oil stocks equal to 65 days' consumption (later extended to 90 days).

Community policy since 1973

After the oil crisis of 1973 the motivation for a Community energy policy was quite different. Instead of oil being too cheap relative to coal, it was both uncertain in supply and increasingly expensive. The immediate crisis revealed the lack of solidarity within the Community; indeed, the OECD-based International Energy Agency (IEA) — established in 1974 — had a more developed and automatic oil-sharing scheme than the EC. Within the Community, what sharing of oil supplies did take place was implemented by the large multinational oil companies (El Agraa, 1985).

Since then there have been three strands to Community energy policy (Swann, 1988). The first was the adoption of Community energy targets and balance sheets to ensure that import dependence is reduced. Although the major responsibility for meeting these targets lies with member-states, the Community has provided financial support — from the EC budget, the New Community Instrument and the European Investment Bank (EIB) — to promote alternatives to oil, especially coal, atomic energy and renewable energy sources. Second, the EC has implemented policies to encourage a rational use of energy, which are concerned with both energy saving and energy pricing, and consist of directives on the thermal efficiency in buildings, support for demonstration projects and endorsement by the Council of Ministers of the principle of realistic energy pricing. The third strand of the Community's energy policy consists of provision for emergency measures.

Irish policy goals

It is possible to identify a number of Irish energy policy objectives, over and above that which is shared by all countries — ensuring adequate supply. One of the most important of these has, traditionally, been the desire to achieve widespread electrification of rural Ireland and to ensure sufficient electricity-generating capacity. Since the foundation of the state these aims were pursued by means of state intervention.

Indigenous energy sources

Although independent Ireland has always imported most of its energy supplies a definite policy goal has been the development of indigenous energy sources. In pursuit of this policy a state-owned company, Bord na Mona, was formed in 1946 to develop and market Ireland's extensive peat deposits. The state-owned electricity generating company supported this policy by building a number of peat-burning generating stations.

The discovery of natural gas off Kinsale in 1974 created new demands on Ireland's energy policy system coming, as it did, in the middle of the 1973/4 oil crisis (Convery, Scott and McCarthy, 1983). Since then the promotion of indigenous supply has focused on this gas field and its use.

Adaptation and conservation

The oil crises of 1973 and 1979 caused Ireland, like other countries, to see the need for adaptation away from fossil fuels. A main thrust of energy policy is to enable this adaptation to happen in a smooth manner. Adaptation includes conservation, and the latter has been an important declared policy objective in Ireland. However, while government has encouraged conservation through exhortation and grants this has, to some extent, been cancelled out by its pricing and tax policies which — by keeping the price of energy and energy-using appliances relatively low — has encouraged energy consumption (Scott, 1980).

A final element of Irish energy policy concerns nuclear power. While Ireland had intended, in the 1970s, to build its own nuclear power plant, policy is now somewhat anti-nuclear. In response to public anxiety about emissions from nuclear power and reprocessing plants on the west coast of Britain, the Irish Government has sought re-assurances from Britain and, in the absence of these, has attempted to influence Community policy on nuclear safety.

Gains and losses to Ireland

It should be clear from these notes on Community and Irish energy policy goals that the effects of Community membership have been positive, but not very significant. First, a major part of Community energy policy — that concerned with the run down of coal-producing regions — was of almost no relevance to Ireland. Second, the Community had very weak solidarity and policy when its member-states, including Ireland, faced energy crises in 1973 and 1979. Third, we should expect that a Community energy policy, however well developed, would have limited significance for Ireland because Ireland is, by Community standards, a very small consumer and producer of energy.

However, when we consider the Community's energy policy since the oil crisis we find a number of effects on Ireland. Community policy to reduce dependence on oil and, in particular, its promotion of alternatives to oil, has complemented Ireland's attempt to develop its indigenous energy sources. Ireland has received EC financial assistance for the exploitation of peat and natural gas. This has consisted of EIB loans of IR£ 35 million to Bord na Mona and IR£ 358 million to the Electricity Supply Board. In addition, Ireland received small amounts from the ERDF (Valoren Programme) and some grant support for rural electrification. The construction of a gas inter-connector between Ireland and other member-states will qualify for assistance under the EC's 'REGEN initiative' under the ERDF.

The Community's rapidly developing environmental policy has complemented Ireland's energy policy in two ways. First, since gas is now regarded as the cleanest fossil fuel it has reinforced the Community's interest in gas. Second, Ireland has benefited from Community assistance for projects in energy research, and demonstration projects in areas such as energy conservation technologies, coal utilization, substitution of hydrocarbons, solar energy, biomass, wind power, geothermal energy and hydroelectric installations. EC finance of some IR£ 25 million has been paid towards Irish projects, and a new programme for 1990–4 – entitled Thermie – was adopted by the Energy Council in May 1990. Other effects of Community environmental policy are discussed in Chapter 10.

Assessment

While membership of the Community has not greatly affected Ireland's energy situation it should be clear that the effects of Community energy policy on Ireland have generally been positive. Although Community policy is not highly developed it has tended to complement Irish energy policy goals. In particular, the Community's interest in promoting alternatives to oil has implied some Community support for Ireland's attempt to develop its indigenous energy sources: peat and natural gas. However, it is important that the scale of these effects be kept in perspective, relative to the effects of the internal market, the CAP, the EMS and Community regional policy.

Bibliography

Convery, F.J., Scott, S. and McCarthy, C. (1983), *Irish Energy Policy*, Dublin: National Economic and Social Council.
El Agraa, A.M. (1985), 'Energy policy', in A.M. El Agraa (ed.), *The Economics of the European Community*, London: Philip Allen.

Scott, S. (1980), *Energy Demand in Ireland, Projections and Policy Issues*, Dublin: Economic and Social Research Institute.
Swann, D. (1988), *The Economics of the Common Market*, London: Penguin.

Chapter 10
Environmental policy
Rory O'Donnell

Introduction

In this chapter we explore the relationship between Community environmental policy and Irish policy. We begin by describing the development of Community policy in this area and note that other Community policies, such as agricultural, regional and energy policies, have significant effects on the environment. We then outline Ireland's environmental policy and identify the environmental issues which have surfaced in Irish political and policy debate. In the final section we assess the impact of Community policy on Ireland. We find that, for a number of reasons, the effect of Community policy depends on the approach of the member-state. We also find that certain Community policies, aided and abetted by the Irish authorities, are actively damaging the Irish environment.

Community environmental policy

The Treaty of Rome did not envisage a common European environmental policy. However, like so much else, the environment was discussed in Paris in 1972, and it thereby entered the Community agenda. There followed a European action programme in 1973. Further programmes were adopted in 1977, 1983 and 1987. By the mid-1980s environmental matters were of major concern in the member-states, and hence in the EC. Only in 1986, with the revision of the Treaty by the Single European Act, did environmental policy formally enter the Community's objectives.

In 1972 the member-states agreed upon a series of environmental goals which still underpin much of Community policy. Among other things these declared that pollution should be restrained at source, that research on environmental problems should be extended, that European citizens had a right to information on pollution problems and that international discussion and co-operation on environmental topics should be encouraged. The various action programmes drawn up since 1973 have employed three sets of instruments: directives, incentives and information. The most widely used instrument has been directives, which list detailed environmental standards and which are binding on member-states.

Since 1973 the EC has issued many directives. These deal with three broad aspects of the environment: air pollution, water quality and soil improvement. In the case of air pollution, directives have set out norms and standards for emissions from traffic, nuclear and non-nuclear electricity generation, noise emissions and other dangers. The Community's directives on the improvement of water have established norms for both household activities and industrial processes. The directives set out quality standards for different types and uses of water, including drinking water, swimming and fresh-water fish. A third group of directives are designed to achieve improvement in the quality of the soil. These lay down norms for emissions into the soil and standards for the use and handling of chemicals.

In considering the environmental impact of the EC it is important to consider not only the Community's stated policy on the environment but also the environmental impact of all its policies. The Community policies which are likely to have had significant environmental effects are the Common Agricultural Policy (CAP) and energy policy. While these are dealt with in two other contributions (Chapters 3 and 9 respectively) it is appropriate to note here that they may well have had effects which contradict, and greatly exceed, those of the Community's environmental policy. Community energy policy has traditionally encouraged alternatives to oil — including the generation of electricity by burning coal. The artificially high agricultural prices created by the CAP induced farmers in several countries to bring more land into production and to produce intensively, thus destroying wildlife habitats and creating effluent and fertilizer pollution.

Until 1986 Community action in the area of the environment took place under the residual powers conferred by Article 235 of the Treaty of Rome. The Single European Act provided for three Articles on the environment to be added to the Treaty. Article 130R sets out the objectives of Community environmental policy (to preserve, protect and improve the quality of the environment; to contribute towards protecting human health; and to ensure a prudent and rational utilization of natural resources), the principles upon which Community action shall be based (similar to those of 1972) and the factors (scientific and regional) which are to be taken into account in formulating policy. Article 130S provides that action on the environment shall require unanimity at the Council of Ministers. Article 130T provides that member-states may introduce more stringent measures than those adopted by the Community.

Ireland's objectives and policy

Background

For a variety of reasons environmental matters have not figured significantly in Irish political or policy debate. Conflict over use of natural resources, which frequently underlies environmental issues, took a very specific form in Ireland — the struggle to achieve ownership of the land. This having been achieved, the society was not receptive to internal challenges to the rights of owner-occupiers. In addition, Ireland did not experience the great growth of industry which, in many other European countries, damaged the environment and forced environmental issues onto the agenda. On the contrary, the major public policies of the independent Irish state were concerned to *increase* population, energy generation, the intensity of agricultural production and the level of industrial activity.

Even in the period since accession to the EC it is hard to identify a clear profile of Irish environmental objectives and policy. This should not be surprising given that a survey of European attitudes to the environment found the Irish to have a low level of environmental awareness and concern. The uncertain place of an environment policy in the public policy system was reflected in the arrangements for the formation and implementation of policy. The Department of the Environment is so called, not because it has responsibility for all environmental policy, but because its original title, the Department of Local Government, would be too ironic given the virtual abolition of democratic local government. It has responsibility for water, sewage and physical planning. Responsibility for the natural environment has migrated from nowhere, through the departments of agriculture, forestry, energy and the marine, and has now settled in the Office of Public Works. This reflects a desire to have a single body deal with all matters of the national 'heritage': inland waterways, national monuments, national parks and, now, wildlife. It can be argued that this is a beneficial arrangement, since it guarantees that these environmental matters are not handled by a department which simultaneously, and predominantly, wants to maximize infrastructural investment and is subject to pressures to allow local 'development'.

Policy issues

Four environmental issues have attracted some interest and have, as a result, entered the political realm. However, the first of these has entered *foreign* policy rather than domestic politics. Anxiety over emissions from nuclear power and reprocessing plants on the west coast of Britain has transmitted itself to politicians who have raised this matter both bilaterally and at Community level (see Chapter 9 on energy policy).

Second, a number of local groups have raised objections to the location of foreign-owned chemical plants. Third, very severe smog in Dublin has, in recent years, become a highly contentious issue. Finally, serious river pollution from farming has threatened those involved in tourism.

With the exception of the first, these are the kinds of issues which the clientilist Irish political system finds it most difficult to deal with — since they involve conflicts which cannot be resolved on an individual basis, or in everyone's favour (see Chapters 20 and 21). However, the past few years have seen favourable developments. The Minister for Industry has indicated that environmental standards will apply to foreign firms — even though they have the backing of the, hitherto, all-powerful, Industrial Development Authority. Some restrictions will be applied on the burning of coal in Dublin; and tougher legislation on agricultural pollution has been passed.

Gains and losses to Ireland

One might assess the gains and losses of Community membership by asking whether Community environmental policy has imposed weaker or tougher standards than Irish policy, and used similar means to achieve environmental objectives. However, given the nature of both Community and national policy, this approach bears little fruit. In general, we find that the many Community directives impose tougher standards than those *in Irish law*. In some cases this has, indeed, brought about improvements in the environment in Ireland. However, in many other cases the relatively unpolluted nature of Ireland means that, regardless of the absence of previous Irish legislation, Ireland already achieved EC standards. Furthermore, many EC directives — such as those on low emission cars and large combustion plants — lay down norms and standards which apply to machinery and installations, rather than behaviour. Ireland tends to import most such machinery and, therefore, obeys the directives automatically. Finally, and most fundamentally, the process of comparing EC directives with Irish legislation misses the main issues.

The three most important issues are the following. First, in the many areas where the Community has issued directives the crucial question in Ireland is *implementation* and *enforcement*. Second, many of the most pressing environmental issues in Ireland are not covered by firm EC directives, but only by Community aspirations. Here national policy, and its interaction with other Community policies, is crucial. Third, some of the environmental problems, and Ireland's policy approach to them, reflect *social* and *economic* problems which require much more than an environment policy for their solution.

Implementation and enforcement

Ireland has a very poor record in implementing and enforcing EC environmental directives. This is not to say that Ireland has a filthy environment — for the reasons outlined above, this is not so — but that those directives which would make a difference are passed into legislation extremely slowly. Then, having become law, the standards are frequently not achieved.

An example is the 1985 directive on environmental impact assessments. Having been canvassed in the Community since the early 1980s, and passed into EC law in 1985, this directive disappeared in Ireland until 1989. Another striking example is the directive on access to environmental information, and many other examples could be cited. While lack of administrative resources may be part of the explanation (see Chapter 20 on government and public policy-making), it seems hard to avoid the conclusion that a conscious effort has been made to forestall any environmental consideration which would interfere with, or even complicate, conventional economic measures — and especially those which might attract support from the structural funds. While there can, of course, be genuine conflicts between economic and environmental objectives, there is a marked tendency to confuse economic objectives with maximization of receipts from the structural funds.

However, where the EC has issued a directive which contains clear norms and standards this is ultimately implemented and can, eventually, be enforced. In several cases this enforcement has required complaints to the Commission, and even legal action.

Aspirations rather than directives

On many subjects Community environmental policy consists more of aspirations than a common policy. Indeed, this can be said of the articles on the environment inserted into the Treaty. It also applies to those bits of environmental policy written into the structural funds and the CAP. Frequently these say that environmental considerations should be 'taken into account' in pursuing national and Community policies. In these cases, Community environmental policy, such as it is, is largely dependent on the attitude of the member-state. It so happens that several very important environmental problems in Ireland arise in this looser area of Community policy, rather than in the areas covered by firm directives. Examples are the problems of soil erosion on the west coast, the registration and preservation of habitats of scientific interest, and the disappearance of peat lands.

In all these cases, and several others, national or Community policy, or both, are directly contributing to environmental destruction. Headage payments for sheep, a special EC support for farmers in disadvantaged areas, is encouraging overstocking on the western hills, and will eventually erode the soil. Addition of new parts of Ireland to the Community's Register of Habitats of Scientific Interest now seem to be resisted by some government departments — on the grounds that it might make the Commission less willing to provide financial support for afforestation. The EC has provided support first for the extraction, and lately for afforestation of Irish peat bogs. Although some Directorates General show considerable interest in these Irish environments, Community policy, as a whole, is harmful to them. This reflects the fact that, to date, the hard core of Community environmental policy is concerned with industrial and agricultural pollution. While this is entirely appropriate in many member-states, it addresses only very partially the environmental problems in less-developed peripheral countries.

Economic problems and conflicts

These and other environmental problems reflect underlying economic and social problems. Consequently, their solution will require more than just an environment policy. A perfect example of this is the soil erosion on Ireland's western hills as a result of overstocking of sheep. The Community's headage payments were intended to address a serious problem: the low incomes of many farmers in disadvantaged areas. This is one instance of a widespread problem in Irish society: the persistence of a sizeable segment of agriculture showing very low farm incomes. This phenomenon is related to the existence of structural problems. A recent study of Ireland's performance and prospects in the EC showed that these structural problems were not, and probably could not, have been reduced by the CAP, and yet they were not seriously addressed by national socio-structural policy. While there is an undoubted Community dimension to the solution of these problems they require, first and foremost, new approaches at the national level.

Assessment

In general, Community environmental directives imply more rigorous environmental standards than existing Irish legislation. However, this statement does not comprehend the key issues concerning EC policy in Ireland. In many areas where the Community has issued directives the crucial question in Ireland is implementation and enforcement. Ireland has a very poor record in implementing and enforcing EC environmental directives. There is some reason to fear that this reflects official reluctance to interfere with conventional economic measures, such as infrastructural projects or investment incentives. However, many of the most pressing environmental issues in Ireland are not covered by firm EC directives.

Indeed, some of these problems are created, or at least aggravated, by other Community policies — such as the CAP and structural funds. Finally, these and other environmental problems often reflect underlying social and economic problems and pressures. Consequently, it would be hopeless, and indefensible, to try to solve them by environmental policies alone, without relieving the underlying social and economic pressures.

Chapter 11
Fiscal and taxation policy
Rory O'Donnell

Introduction

If we define fiscal policy as that concerned with the generation of public revenues and allocation of public expenditures then fiscal policy covers a very wide range of policy instruments. In this sense fiscal policy covers everything which is not either monetary policy or direct regulation. Since most of the components of public expenditure are discussed in detail in the individual entries on economic policies (such as industrial policy, energy policy and transport policy) and on social, educational and cultural policy (for example social security, education and training), we do not adopt this broad definition of fiscal policy in this chapter. Fiscal policy is often defined more narrowly, by reference to the goal of macroeconomic stabilization by means of public finance. Because the impact of EC membership on Ireland's stabilization policy is discussed in the chapter on monetary policy (Chapter 5) we do not deal with stabilization in this contribution. Our concern is primarily with the implications of EC membership for national taxation policies. However, because we are interested in the Community as an emerging *fiscal system* we are reluctant to define the scope of this chapter as taxation policy alone.

The first section surveys the Community's fiscal and taxation policies by noting the extent of convergence, achieved or proposed, in sales taxes, excise duties, corporation taxes and taxes on savings. Section two summarizes the main elements of Irish tax policy and the main features of Ireland's tax system. The final section assesses the effects of Community membership on Ireland's taxation system. To date, these effects are limited and, consequently, much of our discussion focuses on the programme of indirect tax harmonization likely to emerge by 1992. It is not sufficiently recognized that the completion of the internal market will increase the existing pressure for approximation of income and other *direct* taxes in the Community. We close our discussion with an analysis of this, and its implications for the public finance system of the Community as a whole.

Community fiscal/taxation policy

Introduction

At the establishment of the Community the member-countries had very different tax systems. Thus both tax bases and tax rates differed across countries in the five main types of tax: sales tax, excises, corporation tax, personal taxation and social security taxes. Of these five types of taxation the Community can only be said to have a common fiscal/taxation policy in the case of sales taxes, excises and corporation tax. This is because these three can be seen, fairly easily, to have significant implications for the operation and efficiency of the common market. In fact, achievement of a genuine and effective common market and monetary union probably requires a much greater degree of fiscal harmonization than has been recognized to date. This issue is considered in the final section; our intention here is to report the main elements of existing or proposed Community fiscal or taxation policy.

Sales taxes

The creation of the common market required the participating countries to adopt a somewhat similar approach to sales or consumption taxes. The problem did not initially lie in the differences in indirect tax *rates* between member-states; for an approach to taxing goods traded internationally can be adopted — known as the destination principle — which does not lead to any distortion of competition between countries. Instead, the problem lay in the fact that Community countries used two quite different approaches: levying sales or turnover taxes in the 'cascade' and 'value added' systems. The cascade system had a number of drawbacks which impelled the Community to insist that all member-states adopted the value added system. Thus in 1967 directives were adopted laying down that all existing and future member-states must adopt the value added, or VAT, system. Since then, further progress was made towards a Community indirect tax policy. As the Community's own resources came to be drawn more and more from the VAT levied in each member-state, it became clear that the VAT base should be similar in each country. In 1977 a directive was adopted which significantly harmonized the VAT base.

The most recent developments all derive from the decision to complete the internal market by 1992. As was seen in Chapter 2 this involves the removal of all remaining physical, technical and fiscal barriers to the movement of goods between member-countries. In its famous 1985 White Paper, *Completing the Internal Market*, the Commission argued that this requires three developments in the area of VAT. First, the base needs to be fully harmonized by removing the remaining gaps and derogations in certain member-states. Second, the number of rates needs to be harmonized — some countries have only one rate while others have four. Third, the actual tax *rates* need to be harmonized.

It is most important to understand why the harmonization of VAT rates is considered necessary for the completion of the internal market. In the present VAT system — based on the destination principle — the documentation of imports and exports by the customs authorities plays an important role in adjusting VAT so that each good bears only the tax in force in the country in which it is consumed. But there can be little doubt that achievement of a genuine common internal market now requires that customs barriers be removed — since these are an undoubted obstacle to trade. The question then becomes: how can adjustment of VAT on exports and imports be achieved without customs documentation? The Commission argued that whatever system was devised could only work if VAT rates and VAT coverage in the member-states were much closer than they are at present. Thus it proposed harmonization, or at least approximation, of VAT rates. Others argued that an administrative system, for adjusting VAT on commercial exports and imports, could be devised which would work without customs frontiers and without uniformity in VAT rates (Lee, Pearson and Smith, 1988). Although the author sides with the Commission on this issue, this discussion does bring to light two facts which have greatly complicated the recent debate on VAT harmonization. First, harmonization of VAT rates is not, in general, an end in itself but merely a means to an end, i.e. the removal of customs frontiers. Second, the case for harmonization of VAT rates — a major political argument within the Community — turns on a particular judgment on an administrative issue (how to deal with VAT on exports and imports without the use of customs documentation) about which most political leaders will have no opinion. Given its belief that VAT rates must be harmonized, the Commission put forward a detailed plan in 1987. This proposed that member-states operate only two rates of VAT: a standard rate between 14 and 20 per cent and a 'reduced' rate between 4 and 9 per cent, and that zero rates, particularly prevalent in Ireland and the United Kingdom, be abolished. These proposals met serious opposition from member-states, among whom the United Kingdom was the most vocal. The objections varied from loss of national sovereignty, fear of loss of revenue, to fear of political unpopularity. Since the Single European Act had not extended majority voting to fiscal matters, the Commission's original proposals were doomed. In May 1989 the Commission presented revised proposals, suggesting that member-states set any standard rate, subject to a *minimum* of 15 per cent, a reduced rate between 4 and 9 per cent, and retain zero rates on certain items. This involved a major concession to the British case for a more 'market-led' approach to VAT harmonization. These revised proposals are the subject of continuing negotiation at the Council of Finance Ministers.

Excise duties

Different member-states impose very different rates of excise duties on mineral oils, tobacco products and alcohol. These differences undermine the EC internal market in three ways. First, the duties do not apply to exports, and imports of these goods arrive duty free. This system relies on border checks to validate the export and import of dutiable items. Customs frontiers are a non-tariff barrier to trade. Second, differences in excise duties on mineral oils, or other inputs to production, influence the cost of production and therefore distort competition between member-states. Third, differences in excise rates on different products within any particular country can distort competition by taxing imported goods more heavily than domestically produced ones.

As early as 1972 the Commission proposed the harmonization of excise duties, but little progress was made. In its 1985 White Paper on the completion of the internal market the Commission proposed that, after the abolition of frontiers, a new system of administrative control of dutiable products be introduced, along with a considerable measure of approximation of rates of excise duty. In general, the Commission proposed that the new rates on tobacco, mineral oils and alcohol be arithmetic *averages* of existing rates in member-states.

These proposals also met with strong opposition from member-states. The motivation differed depending on whether the proposed duties implied increased or decreased tax revenue for the state in question. In its revised tax harmonization proposals the Commission acknowledged that more flexibility was necessary in order to take account of different rates of tax in member-states — differences which reflect varying priorities accorded to health (alcohol and tobacco), energy conservation and the environment (petroleum products). Consequently, the Commission proposed that the Community policy should specify permissable *ranges* of tax, or minimum rates, rather than precise rates. These proposals are also the subject of ongoing negotiation.

Corporation taxes

It has long been recognized that differences in member-states' approach to the taxation of companies undermines the internal market. First, differences in the rate of corporation tax can induce capital to move from high-tax to low-tax countries, so distorting the allocation of capital. Second, differences in the way in which national systems deal with the taxation of distributed and undistributed profits can imply different degrees of double taxation of dividends. Third, national liquidation taxes and taxes on capital gains can inhibit cross-border mergers and so inhibit the business integration which is an important part of European economic integration. These factors were implicitly recognized in Article

100 of the Treaty of Rome. It noted that approximation of laws may be necessary where discrepancies in the rate of tax, or its method of operation, create distortions in the free movement of capital. Although these problems were recognized at an early stage, the Community has not succeeded in devising a common policy. In 1969 the Commission sent two draft directives to the Council concerning double taxation and mergers. In 1975 the Commission submitted to Council a draft directive on the harmonization of national rates and systems of company taxation; to date none of these directives have been adopted. The urgency of developing a common approach is greatly increased by the recent and impending liberalization of capital movements.

Taxation of savings

Differences in national taxes on the interest accruing to savings accounts can clearly create distortions once money can be moved freely between member-states. In 1989 the Commission accompanied its directive on capital liberalization with proposals for harmonization of national systems for the taxation of savings. The Commission proposed that all member-states apply a 15 per cent withholding tax to interest income, and that member-states strengthen their co-operation to counter tax evasion. The proposed 15 per cent rate, which represents an approximate average of national rates, will be a minimum rate, with states free to impose a higher rate if they wish.

Ireland's fiscal/taxation policy

A state's fiscal or taxation policy reflects its economic and social policies and priorities in a very definite way. Yet looking at the taxation policies in force in Ireland during much of the period of EC membership it is difficult to identify any coherent underlying policy approach. This is the case because, from a certain point in the late 1970s onwards, the Irish tax system evolved by a series of accidents, dictated by political expediency, rather than by design. When this approach led to uncontrollable increases in government deficits and national debt the tax system evolved in response to the imperative of debt reduction. In neither phase would it make much sense to compare Community taxation policy, such as it is, with Irish taxation *policy*.

Perhaps the main policy approach in the Irish taxation system has been that which derives from the state's industrial policy. A major instrument in the package of industrial policy measures assembled in the mid-1960s was the relief from all taxation of profits earned on manufactured exports. This Export Profit Tax Relief (EPTR) is widely agreed to be an important factor in bringing a relatively large number of foreign manufacturing firms to Ireland. One effect of this policy is that taxes on corporations yield a small percentage of total revenue.

A number of other notable features of Irish tax policy can be identified. The first of these is a very heavy reliance on taxes on earned income — especially that of employees — and taxes on expenditure. In addition, there has been a prolonged difficulty, or perhaps reluctance, to incorporate farm incomes into the tax system in a normal way. An important element, since the abolition of domestic rates in the late 1970s, has been the absence of a comprehensive property tax — pushing the tax burden onto earned income. Finally, and perhaps most significantly, ever since the great wave of expediency in the 1970s and early 1980s, the Irish tax system has contained a plethora of allowances, reliefs and exemptions which dramatically erode the tax base and necessitate high tax rates (see NESC, 1987).

Gains and losses of Community membership

Two policy changes

Membership of the Community has brought about two definite changes in Irish taxation policy. First, Ireland had to adopt the value added approach to the taxation of expenditure. This should be viewed as a gain to Ireland — though hardly a significant one. Second, Ireland's export profit tax relief involved an implicit subsidy to manufacturing firms exporting from Ireland. This direct support to Irish exports was viewed as possibly contrary to the Treaty of Rome, and Irish policy was changed accordingly. The zero tax rate on manufactured *exports* was replaced by 10 per cent rate of tax on all manufacturing firms — whether producing for the domestic or foreign market. This still provides an important incentive to industrial development, since the normal rate of corporation tax is considerably higher than 10 per cent. In theory, this remaining industrial policy incentive could, in future, be challenged at Community level. However, it is important to recall that the Community has regional and social as well as internal market objectives and, under these, Ireland has been designated as a priority region. Unless Community regional policy was to become much more centralized than it has been to date, it is hard to see a region's own efforts at industrialization being declared illegal (see Chapter 4).

Indirect tax harmonization

The harmonization or approximation of indirect taxes, due to be achieved by 1992, will have revenue, efficiency and possibly income distribution effects in Ireland. It is possible, in a fairly general sense, to assess whether these effects will be positive or negative.

There seems little doubt that indirect tax approximation will reduce the revenue gathered by the Irish authorities. The reason is simple. In the case of VAT, Ireland will probably have to abandon its 'increased' rate of 25 per cent; this is unlikely to be compensated for by the imposition of VAT on items currently zero rated, such as food — though such an imposition, at a low VAT rate, is possible. In the case of excises, almost any approximation will tend to *reduce* the rates levied on alcohol, and other goods, in Ireland. In assessing whether this loss of revenue will be a gain or loss to Ireland it must be noted that, if the Irish state receives less revenue, then the Irish public pays less tax. Judgment will depend on whether such a reduction in tax revenue, and in public expenditure, is considered desirable or not. Given the sharp reductions in expenditure through the 1980s it is not easy to identify further areas of public provision which could be cut without pain. The Irish Government has argued that it should be compensated by the Community for the loss of revenue which will result from indirect tax approximation. We will see below that this argument, as usually presented, is untenable — but so also is the approach to tax harmonization of the Commission and the other member-states.

The efficiency effects of indirect tax approximation will depend on whether the new system of indirect taxes accords more closely with economic principles than the existing system does. Economic analysis tends to suggest that indirect taxes should be applied at a uniform rate to all goods and services, except for those on which special excises should also be levied. The new set of VAT rates, which are likely to emerge after EC approximation, will involve some move towards the desirable system. This is because there will be fewer VAT rates and some widening of the VAT base. In the case of excise taxes it is less likely that EC approximation will yield a more efficient system. This is certainly so if approximation leads to large reductions in Irish excise duties on alcohol and tobacco. There are sound economic as well as social arguments for the retention of high levels of duty in the Irish case. However, it remains impossible to predict the outcome of negotiations on indirect tax approximation.

Indirect tax harmonization will generate distributional effects in Ireland to the extent that it alters the relative prices of various goods. The greatest distributional effect would arise if Ireland's current zero VAT rate on food was abolished and a substantial rate of VAT imposed. This would decrease the absolute and relative living standards of lower-income households and, in its comprehensive study of the effects of 1992, the National Economic and Social Council has argued that compensatory welfare measures would have to be introduced by the Irish Government. Even if the zero rate of food is retained, as seems likely, the harmonization of indirect tax will generate regressive distributional effects. This will be the case because the harmonization will, almost certainly, reduce the rate of VAT on luxury items which will be of greater benefit to higher-income families.

Direct taxation

The Commission's proposals for the harmonization of taxes on savings will have a definite impact on Ireland. Given the extreme mobility of capital it seems unlikely that Ireland will be able to levy a withholding tax appreciably higher than other countries and especially the UK. This will probably imply a reduction in the rate of withholding tax and, consequently, in the revenue from this source.

However, the 1992 programme will increase not only the mobility of capital but also the mobility of persons within the Community. It is not yet sufficiently recognized that this will greatly increase the existing pressure for approximation of income and other *direct* taxes in the Community, if distortionary tax-induced migration of labour and capital are to be minimized. In the Irish case this amounts to pressure to *reduce* the high average and marginal rates of tax on earned income. This reflects the fact that at present the Irish tax system bears most heavily on mobile means of production, especially labour, and least heavily on immobile factors, such as property.

While pressure for change in Ireland's tax system is to be welcomed, it is necessary also to assess the public finance system of the Community by reference to the principles of public finance. Such an assessment reveals that the tax and expenditure system of the Community defies any rational principles (see NESC, 1989). This is a problem which has existed since the beginning, but current moves to complete the internal market, and to build an economic and monetary union, throw it into sharper relief.

Restraint on the indirect taxes which can be levied by a member-state will restrain its freedom of action for policy purposes to direct taxation. Simultaneously, the increased mobility of labour and capital will inhibit its freedom of action in relation to the rates of direct tax it can levy. In addition, moves to create economic and monetary union will constrain national public sector deficits. Thus, since the public expenditure requirements of member-states are not uniform, pressure towards uniformity of several major sources of tax revenue, when combined with Community restrictions on public sector borrowing, could force some member-states into inappropriate cuts in public expenditure. For example, the pressure to equalize major revenue raising taxes — which the Irish social partners accept as an unavoidable concomitant of integration — could frustrate the pursuit of distribution, adjustment or regional policy objectives.

The problematic aspect of current moves towards tax approximation can be understood by drawing on the concepts of *negative* and *positive* integration. Pressure for more uniformity of several major revenue sources in Community countries, in the context of non-uniformity of expenditure requirements, will both prevent the achievement of a genuine common market — by exacerbating the distortions created by spillover effects — and make even less likely the achievement of other Community objectives, such as cohesion and convergence, by limiting the pursuit of structural and redistributive policies in poorer member-states. The obvious measure of *positive* integration needed to accompany moves towards a Community taxation system is the extension of the role of the Community budget. Such an extension would serve to move the overall system of public finance in the Community in the direction dictated by rational principles and, thereby, assist the achievement of a genuine common market and of other Community objectives.

In view of these considerations its seems indisputable that moves towards tax harmonization, the restriction of the fiscal autonomy of member-states, and the co-ordination of fiscal and monetary policy, should be accompanied by an extension of the fiscal role of the Community. However, two important points must be made in this context. *First*, this argument only holds water if national indirect and direct tax systems are *actually reformed* in such a way as to make them more harmonious — so it is an argument which is as demanding on member-states as it is on the Community as a whole. *Second*, it must be emphasized that these arguments do *not* imply that the Community should engage in fiscal transfers to *compensate* individual member-states for revenue losses associated with harmonization — as has been argued by the Irish Government. Such compensation would be purely *ad hoc*, reflecting, as it would, differences in patterns of taxation in different member-states. In contrast, what is required is the development of a *permanent system* which facilitates integration by balancing the moves towards a common tax system with moves towards a shared revenue and expenditure base. This will involve the Community developing a role in certain expenditure programmes — chosen by reference to the most rigorous principles of public finance — which are currently under unco-ordinated national control.

Conclusion

In this chapter we have surveyed Community fiscal and taxation policy and assessed its impact on Ireland. We have found that the impact of Community membership on Irish taxation policy has, to date, been fairly minor — consisting mainly of a switch to a value added system of sales tax and some modification of fiscal incentives offered to manufacturing industry. However, the completion of the internal market will see major developments in Community fiscal policy which will have significant implications for Ireland. The most definite of these developments will be in the area of indirect tax. The harmonization, or approximation, of indirect tax in the Community will facilitate the removal of frontier controls and will move the Irish system of indirect tax in a desirable direction, but it will also create problems: in particular, a loss of revenue. In addition, the completion of the internal market will increase the pressures for approximation of direct taxes — especially withholding taxes, corporation taxes and income tax — a fact which is not sufficiently recognized or understood in the Community. This evolution towards a Community system of taxation, which will, in many respects, be a highly positive development, could have very harmful effects on some memberstates if it is not accompanied by development of the Community budget. In this way the Community could develop an overall system of public finance which accords more closely with rational principles and which is similar to that found in existing economic and monetary unions. These considerations underline once again the main finding of the modern economics of integration — the close links between economic integration, monetary union and fiscal harmonization (Robson, 1987; NESC, 1989).

Bibliography

Lee, C., Pearson, M. and Smith, S. (1988), *Fiscal Harmonisation: An analysis of the European Commission's proposals*, IFS Report no. 28, London: Institute for Fiscal Studies.

NESC (1987), *A Strategy for Development, 1986–1990*, National Economic and Social Council, Dublin: Government Publications Sales Office.

NESC (1989), *Ireland in the European Community: Performance, prospects and strategy*, Dublin: National Economic and Social Council.

Robson, P. (1987), *The Economics of International Integration*, London: Allen and Unwin.

Chapter 12
Technology policy
Rory O'Donnell

Introduction

Community policy in the area of science and technology developed slowly but is now an important element on the EC's agenda. This slow development of active Community involvement, and the nature of that involvement, mean this area of Community policy has not, to date, generated a significant proportion of the gains and losses experienced by Ireland. However, Community policy may have important effects in the future. This brief entry begins by identifying the nature and scope of Community policy for science and technology. The second section outlines Ireland's objectives and policy. We conclude by identifying the effects on Ireland and assessing whether these are positive or negative.

Community science and technology policy

While the three Treaties (EEC, ECSC and EURATOM) founding the Community provided for joint research and technology projects in specific areas — nuclear energy, coal, steel and agriculture — it cannot be said that the Treaties envisage a common science and technology (S&T) policy. Like so many other declarations of Community intention the need for an EC science and technology policy was first formally identified at the Paris summit of 1972. Following a Commission memorandum the Council of Ministers adopted a programme of action, but limited resources were devoted to this. For many years European co-operation on R&D and new technology proceeded mainly outside the formal institutional and treaty framework of the Community.

Non-EC co-operation on S&T

Since the early 1970s there have been a number of research and technology programmes involving both EC and non-EC states. Examples of these programmes are COST (a general programme of shared research on traffic regulation, oceanography, astronomy, agriculture, food technology, health and the social sciences), CERN (in the field of particle physics), the European Space Agency (ESA) and AIRBUS. While some of these involve purely scientific co-operation others reflect a fairly long-standing anxiety about the technological gap between Europe and the United States.

Development of Community policy

The real birth of EC science and technology policy can be traced to the early 1980s, when this anxiety about the technological gap became acute, as a result of the severe economic difficulties in traditional industries and a patently weak position in the new dynamic high-technology sectors. The Commission proposed that establishment of Europe as a world economic power would require both the removal of barriers within the EC — to generate greater efficiency through competition and scale economics — and temporary protection of Europe's high-technology industries. In 1982 the European Council rejected this approach in favour of one which focused on specific areas of technology where the EC lagged behind, and devoted increased financial resources to programmes of collaboration. It also called for inclusion of science and technology policy in the Treaty of Rome — but endorsed further collaboration with non-Community European countries. Community S&T policy as we know it, and as it affects Ireland, flows from these decisions.

The main instrument of Community research and technology policy is the provision of financial resources to promote co-operation between industrial firms, research centres and universities in all member-states. An important feature of the policy is the so-called 'framework programme'. The framework programme is a multi-annual plan which embraces all the specific EC science and technology programmes and lays down objectives, the type of activities envisaged and the extent of the EC's financial commitment. While individual programmes, such as ESPRIT on information technology, began earlier, the first framework programme ran from 1984 to 1987. Although energy remained very significant, this programme provided extra resources for industrial research.

The revision of the Treaty of Rome by the Single European Act of 1987, added research and technological development to the Community's formal aims and competences. The new Treaty Articles declare that the Community's aim is to strengthen the scientific and technological base of European industry and to enhance its international competitiveness. It states that the EC will pursue this aim by encouraging firms, universities and research centres and by removing non-tariff barriers to business activity. Finally, the Treaty lays down that although the overall framework programme will be decided on the basis of unanimity, individual items will be subject to majority vote.

Following this Treaty revision the second framework programme was agreed in 1988, to run from 1987 to 1991. This provides for action in eight areas: quality of life, information and communication, modernization of industry, biological resources, energy, science and technology for development, marine resources and European scientific co-operation. Although the Commission wanted to allocate ECU 10.2 billion to this framework programme, the Council would only agree to assign ECU 6.5 billion — about 0.2 per cent of Community GDP.

The most famous elements of EC technology policy are individual programmes within this framework programme. The ESPRIT programme promotes co-operation in research on information technology and is jointly funded by the EC and the leading firms in this sector. The RACE programme, launched in 1985, funds research on the creation of an integrated telecommunications system for Europe. The BRITE and EURAM programmes encourage the development of new industrial technologies and materials and their adoption by European firms. Finally, the SCIENCE programme funds joint research in all fields of science by means of bursaries, research grants, training grants and co-operation contracts.

Irish science and technology policy

Three phases of policy formation

Irish S&T policy, and especially the system which formulates policy, has passed through three major phases over the past twenty years. Fitzpatrick *et al.* (1990) identify these as: an institutional phase (up to 1978), an advisory agency stage (1978 to 1987) and a central government phase (1987 to date).

The institutional phase, which began in the 1940s, was characterized by the establishment of specialized statutory state agencies in the areas of industrial research and standards, agriculture and physical planning. In practice, ministers had limited influence on these bodies, and their programmes, which tended to be long-term, were largely determined by the scientists themselves.

The advisory agency phase was one in which a new National Board for Science and Technology (NBST), responding to an OECD review of Irish policy, drew up a national programme for science and technology and strategic sectoral reports. For a number of reasons, these policy reports had less impact than expected, but the NBST did succeed in narrowing the ranges of its R&D programmes, focusing on a few key technologies, and concentrating finance on a few research centres in an effort to build critical mass (Fitzpatrick *et al.*, 1990).

In 1987 the Government reorganized the institutional structure of S&T policy by merging state agencies and centralizing many policy-making powers in government departments. With this new organizational structure policy focused on the key strategic technologies (micro-electronics, information technologies, biotechnologies and automated manufacturing technologies). The emphasis in agricultural research shifted from production support to processing and marketing. In the past year the natural resource areas, such as forestry, marine and food, were added to the list of S&T priorities.

Features of Ireland's R&D activity

Gross expenditure on research and development in Ireland, at almost 1 per cent of GDP, is low by EC standards. This reflects a poor R&D performance in all three sectors: government, business and higher education. However, business outlay on R&D has grown dramatically since 1985 — a period of government retrenchment. Ireland's priorities seem to differ somewhat from other member-states, with no R&D outlay on defence, a higher proportion on industrial production and technology, on agriculture and on social structures.

The low absolute level of R&D activity reflects important features of the Irish economy. A 1985 OECD report on innovation policy in Ireland concluded that 'in terms of innovative orientation Ireland is currently ranked in the bottom quartile of industrialized countries' (OECD, 1985). This is explained by the structure of Irish industry — discussed at some length in a number of chapters in this volume (see Chapters 1, 2 and 7). The low level of R&D on the part of indigenous industry — consisting of small firms trapped in low-technology markets — tends not to be compensated for by foreign-owned industry, which mostly consists of assembly branch plants of corporations who conduct research elsewhere.

Gains and losses to Ireland

An important part of current Community science and technology policy is the initiation of review and evaluation in order to assess the strengths and weaknesses of the policy and to monitor its implementation at national and Community level. Evaluating R&D programmes is not a simple quantitative task, since many of the benefits of research are indirect and long-term — especially its impact on innovation. However, a recent review of the impact of Community policy on Ireland concludes that the policy has brought benefits and that these outweigh the costs (Fitzpatrick *et al.*, 1990). Nevertheless, the study reveals that there are considerable limitations to Ireland's involvement in Community R&D

programmes and to the benefits which these can confer on Ireland. In this final section we briefly explain these findings.

Definite gains

At a most basic level the Community's framework programme for R&D has involved the transfer of significant financial resources to Ireland — nearly ECU 39 million, IR£ 30 million, over the period 1984—8. This constitutes about 5 per cent of total national R&D spending and about 10 per cent of Ireland's official science budget. The consultants undertaking the evaluation considered that 'this resource transfer has, in turn, facilitated a level of research activity in Ireland considerably in excess of what would otherwise have occurred' (Fitzpatrick *et al.*, 1990).

Furthermore, the impact or leverage of this transfer is much larger than these figures might suggest, since EC funding constitutes a much higher proportion of the *discretionary* R&D resources of many public sector bodies, i.e. resources not committed to overheads, salaries, etc. So while Community policy 'has not made any significant economic impact on Ireland', it has had a positive effect on Ireland's technological base by facilitating the upgrading of Irish S&T, the development of new high-technology programmes and centres, the training of Irish researchers and the continuation of R&D at a time of severe national budgetary constraints. A major benefit to Irish researchers has been the development of new R&D co-operation, which has helped shift their focus away from the United States and the United Kingdom, towards other EC countries.

The review also concluded that the first and second Community framework programmes had significant, and generally positive, effects on Irish policy and attitudes — both by influencing stated national policy and by promoting specific R&D activities on the ground. In particular, EC policy reinforced the NBST's advice on international technological trends and provided the broad high-technology focus that underlies all such programmes since the mid-1980s. On the ground, participation in ESPRIT, by far the most important programme for Irish researchers, has encouraged the development of three major centres of excellence in information technology.

Finally, one possible negative effect of Community S&T policy, which was feared in 1984, seems not to have occurred. Fitzpatrick *et al.* found little evidence that Community policy had reinforced the pronounced emigration of scientific and technological personnel from Ireland.

It is important that the effects of S&T programmes are not measured by purely quantifiable, and especially financial magnitudes. The aim of Community policy is to improve the technological level of the European economy and, ultimately, to increase the rate of innovation. Innovation is a dynamic process, dependent on a wide range of factors, which has dynamic effects on the economy and society. It is possible, therefore, that

EC policy will have effects which go well beyond any transfer of funds or increase in the number of programmes, researchers or centres. It is difficult, if not impossible, to measure these dynamic effects but, as will be seen below, there are reasons to believe that, to date, they are not very significant in Ireland.

Qualifications

The undoubted benefits to Ireland of Community technology policy must be qualified in a number of ways. The recent review indicates that 'during the 1984—88 period there was limited direct commercial output or impact on Irish industry arising from the Programme' (Fitzpatrick *et al.*, 1990). Furthermore, the review indicates the reason for this, which in turn reveals some major limitations on the effectiveness of Community policy in Ireland. It is important that these issues be taken into account when assessing Community and national policy and devising new approaches.

The limited commercial impact of Community policy arises from the nature of Irish involvement in Community programmes. An important finding was that most Irish participation in the framework programme has involved non-commercial public-sector bodies. This pattern of involvement results from both the nature of the Community policy and the nature of the Irish industrial and R&D base. First, Community policy is designed to improve the technological competitiveness of the leading EC industries and firms. As such, the framework programme reflects the needs and priorities of large multinational corporations rather than those of a small, peripheral, less-developed member-state like Ireland. Second, the preponderance of non-commercial public-sector bodies among Irish participants reflects those features of the Irish R&D base discussed earlier: the low absolute level of R&D effort in Irish industry, the preponderance of small firms, the concentration in low-technology sectors and the remarkable role played by foreign-owned branch plants in the Irish industrial structure. Thus there is a genuine sense in which Community policy is not suited to Irish needs and Irish industry is not suited to Community policy (Fitzpatrick *et al.*, 1990).

These limitations on the effectiveness of Community R&D policy call for careful thought about future policy at both national and EC level. First, as the recent review says, the framework programme 'cannot be expected to alone provide answers to all technological and economic gaps, i.e. it cannot be blamed for not achieving objectives which it is not designed to achieve' (Fitzpatrick *et al.*, 1990). It can be argued, however, that to date Community R&D policy has not focused sufficiently on natural resources. Second, as in most developmental problems, there is an element of cumulative causation in the technological position of Ireland: structurally weak firms cannot invest in R&D and find it hard to innovate but, without new technologies and innovation, they cannot become structurally stronger. In this sense technology policy confronts the same problems that industrial policy and regional policy confront (see Chapters 7 and 4). But it is important that they do not just replicate one another for, as Fitzpatrick *et al.* say, 'action to overcome more than one aspect of the problem at the same time is clearly required.'

One immediate implication of these findings and arguments is that elements of overall Community science and technology policy, *other than* research and development programmes, may be of greater potential significance to Ireland. For example, the STRIDE programme (to encourage science and technology transfer for regional development) and the SPRINT programme (to encourage transfer of technology to small firms and less-developed regions) seem, on the face of it, more suited to Ireland's science and technology needs. However, to date, the contribution of the SPRINT programme has been very low — a fraction of Ireland's receipts from ESPRIT, RACE or BRITE.

This observation brings us to another possible limitation of Community S&T policy — indeed, of all Community policies with financial instruments. It is possible that the science and technology activity of a small country like Ireland could be tailored to maximize the receipt of EC funding. Where the Community policy in question is not ideally suited to Irish needs this could induce a distortion of national policy. Avoidance of this problem, which could have very harmful direct and indirect effects, requires clear national policy analysis and an understanding among policy-makers and the public that financial receipts from the EC are among the least significant effects of Community membership.

Assessment

A recent review indicates that the scientific and technological impact of the Community's framework programme is positive. 'Ireland would do less research and would have less researchers, less state-of-the-art R&D programmes and less international R&D partnerships, if there were no framework programmes' (Fitzpatrick *et al.*, 1990). However, it is also clear that Community policy has had a limited role in meeting Ireland's needs. This is most clearly demonstrated by the fact that Irish participation in EC programmes and projects consists, very largely, of non-commercial public-sector bodies. This means that the programmes yield very little direct commercial output and have a very limited impact on Irish industry. The low rate of participation of Irish firms reflects both the nature of Community policy and the nature of Ireland's R&D base. Community policy has been framed to meet European needs, which differ significantly from Ireland's. Ireland's poor R&D base reflects a weak industrial structure (see Chapters 1 and 2). Technology policy must be linked with industrial policy and regional policy if they are to succeed in breaking the vicious circle of industrial weakness, relative technological backwardness and regional decline.

Bibliography

Fitzpatrick, J., Wafer, B. and Associates (1990), *Review of the EC Research and Development Framework Programme for Ireland, 1984–88*, Dublin: Fitzpatrick and Associates.

OECD (1985), *Innovation Policy in Ireland*, Paris: Organisation of Economic Co-operation and Development.

PART II: FOREIGN RELATIONS

Chapter 13

INTRODUCTION TO PART II
Patrick Keatinge

The European Community's foreign relations

By virtue of its size and its status in international law the European Community is an important entity in international relations. Recognition of its collective values in a global context was expressed in the *Document on the European Identity*, agreed by the member-states in Copenhagen in December 1973 (*Document on the European Identity*, 1973). This refers in general terms to the effects of economic interdependence, the goals of international peace and security, and the member-states' existing relationships with particular countries and groups of countries throughout the world. The Preamble to the Single European Act subsumes these themes in a statement of purpose, with its reference to 'the responsibility incumbent upon Europe to aim at speaking ever increasingly with one voice and to act with consistency and solidarity in order more effectively to protect its common interests and independence' (Single European Act, 1986).

In practice such aspirations are pursued in three distinct, but closely related, policy frameworks. Foreign policy consultations take place within European Political Co-operation (EPC), as do the Community's general diplomatic relations with third parties. EPC also covers broad aspects of security policy, though given the ambiguity surrounding the latter it is examined separately below in Chapter 15. The other two policy frameworks are more closely associated with the mainstream of the Community's economic activity. Foreign trade policy is conducted by the Commission under the aegis of the original EEC Treaty, as is development co-operation policy, based on the considerable colonial heritage of most member-states.

Ireland's foreign relations

When statehood was gained in 1921 after violent antagonism with a world power, the United Kingdom, its legal basis remained a contentious issue up to the late 1940s. The position of Northern Ireland — seen as the residue of 'the national question' — is still a significant issue, however theoretical in form, while the extent of economic dependence on the United Kingdom was a central determinant of policy up to accession to the EC in 1973. Thus Ireland's foreign relations evolved in the predominantly bilateral setting of 'Anglo-Irish relations' (Keatinge, 1986).

The state's peripheral geo-strategic location permitted a rather isolationist orientation, which was particularly marked in neutrality during the Second World War and in the later abstention from NATO. In both cases the attempt to develop a 'special relationship' with the United States failed to produce leverage to alter Anglo-Irish relations; one by-product of this stalemate was that Ireland remained outside the mainstream of European politics.

By compensation, however, an internationalist orientation also evolved. Although weak in the cases of the League of Nations and the Commonwealth (which was too 'British' for domestic taste) and with regard to the Council of Europe (which was limited in scope), it became more marked once membership of the United Nations was achieved in 1955. This led to distinctive policies with regard to decolonization and Third World issues, disarmament and peacekeeping activities. The quest for EC membership itself, from the initial decision in 1961 to its realization in 1972–3, fits into this diplomatic orientation.

Foreign policy-making is largely concentrated in the relevant government departments, where a pragmatic and discreet policy style has been the rule; comprehensive foreign policy doctrines and strategic rationalizations are noticeable by their absence. The indifference to foreign policy of a poorly organized parliamentary system sustains this emphasis. However, lobbies can be mobilized on specific issues and a recent constitutional judgment (*Crotty* v. *An Taoiseach*, 1987) has brought fundamental foreign policy decisions closer to the unpredictable arena of the referendum (see Chapter 19 on sovereignty and national identity; Chapter 23 on Community law and the Irish legal system).

Bibliography

Crotty v. *An Taoiseach* [1987], *Irish Law Reports* **713**.
Document on the European Identity (1973).
Keatinge, P. (1986), 'Unequal sovereigns: the diplomatic dimension of Anglo-Irish relations', in P.J. Drudy (ed.), *Ireland and Britain since 1922*, Cambridge: Cambridge University Press.
Single European Act (1986), EC *Bulletin*, Supplement 2/1986.

Chapter 14

Foreign policy
Patrick Keatinge

European political co-operation

General goals

The EPC process is in itself an inherent component of the evolving European Union (see Chapter 18). Title III of the Single European Act opens with the commitment 'to endeavour jointly to formulate and implement a European foreign policy' (Single European Act, 1986: Article 30, section 1). However, its operational objectives are more modest. The member-states 'undertake to inform and consult each other on any foreign policy matters of general interest' (Single European Act, 1986: Article 30, section 2). Moreover, the adoption of any common position or action following such consultation depends on a consensus of all the governments. Although the latter are required, 'as far as possible [to] refrain from impeding the formation of a consensus' (Single European Act, 1986: Article 30, section 3c) the judge of what is in fact possible remains the individual member-state.

In practice, EPC has developed in an essentially pragmatic way since its inception in 1970. The routine sharing of information among the member-states' foreign ministries has over time facilitated the formation and articulation of common views on many issues, and in some cases has led to common actions, involving declaratory policy, joint *démarches*, and to a limited extent the granting or withholding of material favours through the Community's trade policy (Ifestos, 1987; Pijpers *et al.* (eds), 1988). But there is nothing automatic about the eventual outcome, in what remains an intergovernmental forum. Significantly, the process lies outside the jurisdiction of the European Court of Justice (Single European Act, 1986: Article 31).

This state of affairs has generally been seen as allowing Ireland to pursue one of its broadest foreign policy goals — the maintenance of formal sovereignty in arriving at foreign policy decisions. However, the Supreme Court's judgment on Title III of the Single European Act did reflect diverging interpretations of the new legal basis of EPC (see Chapter 23). Three of the five judges either implicitly or explicitly adhered to the view that it represented a 'fundamental transformation in the relations between the member-states' and was 'the threshold leading from what has hitherto been essentially an economic Community to what will now also be a political Community' (*Crotty* v. *An Taoiseach*, 1987: 461). On the other hand, the Chief Justice argued that Title III did 'not impose any obligations to cede any national interest in the sphere of foreign policy ... they impose an obligation to listen and consult and grant a right to be heard and consulted' (*Crotty* v. *An Taoiseach*, 1987: 448–9), and this minimalist view was supported by a colleague who pointed to the loose formulation of the obligations in Title III as compared with Title II. Subsequent governments, and the political parties in general, have also favoured this minority interpretation, which *inter alia* avoids heart-searching about the ultimate shape of European Union. If Ireland were to leave the Community even such tentative reservations would hardly arise, for alternative diplomatic groupings are far less ambitious in form or substance than EPC.

A second overall foreign policy goal, the maintenance of diplomatic status, has arguably been enhanced by EC membership. Although one of the smallest states in Western Europe, Ireland enjoys predictable, direct access to the policy elites of all its partners, including the major governments in the EC. The Irish Government, in taking its turn as President of the Council for six months every six years, acts as both political 'manager' and external spokesman of EPC, a role which can provide unprecedented if intangible benefits for a small state, particularly in encouraging relationships with superpowers. Outside the Community Ireland would of course avail of normal bilateral channels, but would often have less claim to serious attention from major governments. The opportunity to play prestige roles in multilateral settings would also be more limited; in thirty-five years as a member of the UN Ireland has twice held a seat on the Security Council but has already had four terms as President of the EC Council in less than half that time.

A third general goal is the enhancement of the state's diplomatic machinery. One of the first effects of membership was an increase in the resources allocated to the Department of Foreign Affairs and to the network of overseas representation, both of which were very sketchy by West European standards (Keatinge, 1978: 210–13, 268–71). EPC requires Ireland to take positions on issues outside its traditional range of interests, but it also provided access to the relevant information collected by its partners, thus permitting a degree of specialization hitherto beyond its reach. The evolving 'group diplomacy', in which EPC relations with other regional groupings have served as a catalyst, also extends Ireland's diplomatic reach. Outside the Community these assets would be eroded through the diminution in the quantity and quality of information and contacts available to an individual small state. Membership of 'like-minded' groups of states, particularly in the context of the UN General Assembly, might provide some compensation, but would be much more limited in scope and probably less cost-effective.

An initial general assessment of Ireland's participation in EPC thus suggests gain rather than loss. The form of the process itself, based as it is on consensus, preserves the basis of external sovereignty, while a small state enjoys obvious advantages in terms of diplomatic status and its general diplomatic capacity. Although the extent to which these benefits are translated into influence with other governments will vary according to particular circumstances, it would be difficult to reject the general proposition that a collective *démarche* on behalf of 300 million people will speak louder than the individual policy advanced by the government of 3.5 million. At the very least this may persuade important third parties to act in a way also favoured by Ireland.

Specific goals

Potentially, EPC covers the entire agenda of international politics, and the profusion of dramatic and persistent conflicts outside Western Europe often obscures the fact that a primary interest is the *political stabilization of Western Europe* itself. This requires first of all a compatibility between the political values of the Community and those embodied in the broader Council of Europe. As a founder-member of the latter in 1949, and as a signatory of its associated European Convention on Human Rights, Ireland has had no quarrel with this objective. On particular occasions when democratic values have been suppressed or threatened by West European regimes, as in Greece up to 1974, and in Portugal and Spain up to 1975, participation in EPC has allowed the Dublin Government to become involved in a serious and ultimately successful attempt to support the emergence of democratic regimes. The partition of Cyprus in 1974, with its echoes of Ireland's own nationality question, has proved much less susceptible to Community influence, but at least membership did not prevent Irish governments from making what contribution they could both in the United Nations and in EPC.

Were Ireland to leave the Community, membership of the Council of Europe would remain as an alternative forum for this type of diplomacy, though one where the instrument of moral persuasion would not be supplemented by extensive possibilities of economic inducement. Irish relations with the non-EC countries in the Council of Europe have taken place along normal bilateral channels and in the UN context, but while friendly and marked by many common characteristics they have not been particularly close. In 1989 Ireland was represented in Stockholm and Vienna, but still had no permanent diplomatic mission in either Oslo or Helsinki. Nor would the European Free Trade Association (EFTA) replace EPC. The EFTA countries' own varied attempts to forge new relationships with the Community reinforce the point that in general terms EFTA as such does not possess a political identity comparable to that of the Twelve.

The *improvement of East–West relations* has been a more obvious, indeed arguably the major, theme in EPC. The formative stage of the Conference on Security and Co-operation in Europe (CSCE) coincided with that of political co-operation; the issues raised in the Helsinki Final Act of 1975 provided much of the substance for the early consultations between the member-states. Subsequently the continuation of the CSCE process itself, as a point of East–West contact at times of tension as well as détente, became an important goal for EPC. Up to 1990 the promotion of liberal-democratic values, expressed in a pluralistic concept of human rights, was one of the major elements in CSCE exchanges, alongside the establishment of ground rules for economic and human exchanges and the broad outline of multilateral security arrangements. At the bilateral level EPC consultations covered relations with individual Communist states, necessarily attributing priority to the Soviet Union and the People's Republic of China. But given the Community's European identity, bilateral issues concerning East European countries have been important, from the Polish crisis of the 1980s to the more general crisis in Eastern Europe at the end of the decade.

Before becoming an EC state in 1973, Ireland pursued a very rudimentary policy on East–West relations. Although its political values were undeniably Western, non-involvement in NATO and the absence of any significant bilateral contact with Communist states ensured that policy was confined mainly to positions taken in the UN General Assembly. Joining the Community was an important catalyst in changing this state of affairs. Ambassadors were at last exchanged with the Soviet Union, partly at least because it would be difficult to envisage performing the role of President of the Council without representation in one of the world's major powers.

The emphasis on the CSCE has also proved to be consistent with Ireland's interests. Apart from its relevance to security goals (see Chapter 15), it provides an ordered framework in which the basic policy principles can be formulated in a systematic way. In particular the focus on human rights has allowed Irish governments to support the position of religious minorities under Communist rule. Participation in a collective approach to Eastern bloc countries, however disappointing its results may have been until very recently, was probably helpful in establishing general guidelines for a state which possessed neither a significant tradition of contacts nor a comprehensive policy. Indeed, participation in EPC may be said to have given Ireland a 'diplomatic education' in East–West relations; it certainly provided a first-hand awareness of the sensitivities and complexities of the positions of those member-states which are by virtue of size or location more directly involved. Even when certain important aspects of East–West relations, such as the relationship between the two German states and the status of Berlin, were deliberately excluded from EPC consultations Irish diplomats and politicians were continuously confronted by West German concerns on the evolution of East—West relations as a whole and by the other member-states' attitudes. Thus when fundamental questions concerning East—West relations arose, as was the case in 1989, Irish policy could be formulated on the basis of the most comprehensive appreciation of the situation possible for a small state.

Outside the EC Ireland would of course be a participant in the CSCE process as of right. So far as the informal 'group diplomacy' of that process is concerned, an alternative caucus to EPC does exist, in the shape of the neutral and non-aligned group of countries (N + N). During the actual review conferences and associated CSCE meetings this might well have served as a useful sounding board for the formulation of national positions and, like EPC, as an instrument of collective influence in trying to reach an agreed outcome. However, consultations between the N + N countries are by no means so intensive and wide-ranging as are EPC contacts, which continue as a matter of routine whether CSCE meetings are taking place or not. Nor does the N + N framework provide direct, continuous access to the major governments in Western Europe. Moreover, the N + N countries depend on bilateral channels for their relations with East European governments and do not share a multilateral framework for this purpose.

Thus as a small state without well-developed links with the Eastern bloc Ireland obtained benefits from EPC membership which would have been more difficult and more expensive to acquire outside it, and this has compensated for the disadvantages of geographical remoteness. In most respects the fundamental positions of the EPC states and the N + N states — each group representing a lowest common denominator — are close to each other, and Ireland has so far not had to face a critical choice of substance by belonging to one rather than the other.

A particularly important aspect of policy on East—West relations is the attitude of the United States, or *'West—West relations'*. This is not directly reflected in the operational structures of EPC, but rather cuts across most of the issues which arise among the specialized official working groups. For the other member-states it is a matter of attempting to provide overall consistency between the general political direction of the Western alliance in its strictly military form (NATO) and of the more amorphous concept of 'the West'. For Ireland, the only EC member not in NATO, this question does not arise. Nevertheless, Ireland does have a highly developed bilateral relationship with the United States, based on the historical experiences of Irish-Americans, attempts to bring American influence to bear on 'the Irish question', and wide-ranging economic and social contacts. Ireland's EC membership has added a further dimension to this 'special relationship', by raising the state's profile in those parts of the bureaucratic maze in Washington which had previously been able to ignore it. This may well have served to increase Ireland's overall diplomatic credibility, and by extension have helped Irish governments in their pursuit of important bilateral objectives. Participation in EPC can also deflect unwanted pressures from the United States; for example, Washington's demands that economic sanctions be imposed against Libya at the beginning of 1986 could be more easily refused in the context of an EPC position than from the more vulnerable stance of a small friendly state which was at the time dependent on the United States for favours on several bilateral issues (Keatinge, 1987). Outside the EC, Ireland might find this type of response more difficult, and the effects of bilateral dependence more marked.

Over the past twenty years EPC has served as an instrument both of crisis-management and of efforts to reach durable settlements in many *regional conflicts outside Europe*, many of which can also be seen as manifestations of North—South conflict. The most important and intractable of these has been the Arab-Israeli conflict, particularly in the aftermath of the October 1973 war with its negative consequences for the supply of oil to most West European countries. The Venice Declaration of 1980, in attempting to provide for the long term interests of both Israel and the Palestinians may have been no more successful than other efforts to establish a settlement, but it did represent a definite convergence of views among the member-states. It was, moreover, a convergence in the direction favoured by Irish governments, with their heavy dependence on oil supplies, an historically-rooted sympathy for the plight of the Palestinians as a dispossessed people, and a concern for the security of the Irish contingent in the United Nations peacekeeping operation in southern Lebanon from 1978 on. Of course these objectives could be pursued outside EPC, through UN and bilateral channels, but without the collective weight, the sources of information and the diplomatic networks open to EC member-states an already precarious policy might prove more costly and hazardous.

The complex of issues in Southern Africa — the conflicts in Angola and Mozambique, the status of Zimbabwe and Namibia, and the central question of apartheid in South Africa itself — has also been a persistent theme in EPC; however, collective action has been limited to a restricted range of economic sanctions agreed with some difficulty in the mid-1980s. The apartheid issue was a noticeable political and moral question in Irish foreign policy well before EC membership was achieved. Given Ireland's anti-imperialist tradition, it is not altogether surprising that an active anti-apartheid lobby with cross-party support has existed since the mid-1960s. Ireland has no formal diplomatic relations with South Africa, a limited range of material interests, and has consistently supported a policy of mandatory sanctions through the UN. Thus in the EPC framework Irish governments tend to be at the 'activist' end of the spectrum so far as common policies are concerned, and in that context have failed to persuade their partners to go as far in this direction (Laffan,

1988). The Irish anti-apartheid lobby, on the other hand, has argued that the Government has used EPC acquiescence as an alibi for its own reluctance to take further national measures. From that point of view involvement in EPC is seen as a negative element. Outside the Community Ireland undoubtedly could take a somewhat stronger stance on unilateral sanctions, but given the cautious, if not conservative, tradition in Irish diplomacy it is by no means certain that it would.

A more recent area of conflict, Central America, has also come into the orbit of EPC consultations. Throughout the 1980s Washington's policies with regard to El Salvador and Nicaragua, particularly with regard to the use of force through proxies, were the cause of tension between the United States and West European governments. Ireland's policy was strongly coloured by moral considerations, articulated by non-governmental organizations with direct experience in the field of development co-operation (see Chapter 17). Based as these were on a distinct tradition of missionary activity, thus drawing on the legitimacy of at least the liberal section of the Catholic Church, there was a considerable measure of cross-party criticism of American policy. EPC offered the possibility of a collective, and arguably constructive, response to this situation, especially through diplomatic and material support for the Contadora peace process in the late 1980s. A contrary view — that EPC was in effect the European branch of the State Department — was voiced by some groups, especially during the referendum campaign on the Single European Act in 1987, but this was not shared by the political establishment as a whole.

The two other serious regional conflicts of the 1980s — the Iran—Iraq War and the conflict in Afghanistan — aroused less passionate involvement by foreign policy lobbies in Ireland. Material interests were limited, though they did exist, particularly with regard to trade with Iraq; Irish missionaries have few roots in the Muslim world. In both cases there seem to have been no obvious incompatibilities between the EPC approach and Ireland's foreign policy goals, and EPC offered the possibility at least of exerting collective influence to limit the use of force and bring about settlements.

Outside EPC Ireland could no doubt pursue similar aims, mainly through the multilateral diplomacy of the United Nations General Assembly. As an individual small state, however, it would probably make little impact in that setting. Operating within an *ad hoc* group of 'like-minded' countries might enhance the Government's influence but such groups do not possess the durability and resources of the EPC group. The non-aligned movement is hardly a viable alternative, being diffuse, fragmented, and essentially non-European in its composition.

The Northern Ireland question

A role for the European Community?

The conflict in Northern Ireland, marked by political violence since 1969, has been one of the major concerns of Irish foreign policy during the state's membership of the European Community. As a conflict of local, religious and national identities with long historical roots it transcends the conventional categories of political demarcation. It can be seen as a sub-national problem (within the United Kingdom) and as a national question with irredentist overtones (within the island of Ireland); it has significant transnational effects, particularly in the operation of terrorist groups, and it is an international issue in the orthodox sense both between the sovereign governments in Dublin and London and with regard to third-party governments.

Both states concerned are members of the European Community, a body whose very existence reflects the goal of reconciling the antagonisms which traditionally divided the European peoples (ECSC Treaty, 1951: preamble). But although the Northern Ireland conflict does have an important foreign policy dimension, which looms particularly large for Ireland, it does not appear on the agenda of EPC, which by convention has excluded bilateral issues between member-states. The effects of membership on this issue are more indirect, being channelled however indistinctly through different parts of the EC system.

Ireland's 'nord-politik'

The Irish state is constitutionally committed to the reunification of the island of Ireland (Constitution of Ireland, 1937: Articles 2, 3). However, in practice this goal — which on the face of it represents a specific territorial dispute between two EC member-states — has been aspirational rather than operational. For the last twenty years the greater part of Dublin's northern policy has consisted of attempts, within the rule of law, to support the position of the minority 'nationalist' community in Northern Ireland, and to encourage the establishment of political dialogue with the majority 'unionists'.

Since 1985 this policy has been pursued within the framework of a formal intergovernmental agreement between Ireland and the United Kingdom, the Anglo-Irish Agreement of 1985. This bilateral arrangement avoids direct confrontation over the historical constitutional issue, and concentrates on the difficult balance between measures of political reconciliation on the one hand and efforts to end terrorist violence on the other.

The European dimension

Initial expectations that an acute conflict affecting two EC member-states would be subsumed over time in the general evolution of West European integration have of course been disappointed; indeed, one reason for excluding the issue from the EPC process was that it might exert a divisive and negative influence on the broader issues of political co-operation. Nevertheless, EC membership has had some positive effects, if of a more marginal nature.

In the first place, Ireland's policy has been aired and has acquired international legitimacy through bilateral contacts with EC partners and through interventions in the European Parliament; moreover; this has been possible even when British governments seemed reluctant to concede that there was an Irish interest in the matter. The Irish Government's strategy of engaging the United Kingdom in a formal bilateral agreement was assisted at an early stage by the endorsement of the European Parliament, through the adoption of the Haagerup Report in March 1984 (EPWD 1-15 26/83). When the Anglo-Irish Agreement was signed the following year the European Parliament gave it an emphatic endorsement.

Community membership has also led to material assistance to Northern Ireland over and above what might normally be derived through the structural funds. Specific cross-border programmes in the late 1970s have been followed by a contribution by the Community as such to the 'International Fund' set up under the Anglo-Irish Agreement. The amounts involved are very modest in relation to the impoverished circumstances prevailing in many parts of Northern Ireland, but can be seen as a token of the potential for further economic improvement at a later stage of integration. Indeed the first intergovernmental review of the Anglo-Irish Agreement in 1989, referring explicitly to the completion of the internal market in 1992, recognizes the common difficulties and opportunities arising for both parts of Ireland and agrees on a common approach (Boyle and Hadden, 1989: 86—7). The transnational and international aspects of security in Northern Ireland have also been alleviated in a modest way through EC membership (Chapter 15).

Finally, the fact that both Ireland and the United Kingdom have been EC member-states during this long period of actual or potential bilateral tension has perhaps had a moderating effect on intergovernmental relations. Ministers and officials have maintained regular contact on an agenda much broader than and not necessarily so potentially antagonistic as that of Northern Ireland, allowing at least for a degree of familiarity and possibly of empathy which may prove helpful. This is illustrated at the highest level, where the practice has been to hold regular meetings between the Irish and British heads of government on the margins of the meetings of the European Council.

Thus EC membership has served to 'internationalize' the Northern

Ireland conflict to a modest extent. Outside the Community Ireland could no doubt continue to exploit other modes of internationalization which have also been developed over the past twenty years, such as the United Nations, the Council of Europe, and bilateral contacts, especially with the United States. It is not likely that such channels would prove to be any more helpful without the additional element of EC membership. In any case, the outcome of the Northern Ireland conflict depends primarily on change at the local level.

Assessment

As an EC member-state Ireland has increased its diplomatic capacity, both in form and in substance. The specific effects of participation in EPC vary from issue to issue, but in general the state's international contacts and influence have been enhanced. The consensus principle ensures that costs are usually marginal. The distinctive elements in Ireland's foreign policy prior to membership have not been significantly altered, and the one policy issue unaffected by EPC, the Northern Ireland conflict, has arguably been influenced positively, if modestly, by other aspects of membership.

Outside the Community Ireland would be one of a group of European small states, several of which are associated with the N+N group in the CSCE. However, Ireland is materially less well endowed than Austria, Finland, Norway, Sweden or Switzerland, and less centrally located. Irish influence in a looser and more tentative group would probably be marginal, and the need for bilateral contacts would be all the greater, with the considerable expense that would entail.

Bibliography

Boyle, K. and Hadden, T. (1989), *The Anglo-Irish Agreement: Text and Official Review*, London: Sweet and Maxwell.
Constitution of Ireland (1937).
Crotty v. An Taoiseach [1987], *Irish Law Reports*, **713**.
European Coal and Steel Community Treaty (1951).
European Parliament Working Document 1-15 26/83, *A Report on the Situation in Northern Ireland*, by N.J. Haagerup.
Ifestos, P. (1987), *European Political Cooperation: Towards a Framework of Supranational Diplomacy?*, Aldershot: Avebury.
Keatinge, P. (1978), *A Place Among the Nations: Issues of Irish Foreign Policy*, Dublin: Institute of Public Administration.
Keatinge, P. (1987), 'Ireland's foreign relations in 1986', in *Irish Studies in International Affairs*, vol. 2, no. 3.
Laffan, B. (1988), *Ireland and South Africa: Irish Government Policy in the 1980s*, Dublin: Trocaire.

Pijpers, A., Regelsberger, E., Wessels, W. (eds) (1988), *European Political Cooperation in the 1980s: A common Foreign Policy for Western Europe?* Dordrecht: Martinus Nijhoff.
Single European Act (1986), EC *Bulletin*, Supplement 2/1986.

Chapter 15

Security policy

Patrick Keatinge

The European Community and security

The role of the European Community with regard to security is incomplete, and its competences are expressed in a tentative, even ambiguous manner. The Single European Act states that the signatories 'consider that closer co-operation on questions of European security would contribute in an essential way to the development of a European identity in external policy matters'. This very general proposition of an aspirational nature is followed immediately by the more modest statement that they are 'ready to co-ordinate their positions more closely on the political and economic aspects of security' (Single European Act, 1986: Article 30, section 6a). There is further reference to the need to maintain the industrial basis of security, and to the existing co-operation between 'certain' member-states in other organizations, namely NATO and the Western European Union (WEU), which is composed of nine European members of NATO.

Differing interpretations of this formulation are possible. In the Irish Supreme Court judgments on the SEA one judge regarded the reference to NATO and the WEU as possibly impinging on the defence policy of an EC state which was not a member of either alliance, but another held that since 'military and defence aspects are not included [they] should accordingly be considered to be excluded' (*Crotty* v. *An Taoiseach*, 1987: 458, 465). To date the latter view seems to be the orthodox one. In practice the 'political and economic aspects of security' encompass the general foreign policy orientations related to international security (covered in European Political Co-operation), the security dimension (broadly defined) of economic sectoral policies under the original treaty framework, and a limited co-ordination of activities related to policing and public order. So far NATO, which is after all led by a non-EC state, has tended to guard its own military prerogatives, almost as much against the 'other alliance' — the WEU — as against the European Community.

Ireland's security: the neutrality reservation

Ireland's security policy matches that of the Community, being equally incomplete and ambiguous in form. This is largely attributable to two factors — the state's peripheral location with regard to the most immediate strategic concerns of European security, and its deliberate, if intermittent, attempts to establish a stance of neutrality. It has been argued that the label 'neutrality' is strictly speaking a misnomer in Ireland's case (Salmon, 1989), and at the very least Ireland has deviated from neutrality norms which up to Austria's EC application in 1989 seemed to be accepted by other West European neutrals (Hakovirta, 1988). Nevertheless, the state's refusal to enter into formal military commitments does set it apart from all other existing EC member-states.

The origins of Irish neutrality may be traced to a desire to distance the new Irish state from the influence of its former British overlord. The actual maintenance of a policy of neutrality during the Second World War, whatever its qualifications, was seen as a demonstration of authentic sovereignty, and the subsequent abstention from NATO in 1949 was formally linked to the continuing partition of the island of Ireland. These justifications of neutrality as an 'un-British activity' persist to some degree, but they have been supplemented in the last ten years by motivations common to the peace movements throughout Western Europe — a rejection of nuclear deterrence, of the institutionalization of inter-bloc antagonism, and of the projection of military force outside Europe (Keatinge, 1984).

The consequent dilemma faced by Irish governments, trying to reconcile such values with a concept of European integration which either neglects or ignores them, has been resolved by the formula that political integration must proceed at the same pace as economic integration, on the implicit assumption that Community defence competences will only be agreed in the final stages of the whole process (Keatinge, 1989a). In the interim, neutrality must be maintained.

In practice, particularly during the 1980s, the proposition that the EC might move gradually into the defence sector, and sooner rather than later, was met by increasingly emphatic assertions of neutrality. These were noticeable by their absence at the time of accession in 1972/3, but the report of the *ad hoc* Committee on Institutional Affairs in 1985 contained a reserve on defence matters by its Irish chairman, Senator James Dooge (*Ad Hoc* Committee, 1985: II, Cb). In 1987 the Government deposited an emphatic national declaration of neutrality with its instrument of ratification of the Single European Act. This stated that the Act did not cover 'the military aspects of security or procurement for military purposes and does not affect Ireland's right to act or refrain from acting in any way which might affect Ireland's international status of military neutrality' (*Ireland Today: Bulletin of the Department of Foreign Affairs*, May–June 1987: 2). Although some politicians, especially in the

Fine Gael and Progressive Democrat parties, have expressed anxiety lest an insistence on neutrality keep Ireland in the second tier of a possible two-tier Community in the future (Keatinge, 1989a: 140), the position to date remains as it has been since accession: EC membership has not compelled Ireland to abandon its stance on neutrality.

Specific effects of EC membership

The effects of the EPC process on Ireland's foreign policy, which are often in themselves an important part of the 'political aspects of security,' are examined elsewhere (Chapter 14). Only in one particular crisis in that context has Irish neutrality emerged as a potentially contentious issue, even if rather tangentially. At an early stage of the *Falkland Islands crisis* in 1982 Ireland joined in the economic sanctions against Argentina, as agreed in EPC and implemented by a regulation under Article 113 of the EEC Treaty. Participation in sanctions had hitherto not been regarded as incompatible with neutrality policy, unlike the position held by other European neutral governments. However, on the eve of hostilities between the newly arrived British task force and the Argentinian invaders the Irish Government declared that in the context of armed conflict support for sanctions was incompatible with military neutrality, and it subsequently opted out of the common action (as did Italy, for different reasons). In the event the compatibility between this decision and the state's obligations under EC law was not tested, and negative political repercussions were primarily bilateral, in the form of poor relations with the United Kingdom, rather than from the other member-states or the Community as a whole.

The impact of EC membership on *national defence policy* is if anything more nebulous. Ireland has received financial assistance for fisheries protection, the burden of which increased significantly with the advent of extended economic zones in the 1970s. The consequent enhancement of Irish naval capabilities does, however, appear to have been limited to the fisheries protection mission; new vessels do not possess a significant anti-submarine warfare capability. Given the failure of Irish governments to publish any comprehensive and detailed statement of national defence policy with respect to external military threats, any further effects of EC membership are impossible to identify.

Irish governments and political groups in general have been more forthcoming on policies concerned with *disarmament and arms control*. EPC provides the primary framework for the co-ordination of the broad approach to security issues in the CSCE process, but the closer such discussions come to specific operational military questions the less significant EPC becomes. During the negotiations concerning confidence and security building measures in the Conference on Disarmament in Europe (CDE) at Stockholm from 1984 to 1986, and in the later extension of these negotiations at Vienna, the NATO caucus was more important than the EPC grouping, thus leaving the Irish delegation to formulate its positions on a national basis. In other arms control fora, especially the United Nations, Ireland continues to pursue policies critical of nuclear deterrence, and therefore in contradiction to its EC partners' formal espousal of nuclear force, as members of NATO or the WEU. Outside the EC Ireland's policies would probably remain unchanged, though in the CSCE framework they could be presented in the neutral and non-aligned (N+N) group.

International peacekeeping operations lie outside the Community's competence (though the participation of some member-states in the Sinai peacekeeping force in 1981 was linked to general EPC support for an Arab-Israeli peace process). For Ireland participation in United Nations peacekeeping has been probably the single most important contribution the state has made to international security since the late 1950s. Fears that EC membership might have negative repercussions on Ireland's credibility as a contributing state have not been realized. Indeed the Irish Government is able, through the EPC process, to help mobilize the collective weight of the member-states in support of peacekeeping operations which are in difficulties; such backing has been evident on several occasions in the case of the United Nations operation in southern Lebanon (UNIFIL).

The threat of *international terrorism* has appeared on the Community agenda with some regularity since the mid-1970s. Meetings of interior and justice ministers and their officials in the 'Trevi group' (a subsidiary channel of EPC) attempt to co-ordinate policies on transnational police operations and, more tentatively, legal questions such as extradition procedures have been raised (Hill, 1988). Ireland has a very direct interest in such developments arising out of terrorist activities, especially by the IRA, in the Northern Ireland conflict (see Chapter 14). Although the primary operational focus in this regard is bilateral (through the Anglo-Irish Agreement of 1985), the IRA has deliberately extended its operations throughout the Community; in the late 1980s the Belgian, French, Spanish and West German authorities were involved, sometimes at the highest political and legal level. Policing and legal actions in response to illegal arms supplies, attacks on British personnel, and extradition cases can all contribute towards the Irish Government's attempt to curb IRA activities in general.

However, given the inevitable paucity of information on such matters it is difficult to assess the extent to which Community membership as such facilitates this task. Obvious successes, such as the capture by French authorities of the arms ship Eksund in 1987, can be seen alongside obvious failures, such as the Belgian-British-Irish confusion over the Ryan extradition in 1988 (Keatinge, 1988, 1989b). National prerogatives, often in constitutional form, weigh heavily on the legal process. Outside the Community Ireland would in any case continue to pursue its objectives through the Anglo-Irish framework and within the context of the Council of Europe's conventions and broader mechanisms such as Interpol.

Assessment

The Community's involvement with security policy, as distinct from foreign policy in general, is at best inchoate. Although any future extension into the field of defence policy proper would probably be divisive in Ireland — even to the extent of provoking a crisis in Ireland's EC membership — the situation pertaining at present has allowed for the continuation of the stance of military neutrality.

Specific gains from membership can be identified in particular aspects of Ireland's security activities. If Ireland were to leave the Community, significant increases in the cost of fishery protection would be incurred, diplomatic support for UN peacekeeping might be marginally more difficult to mobilize, and the fight against IRA terrorism might become more rather than less difficult to co-ordinate.

Bibliography

Ad Hoc Committee on Institutional Affairs (1985), *Report to the European Council*, SN/1187/85 Brussels, 29–30 March.

Crotty v. *An Taoiseach* [1987], *Irish Law Reports*, **713**.

Hakovirta, H. (1988), *East–West Conflict and European Neutrality*, Oxford: Clarendon Press.

Hill, C. (1988), 'European preoccupations with terrorism', in A. Pijpers, E, Regelsberger and W. Wessels, (eds), *European Political Cooperation in the 1980s: A common Foreign Policy for Western Europe?* Dordrecht: Martinus Nijhoff.

Ireland Today: Bulletin of the Department of Foreign Affairs (1987), no. 1037.

Keatinge, P. (1984), *A Singular Stance: Irish Neutrality in the 1980s*, Dublin: Institute of Public Administration.

Keatinge, P. (1988), 'Ireland's foreign relations in 1987', in *Irish Studies in International Affairs*, vol. 2, no. 4.

Keatinge, P. (1989a), 'Ireland and European security — the new cold war and beyond', in D. Keogh (ed.), *Ireland and the Challenge of European Integration*, Cork: Hibernian University Press.

Keatinge, P. (1989b), 'Ireland's foreign relations in 1988', in *Irish Studies in International Affairs*, vol. 2, no. 5.

Salmon, T.C. (1989), *Unneutral Ireland: An Ambivalent and Unique Security Policy*, Oxford: Clarendon Press.

Single European Act (1986), EC *Bulletin*, Supplement 2/1986.

Chapter 16

External trade policy
Rory O'Donnell

Introduction

The external trade policy of the EC, and its effects on member-states, can be viewed as both an issue of foreign relations and of economic policy. Given the nature of Ireland's foreign policy, as explained in Chapter 14, it is most appropriate to focus on the economic dimension of the Community's external trade policy and on its economic significance to Ireland. In this brief entry we begin by describing the EC's external trade policy and then proceed to consider its congruence with Irish policy and its economic effects on Ireland.

Community external trade policy

The customs union

In the face of difficulties confronting political or military integration those who favoured European integration chose to seek an ever closer union by establishing a common market. An important element of a common market is a customs union, which is defined by economists as an area which not only has free internal trade but also a single set of arrangements for trade with non-member countries. Article 113 of the Treaty of Rome requires the Community to have a common commercial policy. Since the achievement of this common policy, in 1968, all matters which are directly to do with external trade policy — such as tariffs, trade agreements and preferential arrangements — are the responsibility of the EC authorities rather than the member-states. However, it has been argued that other matters which have an important, but *indirect* bearing on external trade — such as currency policy, export promotion, approaches to foreign direct investment and the use of economic sanctions and boycotts for political purposes — remain in the hands of the member-states.

In managing the customs union the Community can make use of the common external tariffs, import levies and export subsidies (in the case of agriculture), anti-dumping measures and, of course, a host of non-tariff measures. Using these instruments the Community has pursued its external trade objectives by participating in multilateral tariff negotiations and reaching a series of free trade and preferential trade agreements.

GATT

The Community has participated in several rounds of GATT negotiations. Viewed over the long run these can be seen to have reduced the level of trade protection in manufactured goods — though the pace of tariff reduction varies with the extent of economic difficulties being experienced in the leading industrial nations. The EC has been much less willing to reduce the level of protection for agricultural products and, while this has been, and remains, an important part of EC external trade policy, it is best considered in our section on agricultural policy (Chapter 3).

Trade agreements

The EC has negotiated a network of free trade and preferential trade agreements and these are evidence of an active Community external trade policy. In its early years the EC reached association agreements with Greece, Turkey, Morocco, Tunisia, Malta and Cyprus. Preferential agreements were signed with Spain, Israel, Egypt and Lebanon between 1970 and 1972. In 1963 the Yaounde Convention with eighteen ex-colonies of Belgium and France, was signed.

Trade relations with the state-trading countries — Eastern Europe and the USSR — have proved difficult for the Community in the past, reflecting the very different nature of the planned economies. Since 1972 the Community has attempted to develop an overall approach to trade with the Mediterranean countries. The trade agreements signed under this heading generally permit industrial products, subject to some exceptions, to be imported into the Community duty-free, but restrict the access of agricultural products which are covered by the CAP.

An important element of Community external trade policy are arrangements with less-developed countries. There are two components to this policy, the generalized system of preferences and the Lomé Conventions. These are discussed in more detail in Chapter 17, on development policy. Very briefly, the generalized system of preferences allows duty-free entry, subject to ceilings, to a wide range of manufactured exports from a list of developing countries. The Lomé Conventions have provided non-reciprocal duty-free access to the EC for almost all products originating in a group of particularly underdeveloped countries in Africa and elsewhere (see Chapter 17).

Within these various trade agreements, including the GATT, trade in textiles has generally be subject to a special, more restrictive, regime — the Multi-Fibre Arrangements. These arrangements are considered in more detail in the chapter on industrial policy (Chapter 7).

Ireland's external trade policy

We noted in various sections on economic policy that in order to foster native industry Ireland adopted a policy of trade protection from the early 1930s to the late 1950s. Throughout this period a major policy concern was to secure an outlet for Ireland's agricultural produce. Faced with severe balance-of-payments crises and an upsurge in emigration, policy-makers decided in the late 1950s that further industrialization required export-led growth and greater participation in the international economy. In this sense it can be said that EC membership, in 1973, was the logical outcome of the economic and political policies pursued by successive Irish governments since the 1950s. Official attitudes to the question of membership of the Community reflected fairly closely the strength of belief in Ireland's ability to trade and prosper in a competitive economic environment. In the late 1950s and early 1960s, politicians and government departments, who were later to strongly support membership, expressed considerable doubts about the ability of much of Irish industry to survive in a generalized free trade environment. These fears about the possible effects of EC membership were not inconsistent with a general commitment to an outward looking economic strategy, which was adopted and acted upon in those years. Likewise, the performance of the economy in the years 1958 to 1972 — a period of progressive lowering of protection and the opening of the Irish economy — was crucial in creating confidence in the ability of the Irish economy to maintain economic growth in a competitive European environment (Maher, 1986).

Economic performance in Ireland during the period 1958 to 1972 was significantly better than in the period 1949 to 1958. In particular, Ireland's orientation to the external economy was transformed during the later period. The annual rate of growth in the volume of both exports and imports more than doubled from the earlier period. Of more significance even than the increased growth of Ireland's foreign trade was the rapid *diversification* of market outlets which accompanied the country's export growth. In 1958 almost 80 per cent of Ireland's manufactured exports were to the United Kingdom; by 1972 this share had fallen to 58 per cent (see Table 16.1). This was achieved by rapid growth of manufactured exports to the EC-six and the United States.

These positive economic trends were quickly ascertained, and Maher

Table 16.1 *Geographical structure of Irish trade: exports (percentage shares)*

Destination	1955	1960	1970	1980	1989
United Kingdom	89.1	74.7	62.4	43.2	33.5
Other EC	4.5	6.0	12.6	32.1	40.7
Total EC	93.6	80.9	75.0	75.3	74.2
EFTA	0.0	1.1	1.5	3.7	5.6
State-trading	0.0	0.1	0.7	1.2	0.6
North America	3.0	8.3	14.5	6.6	8.6
Other	2.8	9.7	8.3	13.2	10.9
Total	100.0	100.0	100.0	100.0	100.0

Source: Trade Statistics of Ireland.

argues that the rapid economic growth in 1959 and 1960 played a significant part in the decision, in 1961, to apply for membership of the EC (Maher, 1986). Indeed, as the 1960s progressed it became *necessary* for Irish officials to portray the economy as dynamic and capable of success in international competition. This arose because the six members of the EC had grave doubts about Ireland's economic suitability for membership. Irish officials and ministers went to considerable lengths to reassure other governments of the country's commitment to membership and economic suitability for it. The first they did by undertaking progressive reductions of tariffs (either unilaterally, as in 1963 and 1964, or under the Anglo-Irish free trade area agreement after 1965); the second they were able to do by showing that, as protection was progressively reduced, the Irish economy sustained its rapid growth of output and, in particular, exports (NESC, 1989).

The need to highlight the economic successes in the 1960s did not blind officials and ministers to the difficulties which might be faced in free trade. Their response is discussed in the introduction to the economic policy section (Chapter 1) and in the chapter on industrial policy (Chapter 7).

Since 1973 Ireland has generally supported the main thrust of EC external trade policy — especially the Community's reluctance to open the internal market to free competition in agricultural products.

Gains and losses to Ireland

Changes in trade regime

Given the changes in Irish trade policy before 1973, and especially the signing of a comprehensive free trade agreement with the United Kingdom in 1965, it can be said that adherence to Community external trade policy was a continuation of the approach adopted by Ireland from 1958. Yet membership of the Community did imply significant changes in Ireland's external trade regime; these have been identified in a comprehensive study of the implications of EC external trade policy for Ireland (Matthews, 1980). First, since the Community's common external tariff was lower than Ireland's, joining the EC meant a slight reduction in the level of protection against imports from countries like the United States and Japan. Second, simultaneous with Ireland's accession, the EC entered free trade agreements with the EFTA countries and this implied increased Irish exposure to manufactured imports from EFTA and duty-free access to EFTA markets. Third, Ireland's existing trading agreements with Bulgaria, Romania, Czechoslovakia and the USSR lapsed after 1974. Fourth, the generalized system of preferences and the Lomé Conventions removed some of the barriers to trade between Ireland and the developing and less-developed countries. Fifth, the continuation of limits on textile imports from low-cost suppliers provided a significant protection to Irish industry. Finally, membership of the EC implied a dramatic change in the external trade regime of Irish agriculture. Imports from third countries were subjected to duties and levies and Irish exports benefited from export refunds. Our concern is to make an assessment of the economic gains and losses which follows these changes in trade regime or trade policy.

Economic effects

In his analysis of the implications of EC external trade policy, Matthews argues that the effects have generally been positive — but not very significant. This conclusion can be illustrated by reference to the geographical structure of Ireland's trade — summarized in Tables 16.1 and 16.2.

Table 16.1 shows the geographical structure of Irish exports in selected years from 1955 to the present. Several features of these data are noteworthy. First, the diversification of Ireland's exports, evident in the 1960s, continued after EC accession. Indeed, dependence on the UK market as an outlet for Ireland's exports decreased dramatically — especially since 1973. Second, despite an enormous increase in the share of Irish exports going to EC countries *other than* the United Kingdom, Irish exports to the *total* EC have decreased from 93.6 per cent, in 1955, to 74.2 per cent, in 1989; these figures illustrate the fact that Irish exports to non-EC countries have grown very considerably. This reflects much increased penetration of the North American markets and the opening of new export markets in the Middle East and in the less-developed countries (Matthews, 1980). Such diversification, and especially the increased share of exports to non-EC markets, suggests that the EC's external trade policy has facilitated rather than harmed Ireland.

Table 16.2 *Geographical structure of Irish trade: imports (percentage shares)*

Origin	1955	1960	1970	1980	1989
United Kingdom	52.6	49.5	52.1	50.8	40.9
Other EC	12.0	13.6	17.3	20.1	24.5
Total EC	64.6	63.1	69.4	70.9	65.4
EFTA	5.1	4.5	4.5	4.3	3.8
State-trading	0.8	1.1	2.0	1.3	1.1
North America	12.0	10.3	8.8	10.1	16.8
Other	17.5	20.8	15.3	13.5	12.7
Total	100.0	100.0	100.0	100.0	100.0

Source: Trade Statistics of Ireland.

This suggestion is strengthened to a definite conclusion when we consider the geographical structure of Irish imports from 1955 to the present (Table 16.2). The most striking feature of these data is that, overall, the origin of Ireland's imports shows much less change. The United Kingdom never provided as large a share of Irish imports as it took of Irish exports — but neither has that share declined as rapidly. In the case of imports, the decline in the UK share is fully offset by the increase in the 'other EC' share — such that a higher proportion of what Ireland imports now comes from Community countries than was the case before Ireland's accession. While this might not be surprising it does, by definition, mean that non-EC imports into Ireland have not increased as a share of total imports. It is this that confirms our earlier suggestion that conforming to EC external trade policy since 1973 has provided marginally more opportunities than threats to Ireland.

The threat from low-cost producers

A question that naturally arises is whether the Community's trade policy towards less-developed countries — the generalized system of preferences and Lomé Conventions — has not exposed Irish manufacturing, especially the weak indigenous sector, to low-cost competition from poorer countries and been responsible for the very severe adjustment problems documented in Chapter 2. All studies on this question have concluded that, on balance, Ireland has probably gained rather than lost from the operation of the EC's preferential arrangements with third countries. Table 16.2 shows that in 1989, 12.7 per cent of Ireland's imports came from countries other than North America, the Eastern bloc, EFTA and the EC. This 'other' category includes not only the less-developed countries but also Japan and OPEC. Matthews' detailed investigation shows that a small proportion of industrial job losses can be attributed to imports from low-cost producers — a conclusion confirmed by O'Malley (1985). The recent NESC study on the performance and prospects of Ireland in the EC concluded that, even in the case of textiles, clothing and footwear, it is not easy to ascribe Ireland's specialization *out* of these industries to competition from the less-developed economies specializing into them. Indeed, looking at the detailed statistics of Ireland's imports of, say, clothing, the predominance of the United Kingdom, Germany and, to a lesser extent, Italy is quite striking (NESC, 1989).

The effects of EC external trade policy on Irish agriculture are considered in Chapter 2.

Assessment

Although Ireland had, since the early 1960s, adopted a trade policy which was favourable to the freeing of trade, accession to the Community in 1973 did involve a major change in Ireland's external trade regime or trade policy. In general, this change involved a reduction in barriers to trade in manufactured goods between Ireland and non-EC countries. Our concern in this chapter has been to ascertain the gains and losses resulting from the change. Studies of this question have found that, on balance, Ireland has gained from greater access to the third-country markets. We have illustrated this argument by reference to the changing geographical pattern of Irish trade. Furthermore, there seems little evidence to support the view that imports from low-cost Third-World producers have been responsible for a significant proportion of Ireland's painful adjustment to free trade in the past two decades. If Ireland had never joined the EC she could, of course, have reduced tariffs unilaterally and achieved some of the benefits outlined above. But there are two reasons why Ireland's external trade policy would have been, and still would be, less successful outside the EC. First, given its small size Ireland could not have achieved the reciprocal tariff reductions negotiated by the EC. Second, on its own, Ireland could never have negotiated general tariff reductions in conjunction with continuation of high levels of agricultural protection.

Bibliography

Maher, D.J. (1986), *The Tortuous Path: The Course of Ireland's Entry into the EEC 1948–73*, Dublin: Institute of Public Administration.
Matthews, A. (1980), *The European Community's External Trade Policy: Implications for Ireland*, Dublin: Irish Council of the European Movement.
NESC (1989), *Ireland in the European Community: Performance, Prospects and Strategy*, Dublin: National Economic and Social Council.
O'Malley, E. (1985), 'The performance of Irish indigenous industry: some lessons from the 1980s', in J. Fitzpatrick and J. Kelly (eds), *Perspectives on Irish Industry*, Dublin: Irish Management Institute.

Chapter 17

Development policy
Helen O'Neill

The EC's development co-operation policy

From its foundation in 1957 the EC has had a 'special relationship' with at least some less-developed countries (LDCs). At first this took the form of association agreements between the EC-six and the colonies and former colonies of some of its member-states. After the first enlargement in 1973, which brought in Denmark, Ireland and the United Kingdom, a fundamental overhaul of the 'special relationship' between the EC and developing countries was seen as necessary, primarily in order to accommodate the United Kingdom's own special relationships with its former colonies. A second reason was in order to improve the trade concessions offered by the EC to their 'special partners', since the concessions provided up to the early 1970s had been reduced in relative terms as a result of the introduction in 1972 of the EC's generalized system of preferences which extended trade concessions to almost all developing countries.

Today the EC as a grouping has a development programme and the individual member-states have their own national programmes. If added together, the Community and its member-states constitute the largest source of official development assistance in the world.

The Lomé Convention

After protracted negotiations, the first (1975–80) of the Lomé Conventions was agreed between the EC and forty-six (now sixty-six) partners in the developing countries of Africa, the Caribbean and the Pacific (ACP). Other, but significantly less-comprehensive, development co-operation arrangements, have since been signed between the EC and groups of developing countries in the Mediterranean region, the Middle East, Asia and Latin America. But the EC-ACP partnership, embodied in the Lomé Convention remains the centrepiece of the EC's development policy. It is a contractual arrangement, agreed between two groups of countries, the EC and the ACPs, who are perceived as partners. Within the Convention, the ACP states receive financial aid and non-reciprocal duty-free access to the EC market for almost all their exports. Part of the financial aid is allocated to a fund to assist in stabilizing export earnings (STABEX) and to develop mineral production (SYSMIN). Food aid and emergency aid are other important elements.

As new needs arose, and particularly as economic and social conditions deteriorated in Africa in the 1980s, the predominantly project approach of the earlier Conventions was replaced in Lomé III (1985—90) by a newer 'programming' approach which focuses on the key sectors which satisfy basic needs for the poorest, such as agriculture and rural development, primary health care and education.

Structural adjustment

Recently, responding to the profoundly deteriorating situation in sub-Saharan Africa (SSA), the EC introduced an important initiative in the form of a 'Special community programme to aid certain highly-indebted low-income countries in sub-Saharan Africa'. During 1988 and 1989 the EC is making available ECU 500 million in the form of quick-disbursing aid for import support for sectoral programmes in the poorest and most debt-distressed African countries. Some of these funds can be used for general balance-of-payments support provided the recipient countries are undertaking economic reform, or structural adjustment programmes. How significant such structural adjustment funding will be in the fourth Lomé Convention (beginning in 1990), or whether the conditions attaching to such funding will be the same as World Bank/IMF conditionality for structural adjustment lending, was the subject of some debate among the EC member-states at the end of 1989.

Ireland's development co-operation policy

Up until 1973, when Ireland joined the EC, its links with developing countries had been mainly missionary-based, with a geographical concentration on English-speaking Africa. Official financial contributions were very small. During the 1950s they arose as a consequence of joining the UN (1955) and the World Bank (1957). In the 1960s, multilateral transfers were broadened to include the International Development Association (from 1960), the World Food Programme (from 1962) and Disaster Relief (from 1967). On the bilateral side, some technical assistance was given to Zambia in 1965—6. An official bilateral aid programme was launched in 1974.

That the bilateral programme was launched so soon after accession to the EC and that total official development assistance (ODA) began to increase substantially from that time was no coincidence. Rather, it might be described as the consequence of a benign conjuncture of circumstances. A few months after Ireland joined the EC a Coalition Government with a Minister for Foreign Affairs deeply committed to development issues came to power. The fact that the country had just joined the EC, which already had a coherent development policy of its own, probably helped to nudge the Government towards the establishment of an Irish programme and, indeed, probably resulted in its size being somewhat bigger than it might otherwise have been.

Objectives of Ireland's development policy

It is not surprising, given the widespread realization that it was the voluntary (and most especially the missionary) sector which pioneered Ireland's involvement with the Third World, that a strong humanitarian motivation is usually described as underlining the programme.

In official documents it is always stated that the primary objective is to promote the development of developing countries.[1] The broadening of foreign policy in general is another objective. Once launched, aid to the Third World was perceived to be one of the 'basic objectives of Irish foreign policy'.[2] Subsequent official statements described development co-operation as being 'an integral and increasingly important part of our international relations',[3] and 'a new dimension to this whole area of our external relations'.[4]

Support for various elements of the new international economic order (NIEO) during the 1970s — most notably support from within the progressive 'like-minded' group of developed countries for the establishment of the common fund to stabilize primary commodity prices, and frequent references in official speeches to the existence of mutuality of interests between rich and poor countries — suggest that Irish development policy in its widest interpretation is also aimed at improving North—South relations and promoting a more just and peaceful world.

The production of direct economic benefits for Ireland is not seen as an objective of the Irish bilateral aid programme. None the less, several firms, most notably in the services sector, have benefited from it because the programme has a technical assistance bias. Economic benefits are expected — and obtained — more from participation of Irish concerns in the projects of the multilateral organizations, including the World Bank and the EC, although it is acknowledged that the early experience gained by Irish firms from working on projects in the bilateral programme has been of considerable assistance to them in gaining contracts from the multilateral institutions.

Objectives relating to the volume of Irish aid have generally been vague. Although the Government accepts the UN target of 0.7 per cent of GNP as an objective, no time horizon has been specified and earlier commitments to specific annual increases in ODA are no longer made. A statement by the Taoiseach (Prime Minister) in the Dail (Parliament) on 23 November 1989 that the Government would work towards the achievement of the target 'as economic circumstances permit'[5] is reminiscent of a 1963 statement that official aid would increase 'according as our own economic capacity grows'.[6]

Principles of Ireland's development policy

Among the main principles underlying any country's ODA programme are those relating to the multilateral/bilateral distribution and, within the bilateral programme, to geographic and sectoral distribution. On the first, in Ireland's case, although no target has been set, a policy decision was taken in 1979 to build up the relative importance of the bilateral side. As regards geographic distribution, the focus has always been on Africa and the criteria used in choosing the four 'priority' countries (Lesotho, Tanzania, Zambia and Sudan) have included relative poverty, ability to absorb and make effective use of aid, and suitability of social structures and policies to facilitate the flow of assistance to the 'neediest sectors'.

Effects of EC membership on Ireland's development policy

In considering the effects of EC membership on the principles underlying Ireland's development policy, it is appropriate to distinguish first between the effects which membership had on the establishment of principles and, second, the effects which membership has had on their realization.

Establishment of principles

It is unlikely that EC membership had any effect on the establishment of principles. Until Ireland joined the EC, almost all of its tiny amount of ODA payments were multilateral and paid through the UN system. The establishment of a bilateral programme after 1973 was, in effect and simultaneously, a statement of intent to reduce the relative importance of the multilateral contribution. As to geographic and sectoral distribution, although the focuses in the case of the Irish programme are rather similar to those of the EC, the choices in the Irish case were clearly made without regard to the EC programme. Ireland's early pre-EC links with developing countries had been mainly with English-speaking Africa. The selection of education, agriculture and rural development, and primary health care as the sectoral focuses was determined not only by perceived need within those sectors in Africa but also by what was seen to be

Ireland's special interests and competence in the delivery of aid. Since 1973, however, new concerns have become important. The most important of these are the role of women in development and the impact on the environment of various strategies of development. Because both of these concerns have become important at the level of the EC's own development policy, sensitivity to them within Ireland's official programme has undoubtedly increased.

Realization of principles

After 1973, the proportion of Irish ODA devoted to multilateral flows began to fall steadily and significantly. From 100 per cent in 1960, multilateral payments fell to 55 per cent by 1986. However, since that date they have begun to climb again relative to bilateral flows. In 1989, the ratio was back to 64:36 and the 1990 estimates suggest that ratio is being maintained at least in the short term. As already noted, relative decreases or increases in multilateral flows are determined by what happens to the bilateral programme. Almost all the multilateral flows are mandatory or assessed payments to the UN and the EC. When the bilateral programme was increasing (up to 1986), the multilateral/bilateral ratio was falling. Once the bilateral programme began to be cut, the ratio began to rise again. Among EC member-states, and among the members of the OECD's Development Assistance Committee (DAC), Ireland has the highest ratio of multilateral to bilateral flows. The EC has probably had very little influence on the development of this overall ratio since, unlike the DAC, it does not issue regular reports on the bilateral development programmes of member-states, nor does it issue recommendations on them.

Within the multilateral side of the Irish ODA programme, membership of the EC has had a dramatic impact on relative distributions. The World Bank, and the UN and its agencies has been replaced by the EC as the chief conduit of that part of ODA flows which Ireland expands multilaterally.

The Community's own development programme — as distinct from the individual programmes of the member-states — draws its funding from three sources. First, the European Development Fund (EDF) which finances the EC-ACP Lomé Convention. The fund provides grants for all financial, technical and emergency assistance under the Convention, as well as funding for STABEX and SYSMIN. In 1988, the total allocated to the fund by member-states was ECU 1,000 million (IR£ 775 million), of which Ireland's share was 0.59 per cent (IR£ 4.571 million). Second, the General Budget of the EC, of which 3 per cent was allocated for development co-operation in 1988, providing grant aid for all financial and technical assistance to extra-ACP developing countries (that is, those in Asia, Latin America and the Mediterranean countries) and funds for the EC's food aid programme. In 1988, ECU 1464.9 million (IR£ 1,139.7 million) from the EC general budget was spend on development co-operation, of which Ireland's calculated share was IR£ 8.4 million. Third, the European Investment Bank. Ireland's contributions to the EDF and the budget were low to begin with but after a few years they had built up to its full calculated share. In monetary terms they grew from IR£ 400,000 in 1975 to IR£ 6.7 million in 1980 and IR£ 14.7 million in 1989.

Ireland's contributions to the World Bank and the UN and its agencies grew steadily up to 1987 (IR£ 10.4 million), but have fallen since then (IR£ 6.7 million in 1989 and 1990). As is the case with the bilateral programme, the largely non-mandatory payments to the UN agencies have been a major casualty of the ODA cut-backs since 1986.

As already noted, Ireland's choices in the geographic and sectoral distribution of ODA funds were not determined by, but none the less largely reflect, those of the EC's own programme. Frequent consultation among the member-states, both in Brussels and 'on the ground' in Africa probably tends to reinforce convergence of approach, especially at the sectoral level. As to new initiatives, as already noted, participation in discussions on women in development (WID) has increased Ireland's sensitivity to this issue. So far, however, beyond including women as an important target group whose interests must be taken into account at the appraisal stage of all projects, very little has been spent on WID within the Irish bilateral programme.

Realization of objectives

Earlier, the main objectives of Irish development policy were seen to be, in order, the promotion of development in the assisted LDCs, the improvement of North—South relations, the broadening of the foreign policy agenda and (marginally and indirectly) the production of economic benefits for Ireland. To accomplish these objectives, increased funds were clearly needed. Did EC membership promote the allocation of increased funding to development co-operation?

Growth in total ODA flows

Since joining the EC, total ODA from Ireland increased steadily and significantly, from IR£ 1.5 million in 1974, IR£ 8.4 million in 1978, IR£ 24.6 million in 1983 and IR£ 40.5 million in 1986. Since then it has declined in real terms and as a proportion of GNP (from 0.25 per cent in 1986 to 0.17 per cent in 1989). Meanwhile, the bilateral programme, having risen up to 1986, began to fall in nominal terms and as a proportion of total ODA from 1987. Contributions to the EC's development programme have risen over the same period, from IR£ 400,000 in 1975 to IR£ 14.7 million in 1989. The decline in overall ODA flows reflected the decline in overall public expenditure which began in 1987 as the Government sought to correct the public finances and control the growth of Ireland's national debt.

Indeed, ODA was cut disproportionately — 30 per cent in 1988 compared with overall public expenditure cuts of 7 per cent that year. Has the continued growth in contributions to the EC development programme, in a period of public expenditure cuts, been the cause of the fall in the size of Ireland's bilateral aid? Has Ireland moved from a position where the establishment and growth of its bilateral programme was promoted by EC membership to one where it is now constrained by it? This does not appear to be the case. The single biggest impact on the size of ODA flows is the Government's overall budgetary strategy. In the period when government was committed to certain annual percentage increases in total ODA, very large increases or decreases in contributions to the EDF would have impacted on the size of the bilateral programme. In general, however, changes in EDF contributions were not such as to have had a noticeable effect on the bilateral side.

Unlike the DAC, which issues regular — and often critical — reports on its members' performances, the EC does not formally examine or report on the development programmes of its member-states. Much less are member-states criticized if their bilateral programmes decline. Development policy is only one of a number of policy headings in the total EC list; there are so many trade-offs to be taken into account that criticism of other member-states' performances under any single heading are usually very risky.

In any case, on a scale from 'generous' to 'parsimonious', Ireland would be classified as middle-ranking when it comes to agreement among the member-states on the size of the EDF. It would seem that the Department of Foreign Affairs, which is responsible for the development policy, is in a stronger position *vis-à-vis* the Department of Finance when calling for increased funds for the Lomé Convention (and thus the EDF) than it is when trying to increase or even maintain the size of its bilateral aid programme.

Promotion of development in LDCs

An evaluation of the impact of Irish aid on the developing countries it assists is beyond the scope of this chapter. Even more so is an assessment of the effects of EC membership on the effectiveness of Irish aid as an instrument of development. Instead, three issues which are important where Irish and EC development policies interface will be briefly considered. Those issues are: aid to the poorest; structural adjustment; and ACP exports to the EC. All three are critical for development prospects in Africa in the 1990s.

Assisting the poorest

As already noted, from a sector point of view, Ireland's bilateral aid is focused on education, rural development, and primary health care. Aid to those sectors could be expected to promote the welfare of poor groups, if not the very poorest. The latter are notoriously difficult to reach, especially through official aid programmes. Non-governmental organizations (NGOs) tend to be more effective in helping the poorest. Co-financing of NGOs has been an effective element in the Irish bilateral aid programme for a number of years. Total expenditure under this heading has been small in recent years (about IR£ 500,000 in both 1988 and 1989). However, the effectiveness of these organizations and the overall effectiveness of both the Irish aid programme and that of the EC has been promoted by grants to them from the EC's own co-financing scheme with NGOs. Between 1976 and 1988, a total of ECU 10.9 million has been received by Irish NGOs from the EC, undoubtedly assisting them to improve levels of living among the poorest groups in the developing countries.

Structural adjustment

As already noted, the special community programme for sub-Saharan Africa (SSA) was established in 1988 to provide quick-disbursing aid for import support for SSA's poorest and most indebted countries.

It has also been noted that some of the funds can be used for general balance-of-payments support, as distinct from sector-specific imports but, in such cases, a condition is that an economic reform programme should be in place in the recipient country. Debate among the EC member-states has centred around whether it is necessary for the country to have a structural adjustment programme agreed with the World Bank or, if not, what sort of reform programme should the EC demand as a condition attaching to these funds. In other words, could and should EC 'conditionality' in the case of non-project aid be different from that of the World Bank and IMF? And, further, what proportion of funds from the Lomé Convention should be devoted to structural adjustment loans in future?

The EC member-states were divided on these issues in 1988 and 1989. Ireland's view was that it would be unwise for the EC to devote a significant proportion of EDF funds to structural adjustment loans; in its view, the coherence of the EC's development programme would be jeopardized if too high a proportion of EC aid were given to structural adjustment loans. Ireland also supported a more independent line on the structural adjustment issue itself. As a result, dialogue between the EC and the World Bank and IMF on the whole question of conditionality and structural adjustment loans is expected to result in some modification of the approach taken to date on this issue by the Bretton Woods institutions.

ACP exports to the EC

When it comes to the interface of development policy and trade policy, Ireland's foreign policy, in common with that of many donor countries, and even the EC itself, displays a certain lack of coherence. A classic example is the giving of aid for the development of industry and agriculture, followed by the raising of protectionist walls against exports to the donor country from the assisted sectors. In Ireland's case, trade policy towards developing countries varies according to sector. In the case of imports of textiles and clothing from LDCs — that is, products covered by the Multi-Fibre Arrangement — Ireland is consciously protectionist because of the continued importance of the sector in employment terms domestically. As regards imports of other manufacturers, the country is relatively liberal. Overall, membership of the EC probably exercises a restraining hand on the protectionist tendencies that exist *vis-à-vis* imports of manufactures, especially in 'sensitive' sectors such as textiles and clothing. As to imports of agricultural products, Ireland is strongly supportive of the Common Agricultural Policy (CAP) and against derogations when it comes to imports of CAP-related products from developing countries. In this case, membership of the EC, which carries CAP benefits with it, probably allows a more protectionist approach to be taken towards developing countries (see Chapter 3 on agricultural policy).

Improvement of North–South relations

Ireland has been a member of the so-called 'like-minded group' of industrialized countries since its inception in 1976 and was thus one of the countries pushing for the new international economic order (NIEO) and improvements in North–South relations in the late 1970s. With the Dutch and French, it was active in the early days of the negotiations for the establishment of the common fund to stabilize primary commodity prices. As negotiations on the fund and on other NIEO issues proceeded, the views of both the more 'hardline' Northern countries (including some EC member-states) and of the 'like-minded' group came closer together. It could be said that for the EC member-states as a whole, their membership of the EC had a moderating influence on all of them. Nevertheless, even today, differences of approach are still discernible on North–South issues, as already noted earlier in relation to structural adjustment financing under Lomé. At the wider level of discussions on North–South issues in the UN (the so-called 'North–South dialogue') the EC tries to arrive at a consensus view, the product of discussions where individual member-states, and the EC as a group, mutually influence each other.

Broadening of Ireland's foreign policy

Ireland's development policy has helped to open up new areas for consideration within its overall foreign policy. The focus in its development policy is Africa. One consequence of EC membership is that, given the global reach of the Community's development-related links, Ireland's foreign policy has had to take account of countries such as those in Central America which, in a purely bilateral context, it would not otherwise have done. In foreign policy terms, the costs are purely financial; the benefits are a broadening of the international links in ways not possible either bilaterally for a small country or multilaterally as a member of the UN.

Economic returns to Ireland

Although the production of direct economic returns has never been an objective of Irish development policy, many firms (most notably in the public sector) and individuals have benefited from the programme. Since Ireland's bilateral aid is provided mainly in the form of technical assistance, economic returns tended to come initially from participation in the bilateral programme, the money from which, although officially untied to the purchase of Irish goods, none the less used Irish personnel almost exclusively.

Later on, experience with the bilateral programme helped Irish firms and individuals to obtain technical assistance contracts with the multilateral organizations. EC membership opened up EC contracts to them. Overall, then, EC membership has been instrumental in building up an international consultancy sub-sector within the export services sector.

Concluding remarks

Membership of the EC probably helped to get Ireland's bilateral aid programme underway in 1974. Although the programme's early sectoral focus was largely domestically-determined, subsequent developments were in part influenced by EC membership. On policy issues, influences have been bi-directional. In relation to trade with developing countries, the influence of the EC on Ireland is greater than the influence of Ireland on the EC. On issues relating to the wider North—South dialogue and some policy issues within the Lomé Convention, Ireland's influence on EC policy has not been insignificant.

Having a development policy has helped to broaden Irish foreign policy generally. And if Ireland was to leave the EC what effect would that have on its development policy? EC membership has undoubtedly been instrumental in promoting Ireland's own development since 1973. If Ireland were to leave the EC, per capita income would fall and perhaps the country would feel that it could no longer afford a development programme at all. As a member of the world's largest trading bloc, it can hardly sustain such an argument.

Notes

1. Brian Lenihan, TD, Minister for Foreign Affairs, address to the inaugural meeting of the National Advisory Council on Development Co-operation, 31 March 1980, p. 7.
2. Garrett FitzGerald, TD, Minister for Foreign Affairs, Parliamentary Debates, Dail Eireann, Official Report, vol. 265, p. 742, 1973.
3. Michael O'Kennedy, TD, Minister for Foreign Affairs, address to the Annual General Meeting of DEVCO, the State Agencies Development Co-operation Organization, 12 February 1979, p. 2.
4. Jim O'Keeffe, TD, Minister of State for Development Co-operation, address to the National Advisory Council on Development Co-operation, 30 July 1981, p. 1.
5. An Taoiseach, Charles Haughey, TD, in answer to a question in the Dail on 23 November 1989, as reported in *The Irish Times*, 24 November 1989.
6. Ireland, *The Second Programme for Economic Expansion*, Dublin: Government Publications, 1963, p. 16.

Bibliography

Department of Foreign Affairs, *Ireland's Development Assistance*, Dublin, various years.
FitzGerald, Garrett (1988), 'Ireland's development policy: aid and trade', *Studies*, autumn, pp. 328—41.
O'Neill, Helen (1984), 'Ireland's aid: performance and policies', in Olav Stokke (ed.), *European Development Assistance: Policies and Performance*, vol. 1, Tilburg and Oslo: EADI and NUPI, pp. 239—61.
O'Neill, Helen (1985), 'Ireland, Europe and the Third World: the question of aid', *Journal of the Statistical and Social Enquiry Society of Ireland*, pp. 137—48.
Sutton, Mary (1989), 'The European Community and the Third World — Ireland's role', *Studies*, autumn, pp. 262—73.

PART III: POLITICAL AND LEGAL SYSTEMS

Chapter 18
Introduction to Part III
Brigid Laffan

After the Second World War a myriad of political, economic, social and defence organizations mushroomed in Western Europe. These organizations are both a manifestation of growing interdependence among states and have contributed to this interdependence. All of the countries of Western Europe are embedded in a web of cross-national and trans-national links that blur the boundaries between them as sovereign independent states. It is possible to talk of a fourth level of government that is additional to national political structures. The European Community is unique in the pantheon of West European organizations because of its legal order, institutional structure, policy scope and the ultimate goal of European Union. The European Community has a special effect on the political, administrative and legal structures of its member countries. The purpose of this section is to analyse the impact of EC membership on Ireland's political and legal system.

European Community goals

The European Community is not an international organization in the classical or traditional sense of the word. Yet it is based on a Treaty framework and involves commitments by formally sovereign states. Participation in the European Community involves intensive co-operation across a range of policy issues, not found in most international organizations. Collaboration takes place within a sophisticated institutional framework and agreements are usually embodied in law. By joining the European Community, a country opts for participation in extensive multilateral co-operation and extra-national law-making which erodes formal legal sovereignty. We must be mindful that the nature of the contemporary international system, characterized by a high level of interdependence, itself erodes sovereignty. None the less, the European Community has substantial and special effects on the sovereignty of its members. These effects are assessed in the section on the impact of EC membership on the legal system.

The ultimate goal of the European Community goes beyond that found in conventional international treaties. The Preamble to the Rome Treaty (EEC, 1957) speaks of 'ever closer union among the peoples of Europe'. In the Single European Act (1986), the member-states express their intention to 'transform relations as a whole among their States into a European Union'. Although the precise meaning of this term has never been elaborated and there remain EC member-states fundamentally opposed to such a Union, it provides part of the ideological underpinning of the Community edifice and serves to justify political action (Pryce, 1987: 275). Economic and monetary union which is currently being explored by the European Council following the presentation of the Delors Report on EMU in April 1989 is an intrinsic part of such a union. The Delors Committee regards EMU as a natural consequence of attempts to complete the internal market and a 'quantum jump' which goes beyond the single market programme (Delors Report, 1989). The Madrid European Council in June 1989 agreed to the first stage of EMU and the Strasbourg European Council of December 1989 went further to envisage the convening of an intergovernmental conference on EMU at the end of 1990. There is considerable debate in the Community concerning the institutional changes that should accompany moves towards EMU; the powers of the European Parliament and the Commission are part of the current agenda. A profound transformation in relations among the EC member-states may occur because economic union requires the transfer of significant decision-making powers to the centre. Such a transfer must be accompanied by new political structures.

Bibliography

Delors, J. (1989), Report on Economic and Monetary Union, submitted to European Council.
EEC Treaty (1957).
Pryce, R. (ed.) (1987), *The Dynamics of European Union*, London: Croom Helm.
Single European Act (1986), EC *Bulletin*, Supplement 2/1986.

Chapter 19

Sovereignty and national identity

Brigid Laffan

This section explores sovereignty as an issue in the political debate concerning EC membership and assesses whether or not attachment to the notion of sovereignty affects attitudes to the development of the Community. Ireland's acquisition of statehood in 1921 makes the country the youngest state among the EC members. The formation of the Irish state in that year did not finally settle the issue of independence because the Treaty made provision for continuing links with Britain and was thus less than full independence. Full sovereignty was not vested in the state until the adoption of a new constitution in 1937. The recent acquisition of statehood together with a continuing preoccupation with constitutional issues would lead us to expect a cautious attitude towards political integration and a desire to protect recently acquired autonomy. Paradoxically, there is less preoccupation with the issue of sovereignty in Ireland than in Denmark or Britain who also joined in 1973. Why is this so?

The main reason for this strange paradox is a deep-rooted view of the European Community as essentially an economic entity. A preoccupation with the economic dimension of EC co-operation characterizes Ireland's approach to European integration for a number of reasons. First, Ireland's level of economic development is well below that of the Community average. A perception of economic vulnerability and resource shortage moulds the thinking of Irish politicians and civil servants. Second, Ireland's first application for membership in 1961 stemmed from a change in foreign economic policy based on a desire to move towards free trade and export-led economic growth. Access to multilateral trading groupings was important for the successful implementation of this policy change. Third, non-involvement in the Second World War isolated Ireland from the shared experiences that led political leaders on continental Europe to opt for co-operation. Thus attention is focused primarily although not exclusively on the European Community as an economic entity. Attention to the political dimension of the European Community is related to the protection of neutrality and to a loosening of the ties with Britain.

The Irish electorate was given two opportunities to express its views about EC membership; in 1972 prior to accession to the Community and again in 1987 when the ratification of the Single European Act was the occasion of a second referendum. The 1972 referendum was required because of the need to render EC membership constitutional. Sovereignty was an issue, although not a central one, in the debate on membership. The opponents of membership, drawn mostly from the left of the political spectrum, argued that the country's accession to the Community would involve an erosion of sovereignty and would in the long term restrict the country's ability to pursue an independent and neutral foreign policy. The anti-marketeers operated under an umbrella organization called the Common Market Study Group, later to become the Irish Sovereignty Movement. Proponents of membership, which included the two main political parties, Fianna Fáil and Fine Gael, together with employers' organizations and the farming lobby presented an alternative view of the impact of the EC on sovereignty. While accepting that all international co-operation involved some diminution of sovereignty, according to the pro-marketeers, such limitations on national freedom would be more than counterbalanced by the influence Ireland could bring to bear on the formulation of EC policies. The sharing or pooling of sovereignty was emphasized. This notion that Ireland may in fact have greater control over its destiny inside rather than outside the Community was persuasive, given Ireland's continued dependence on Britain despite formal independence. Accession to the Community offered the prospect of reduced economic dependence on Ireland's major trading partner and a multilateral framework for the pursuit of economic and foreign policy goals. The strong political position of the pro-market forces ensured that there was an overwhelming vote in favour of membership; 83 per cent of those voting opted for a 'yes' vote. There was a high correlation between a 'yes' vote and support for Fianna Fáil and Fine Gael in the elections which preceded and succeeded the 1972 referendum (Coakley, 1983: 51).

Sovereignty was raised again during the referendum on the ratification of the Single European Act in 1987. This referendum was necessitated by a successful challenge in the Supreme Court on the constitutionality of the SEA. The judgments on the case dealt specifically with sovereignty in foreign policy and are covered in Chapter 23 on the legal system. Unlike the 1972 referendum, the debate on this occasion was dominated by political issues. There were a large and diverse range of groups urging a 'no' vote. The Irish Sovereignty Movement opposed the SEA as a further diminution of Ireland's sovereignty and its freedom to pursue an independent foreign policy. This traditional voice of opposition was joined by environmentalists, peace groups and Third-World activists. European Political Co-operation would lead inexorably to a common European foreign policy and would render Irish neutrality meaningless according to those against ratification of the SEA. The supporters of the

Act came from the proponents of Ireland's membership of the Community fifteen years earlier. The main issue of the pro-campaign was Ireland's continued membership of the Community. Again the referendum was carried (69.9 per cent voted 'yes' and 30.1 per cent voted 'no') although the turnout of 44.1 per cent was the second lowest ever for a referendum. This suggests that the enthusiasm for the Community so evident in 1972 had been dampened by economic recession and the realities of membership (Gallagher, 1988; Keatinge, 1988).

Bibliography

Coakley, J. (1983), 'The European dimension in Irish public opinion 1972–1982', in D. Coombes (ed.), *Ireland and the European Communities: Ten Years of Membership*, Dublin: Gill and Macmillan.

Gallagher, M. (1988), 'The Single European Act referendum', *Irish Political Studies*, vol. 3.

Keatinge, P. (1988), 'Ireland's foreign relations in 1987', *Irish Studies in International Affairs*, vol. 2.

Chapter 20

Government and administration

Brigid Laffan

Ireland is a parliamentary democracy governed by a written constitution that specifies the powers and competences of the President, the Executive, the Parliament and the Judiciary. The President exercises a reserve role in the political system. Executive powers reside in the government of the day which must command a majority in Parliament. The President has a number of discretionary powers although in practice he or she acts on the advice and authority of the government. The Taoiseach or Prime Minister is formally appointed by the President although nominated by Dail Eireann, the lower house of a bicameral legislature. The government consists of not more than fifteen ministers who are responsible for one or more departments of central government. Each minister is accountable to the Parliament for the activities of his department and the Cabinet as a whole is governed by collective responsibility.

Adaptation to the demand of EC membership was perhaps the greatest challenge faced by the Irish civil and public service since the foundation of the state. Paradoxically, the creation of the state may have been less demanding because a very high proportion of the then civil service transferred to the service of the new state. Ireland inherited a well-established administrative apparatus. In contrast, membership of the EC came at a time when there was widespread questioning of the capacity of Ireland's public administration to cope with the demands of an industrializing and urbanizing society.

Community membership placed a heavy burden on the Irish public sector for which it was relatively unprepared. Little strategic thinking concerning the need for administrative adaptation took place until membership became a reality. This was partly because of an interdepartmental battle on the question of responsibility for the co-ordination of EC policy. During the accession negotiations the Departments of Finance and Foreign Affairs had joint responsibility for the negotiations. The Department of Foreign Affairs was isolated from the initial decision to apply for membership in 1961, a decision taken by a small group of finance officials and the Taoiseach of the day, Mr Sean Lemass. After accession, responsibility for the day-to-day co-ordination of EC policy was assigned to the Department of Foreign Affairs by the Cabinet (Burns and Salmon, 1977).

EC membership required expansion in a number of areas of the civil service, notably, the Departments of Foreign Affairs and Agriculture together with the Revenue Commissioners. In the Department of Foreign Affairs, the economic division which is responsible for EC matters almost trebled in size between 1970 and the mid-1970s. The political division, which is responsible for European Political Co-ordination, underwent a similar transformation. The Irish permanent representation in Brussels emerged as the largest overseas mission. For Ireland, the presidency of the Council of Ministers in 1975 served as the final apprenticeship for the public service in its adaptation to EC membership. The demands of the presidency ensured that departmental responsibility for policy areas was clearly delineated so that chairmanship of Council working groups was assured. Management of the Council agenda and the calendar of meetings made Irish politicians and officials *au fait* with the nuts and bolts of the Community's policy process. A six-month stint made the servicing of the normal workload attached to Community business less daunting. The experience of the presidency had a beneficial effect on the psychological environment of national policy-makers. Thereafter, the Community became an accepted if complicating factor in national decision-making.

The management of Community business

The coherence of public policy is the responsibility of the Cabinet which stands at the pinnacle of the Irish system of government. The Cabinet keeps an overview of Irish policy and takes decisions when a memorandum is received from a department. Government memoranda are used to inform the Cabinet on all major issues that will reach the Council of Ministers. From time to time a Cabinet sub-committee is established to deal with major dossiers, notably the intergovernmental conference leading to the Single European Act. In autumn 1987, the present Taoiseach, Mr Charles Haughey, set up the Committee of Ministers and Secretaries to oversee Ireland's preparations for the completion of the internal market and the reform of the structural funds. This committee met almost every week until Ireland submitted its *National Development Plan* to Brussels in March 1989. The establishment of this committee and the frequency of its meetings indicates the importance attached to EC developments in the post-Single European Act era by the Government. The Departments of Foreign Affairs, Agriculture, Industry and Commerce, Finance and the Taoiseach's Department are the leading ministries in the management of EC policy. Each ministry is responsible for those areas of EC policy that fall within its domain while the economic division of the Department of Foreign Affairs keeps a watchful brief over the flow of proposals through the Council system in all policy areas and directs the flow of information to and from the permanent representation.

At administrative level the European Communities Committee which predates EC membership is the main institutional device for formulating national positions and resolving interdepartmental conflict. Formerly, it met at secretary level but now meets at assistant-secretary level; representatives of the Departments of Foreign Affairs, Agriculture, Finance, Industry and Commerce, Labour and the Taoiseach's Department attend. Up to March 1987, it was chaired by the Deputy Secretary of Foreign Affairs and serviced by that department. Responsibility was transferred to the Taoiseach's Department when the present Taoiseach, Mr Charles Haughey, designated a portfolio for the co-ordination of EC policy which is held by a Minister for State in his department. The committee is therefore no longer a purely administrative committee but spans the administrative/political divide. Foreign Affairs continues to exercise its role as an overseer of all EC policies but the Taoiseach's Department plays an important part in setting priorities and in co-ordinating major negotiations. The establishment of the high level committee of ministers and secretaries in autumn 1987 underlines this. The European Bureau, set up to co-ordinate the Government's information campaign (EUROPEN) on 1992 is attached to the Taoiseach's Department. The bureau is responsible for a public awareness campaign and for a number of sectoral studies that examine in detail the implications of the internal market programme for specific branches of the economy.

Ireland's permanent representation in Brussels is accorded a high status in the policy process because of the small size of central government. A period working in the unit is perceived as useful from a career perspective both by diplomats and members of the home civil service. The permanent representative and his deputy are always career diplomats from Foreign Affairs. This department supplies the lion's share of remaining officials, usually about 45 per cent. The need to provide detailed coverage of the substantive areas of EC policy ensures that the remaining officials are drawn from the domestic departments. It is difficult to establish what the balance of influence is between the representation and the administration in Dublin. By and large, the preparation of dossiers and administrative co-ordination remains the prerogative of the national bureaucracy. The representation provides invaluable information concerning the attitudes of other delegations to a particular dossier and possible negotiating scenarios. The status of the permanent representative also ensures that his views carry considerable weight in the formation of policy responses.

Ireland's policy style

The system of policy formation on European Community issues in Ireland differs markedly from the other member-states in a number of important respects. It is much less institutionalized than in other member-states; there are far fewer co-ordinating committees and those that exist meet less frequently than their counterparts. Written requests for information and telephone contacts are more prevalent than formal policy groups. It is necessary to assess and explain this apparent difference between Ireland and the other member-states. An understanding may be found in the small size of the bureaucracy and the country's administrative culture. Administrative adaptation to EC membership has been pragmatic and *ad hoc*. Pragmatism permeates the country's administrative culture and leads to a policy style which concentrates on clear sight over short distances. Policy-making is highly reactive as position papers are worked out at each stage of the negotiating process. The small size of the bureaucracy leads to a less formal approach to policy-making; civil servants working on the Community know their counterparts in other government departments and deal with many issues over the telephone. Size has implications not only for the policy process but also for the range of interests that must be accommodated for EC negotiations. Interests may be aggregated with greater ease in a small country than in a larger one; the potential for competing claims and conflict is reduced. Irish policy-makers have found it reasonably easy to establish major priorities for the purposes of EC negotiations.

The management of EC business is weak in a number of respects. First, the system has a limited capacity to evaluate the extensive flow of legislative proposals from the Commission and the balance within and between policy sectors. The Irish system of public administration is characterized by a high degree of departmental autonomy. Individual departments guard their policy domains to the neglect of linkages between issues. The implementation of the directive on the mutual recognition of diplomas involves a large number of government departments with diverse interests. A balanced approach to this directive requires the establishment of an interdepartmental policy group but none has been established to date. Second, the 'in-tray' 'out-tray' approach to policy-making weakens the system's capacity to think in the medium to longer term. The Department of Foreign Affairs has neither the resources nor the inclination to assess the development of Community policies from a medium-term perspective. The permanent representation cannot assume a role of this nature. At best it acts as an early warning system for national officials. The European Communities Committee which is supposed to adopt a strategic approach has not always done so. The fact that it did not meet at all for a period in 1984/5 highlights a lacuna in strategic thinking about the Community at a time when there were major institutional and policy issues on the EC agenda. The creation of a ministerial post for the co-ordination of EC matters in March 1987 by the Taoiseach suggests that he was unhappy with the management of EC business, particularly with the role of the Department of Foreign Affairs. The establishment of a high-level committee of ministers and secretaries chaired by the Taoiseach himself in the latter half of 1987 may be interpreted as an attempt to up-grade co-ordination on 'high policy' issues and to involve the Taoiseach's Department more intimately in the process of co-ordination. The Government's decision to ask the National Economic and Social Council (NESC) to undertake a study of Ireland's membership of the Community and to assess future policy developments suggests that a more considered approach is being taken on the completion of the internal market and cohesion. The NESC Report, published in September 1989, emphasizes Ireland's need to develop a strategic approach to the development of the Community and stresses that EC membership does not reduce the need for clear Irish policy aims and methods (NESC, 1989). Third, there is little thinking in the Irish public service about the development and powers of EC institutions. Irish policy-makers made only one submission to the SEA intergovernmental conference, a rather short document on cohesion. In view of a new intergovernmental conference on the horizon to discuss EMU and related institutional issues, it is important that there is consideration of these matters in Ireland.

The Single European Act which expanded the use of majority voting in the Council and enlarged the role of the European Parliament and the Commission's implementing powers alters the 'rules of the game' in EC policy-making in a very profound sense. The successful expansion in the use of majority voting in the Council and the change in the Council's internal rules of procedure has greatly accelerated the speed of decision-making and has broken the ingrained habits of twenty years. The search for consensus no longer delays discussions in the working groups. For example, in the 1970s, it took four-and-a-half years to get agreement on the supplies directive for public procurement. It took only one-and-a-half years to substantially reinforce this directive in the post-SEA era. National administrations have had to respond to these changes. The speed of decision-making requires a much faster assessment of Commission proposals at national level. Reservations will no longer keep an item on the Council's agenda. Once a qualified majority is assembled in the Council, a decision is taken. Negotiators can no longer rely only on their own instructions but must work in tandem with other delegations. While 'corridor diplomacy' and contacts at the margins of meetings has always been an important aspect of EC policy-making, its saliency is increased when each member-state is attempting to participate in a qualified majority or to construct a blocking minority. The absence of a strong tradition of continental languages in the Irish civil service militates against 'corridor diplomacy' with the French-speaking countries of the South. This is partly offset by the ease with which Irish people establish personal contacts. The embargo on public sector employment which has reduced the size of the civil service has had an impact on the management of EC business, notably on the implementation of EC law (Laffan, 1990).

Local and regional government

Ireland is a unitary state with a two-tier system of government at central and local levels. There is no system of representative regional government in the country. Local authorities are affected by EC policies that impinge on those areas for which they have responsibility, notably, environmental directives, public procurement, public health and safety and EC financial instruments for the lesser-developed parts of the Community. The European Regional Development Fund (ERDF) is the main budgetary item of interest to local authorities. Prior to the establishment of the ERDF in 1975 there were great expectations among Irish local authorities concerning possible financial flows from the fund. In the event, the ERDF has been managed and administered in a highly centralized manner in Ireland with the Department of Finance using the fund as reimbursement for expenditure through the public capital programme (PCP). This was possible because the entire state is regarded as one region for the purposes of ERDF monies. Local authorities have not received ERDF monies directly and have had no input into the planning of ERDF applications.

The reform of the structural funds, necessitated by the Single European Act (SEA), has led to changes in Ireland concerning the management of financial transfers from the Community and the role of sub-national government. The reform of the funds has as a major focus the development of 'partnerships' between the Community, national, regional and local levels in the policy process. In addition, the Commission is moving away from financing projects to programmes of a geographic or sectoral nature. The emphasis on partnerships and programmes poses problems for Ireland for two reasons. First, the regional tier of government is weak; in 1963, the Government established nine regional development organizations (RDOs) on a non-statutory basis to act as a focus for local development agencies and local government. The RDOs had little or no administrative back-up and no power. They were abolished in 1987 as a cost-cutting exercise. The policy scope of local government is extremely narrow in Ireland and there is no form of local taxation. Second, Ireland did not move towards the programme approach for structural fund monies in the 1980s as the Commission stressed its desire to alter the grant-awarding procedures. Consequently, Irish officials had little experience of the development and implementation of programmes prior to the 1989 reform of the funds.

In October 1987, in an attempt to demonstrate a willingness to adopt a programme approach, the Government announced the commencement of pilot programmes for Dublin, Cork and the West. The announcement of three pilot programmes served only to fuel local rivalry as those areas excluded from the proposal felt that they would not get a fair share of the EC structural-fund cake. The reform of the funds became a sensitive issue on the political agenda; the opposition parties, interest organizations and local politicians were virulent in their protests about the management of the reform. The Government felt the need to adopt a global approach and in August 1988 an announcement was made dividing the country into seven regions which would serve as the basis for the development of programmes for structural fund purposes; the regions had no wider mandate than this.

In each region, a working group was established of local authority administrators, representatives of state-sponsored bodies and central government departments. The working groups were chaired and serviced by the Department of Finance. The announcement led to conflict concerning the geographical breakdown and the absence of elected local representatives on the working groups. This led to a third Government decision to set up a second committee in each region consisting of all the relevant interest organizations and local politicians. Some of the working groups had not completed their deliberations when Ireland submitted its *National Development Plan* to Brussels in March 1989. The Commission is unhappy with the involvement of local and community bodies in the administration of the increased structural fund monies (Commissioner Bruce Millan, *The Irish Times*, 21 September 1989). At the insistence of the Commission the working groups and the advisory groups are to be merged and given a role monitoring the implementation of the plan in their areas. The management of EC monies and the reform of the structural funds is entangled in a debate about the role and structure of subnational government in Ireland. Local politicians regard the Commission as a potential source of pressure on the Government for greater dialogue across all levels of government (Laffan, 1989). The presence of a Commission official on the monitoring committees for the operational programmes will facilitate dialogue between Brussels and local groups.

Bibliography

Burns, B. and Salmon, T. (1977), 'Policy-making coordination in Ireland on European Community issues', *Journal of Common Market Studies*, vol. 15, (June).

Laffan, B. (1989), 'While you are over there in Brussels, get us a grant: the management of the structural funds in Ireland', *Irish Political Studies*, vol. 4.

Laffan, B. (1990), 'Putting EC law into practice: the Irish experience', *Administration*, vol. 37, (no. 3).

NESC (1989), *Ireland in the European Community: Performance, Prospects and Strategy*, Dublin: Pl. 6662.

Chapter 21

The political process
Brigid Laffan

The party system

Irish political parties do not readily fit into the normal pattern of European political families; the party system is dominated by two large parties, Fianna Fáil and Fine Gael which have their origins in the Sinn Fein movement and the quest for independence. Cumann na nGaedheal (later Fine Gael) and Fianna Fáil were founded by rival leaders of the independence movement. These parties gained a foothold during the critical time in the formation of the party system and retained their dominant position. Fianna Fáil is since 1933 the only party to form a single-party government and held power for thirty-eight of the forty-nine years between 1932 and 1981. The Labour party is a minor party that has participated in government with Fine Gael on a number of occasions to provide the electorate with an alternative to FF rule. There are two other minor parties in the Dail, the Workers' party which lies to the left of the Labour party and the Progressive Democrats, founded in 1985 by a former FF cabinet minister, Mr Desmond O'Malley.

The issue of EC membership did not lead to internal splits in the country's political parties. The two main parties campaigned in favour of membership and delivered the vote, as noted above in the section on the EC referendum. The Labour party provided the parliamentary opposition to membership; although the party had favoured membership during the 1960s, the 1971 Party Conference voted against full membership but advocated some form of association. Fianna Fáil lost a general election in 1973 just after Ireland's accession to the Community and were replaced by a coalition of FG and Labour who had fought on opposite sides of the referendum campaign. Surprisingly this did not lead to policy disputes in the Government as the Labour party accepted the verdict of the referendum and adjusted to the reality of Ireland's involvement in the Community.

Although there are differences among the parties in their approach to the European Community, a distinctive Irish approach is discernable.

Ireland's experience as a small peripheral less-developed economy shapes its approach to the Community. The defence of the CAP, the politics of redistribution and the need to ensure that sectoral developments are appropriate to Irish circumstances dominate Ireland's EC agenda. A recurring concern in Ireland's 'European' policy is the need to ensure that political co-operation advances only on the basis of agreement on economic co-operation. The defence of neutrality is a permanent theme in the debate about Europe. Governments of every hue operate within these broad parameters.

As the party that negotiated the terms of Ireland's accession Fianna Fáil appears less enthusiastic about the Community when in opposition. It attaches considerable importance to the 'veto' as a protection of the rights of small countries and is loath to give too much power to the European Parliament because of the country's sparse representation (fifteen seats) in that assembly. The impact of the SEA on the 'veto' has never been acknowledged. The Fianna Fáil leader, Mr Charles J. Haughey, adopted a hostile approach to the Single European Act (SEA) and was highly critical of the Government's management of the negotiations. In the Dail, Mr Haughey expressed doubts about the institutional changes embodied in the Act and the impact of the SEA on Ireland's neutrality. In the event, the referendum necessitated by the *Crotty* case took place during Fianna Fáil's period in office after the 1987 election. This tempered the party's hostility towards the Act and highlighted once again how the rhetoric of opposition changes in government. Mr Haughey accepted the basic thrust of the NESC report which called for the fullest measure of economic integration and is strongly federalist in character (ICEM Conference, 2 October 1989). This represents a considerable reassessment of Fianna Fáil policy towards the European Community.

Fine Gael would regard itself as a very *communautaire* party; Dr Garrett FitzGerald was appointed Foreign Minister in the 1973 Coalition Government and had responsibility for Ireland's first presidency in 1975. Dr FitzGerald, himself a committed European, set out to develop a distinctive Irish approach to the Community. Because of the high degree of congruence between developments in the EC and Irish interests during the first years of membership, Ireland appeared enthusiastic and *communautaire*. In the 1980s, a period of electoral instability and negotiations on the Anglo-Irish Agreement relegated EC issues to a peripheral place on the agenda. Mr Peter Barry of Fine Gael who was Minister for Foreign Affairs from 1982 to 1987 devoted considerable energy to the Anglo-Irish Agreement and displayed little sustained interest in the European Community. When Dr FitzGerald retired from the leadership of Fine Gael, he was replaced by Mr Alan Dukes, who has extensive European experience. He was in charge of the Irish Business Bureau in Brussels and was *chef de cabinet* to a former Irish Commissioner.

The Labour party accepted in the verdict of the electorate in 1973 and adjusted to the reality of EC membership. Its grassroots remained somewhat hostile to the Community. Although it was in government when Ireland signed the Single European Act in 1986, it was unable to support the ratification of the Act in the 1987 referendum. Its Administrative Council, in a bid to ensure that it did not oppose the constitutional amendment, decided that individual members of the party were free to support or oppose the amendment. The Workers' party opposed the referendum but altered its 'European' policy since then; at the 1989 party conference, the leader of the party, Mr P. De Rossa, spoke of a 'democratic socialist united Europe' (*The Irish Times*, 10 April 1989). Both left-wing parties stress the need for a social charter and the redistribution of resources from the richer to the poorer parts of the Community.

Irish political parties have found a niche for themselves in the European Parliament. The Labour party as a member of the Socialist International and the Confederation of European Socialists had a history of transnational party co-operation; it automatically joined the Socialist grouping of the European Parliament. In the first directly elected Parliament the Labour party had four seats. The loss of these seats in the 1984 direct elections weakened the party's day-to-day links with the Socialist grouping although it maintained observer status in the group. Its international links predate EC membership and survived the absence of representation in the European Parliament between 1984 and 1989.

The two main conservative parties were faced with a real dilemma when choosing partners in the European Parliament. It was imperative for both parties to join different groups so that electoral competition at domestic level could continue. In what was regarded as an astute move, Fine Gael opted for the Christian Democratic Group (European Peoples Party) prior to accession. This gave Fine Gael membership of one of the mainstream political groupings in the Parliament. Dr Garrett FitzGerald, when Foreign Minister and Taoiseach forged close links with his Christian Democratic colleagues in other member-states. Membership of the EPP has not been without its problems for Fine Gael; it is one of the groups most committed to the development of a defence and security dimension to European co-operation. There is tension in the Fine Gael group between the majority of MEPs who seek a let-out clause on neutrality and one or two who endorse the development of EC security and defence policies.

Fianna Fáil was left without a party grouping for its first six months in the European Parliament. The privileges associated with group status led the party to join with the French Gaullists to form the European Progressive Democrats or the European Democratic Alliance, as it is now called. The EDA is based on a pragmatic attachment because both parties had difficulties in aligning themselves with the traditional political families in the Parliament. The two parties agree to differ on many policy issues although they are both committed to defence of the CAP. It has never been an easy alliance and on a number of occasions there have been discussions within Fianna Fáil on possible alternatives. After Spanish accession talks were held with a number of their MEPs but nothing materialized. Fianna Fáil will continue its involvement with the Gaullists in the absence of an alternative. There is no evidence of a cross-fertilization of ideas from one branch of the grouping to the other and no apparent impact at domestic level.

The Progressive Democrats contesting the European elections for the first time in June 1989 joined the Liberal grouping and are represented in that grouping by Mr Pat Cox MEP who took a seat in Munster. Before that, Mr T.J. Maher participated in the Liberal group although he is not involved in a party at national level. The Workers' party joined 'Left Unity', a breakaway group of Communists, when it won its first EP seat in June 1989. Membership of the Socialist group was precluded because of the Labour party's prior involvement with the group and the attitude of Mr John Hume of the SDLP in Northern Ireland.

Elections to the European Parliament are now part of the political calender in the member-states as they provide an opportunity for party competition. Although they are not as significant as general elections because the governance of the country is not at stake, European Parliament elections have acted as mid-term tests of the incumbent government in 1979, 1984 and 1989. In 1979 the incumbent Fianna Fáil Government faced the electorate at the end of a protracted postal dispute and performed badly as a result. The then Taoiseach, Mr Jack Lynch, resigned within six months of the election — the performance of his party during the European elections influenced his decision to resign. In 1984, domestic circumstances for the Coalition Government were even graver with high unemployment, a rising public debt and heavy taxation. The Labour party, the junior party in the coalition, lost all four of its EP seats, which was interpreted by opponents of coalition within the party as a result of its involvement with Fine Gael (Collins, 1986).

Ireland is divided into four constituencies for the purposes of the Euro-elections: Leinster (three seats), Munster (five seats), Connaught/Ulster (three seats) and Dublin (four seats). In the absence of agreement on a common electoral system for the Community as a whole, the system of proportional representation called the STV or single transferable vote system used for both local and national elections is used for the Euro-elections. The single transferable vote gives each elector one vote which is exercised by indicating on the ballot paper the candidates preferred in order of preference, regardless of party, in multi-member constituencies. The 1977 European Assembly Act gives all Irish citizens and nationals of other EC countries a vote in the European elections provided they are ordinarily resident in the state. Although membership of the EC has had no impact on the country's electoral system, its influence could be sizeable; a common European electoral system is likely to be akin to the continental list system rather than the Anglo-Saxon form of PR found in Ireland. The experience of working with the list system, which would give the party leaderships a greater say over the selection of candidates than they currently have, could fuel demands for electoral reform.

The political parties fared differently in the three elections. In 1979 the Labour party did particularly well winning four seats with just 14 per cent of the first preference vote; all four seats were lost in the subsequent election. Fianna Fáil won five seats in 1979 which was a poor performance for a party which aspires to win an overall majority and frequently does. Fine Gael won four seats. Two well-known independents were able to mobilize a high vote and headed the poll in their respective constituencies. In 1984, Fianna Fáil set out to reverse the 1979 result and to gain a majority of the fifteen seats. The Euro-election was regarded as a run up to the next general election by party strategists. By winning eight seats, the party succeeded in their goal. The Labour party lost all four of its seats, two of which were won by Fine Gael their coalition partner. This exacerbated tensions within the coalition for the next two years. Table 21.1 gives the results of the 1979 and 1984 direct elections.

Table 21.1 *Results of the 1979 and 1984 European elections*

Party	1979 Seats	%	1984 Seats	%
Fianna Fáil	5	34.68	8	39.17
Fine Gael	4	33.13	6	32.21
Labour	4	14.48	0	8.36
Independents	2	—	1	—

Source: European Parliament Election Results, December 1984, Dublin: EP Office, p. 14.

The June 1989 Euro-elections were completely overshadowed by the calling of a general election on the same day. The quest for domestic political power relegated the Euro-elections to that of a sideshow at the margins of the campaign. The campaign for the European elections had started well before the decision to have a general election on the same day. The minority Fianna Fáil Government decided to use the occasion of the Euro-election to go the hustings in search of a majority of seats in the Dail. One beneficial side effect of the general election was that voter turn-out rose from the low of 47 per cent in 1984 to 68 per cent in 1989. The disadvantage was the relegation of issues relating to the implementation of the European Community's programmes on the internal market and cohesion to the margins. All political parties contesting the Euro-elections issued special manifestos setting out with greater or less detail the main priorities on the development of the Community. The Fianna Fáil manifesto emphasized the importance of the *National Development Plan* 1989—93, which looks for IR£ 3.4 billion from the Community for Ireland. Details are presented in the manifesto of the regional breakdown of proposed expenditure. The protection of neutrality is again highlighted. The Fine Gael manifesto is a very short document which sets out in very general terms the importance Fine Gael attaches to recent developments in the Community. The absence of any reference to European Political Co-operation is striking. Both the Labour party and the Workers' party stress the social dimension of the internal market and the need to ensure that the benefits of the completed market do not go only to the more advanced areas of the Community. The Progressive Democrats pay considerable attention to the role of the European Parliament and is the only party to conclude that the legislative power of the Parliament is inadequate even after its increased role in the Single European Act. The need to strengthen links between the national and European Parliaments is emphasized in the PD's document.

In 1989, as in 1979 and 1984, the government of the day suffered. Fianna Fáil in losing two seats in 1989 failed to maintain a majority of EP seats, a feat achieved in 1984. The party's poor performance in the general election manifested itself also in the results of the European elections. Fine Gael, the other major party, also lost two seats; in fact its percentage share of the vote fell by 10.6 per cent on the 1984 figures. The political consequences of this are not grave because the party increased its share of both the vote and seats in the general election. The Progressive Democrats performed significantly better in the European elections than they did in the general election by winning a seat in the Munster constituency. The swing to the left in the general election manifested itself also in the European elections. The Labour party returns to the Socialist group with one representative and the leader of the Workers' party, Mr P. De Rossa gives his party its first representation in the European Parliament. Mr T.J. Maher continues to hold his seat in Munster and Mr Neil Blaney, a former Fianna Fáil minister, regained his seat in Connaught/Ulster. The Green party polled well in Dublin with 8 per cent of the vote and in Leinster with 6 per cent of the vote. If they manage to double this vote in the next European elections they will win a seat. See Table 21.2 for the results of the 1989 election.

The 'dual mandate' is a source of tension for the country's political parties. After the 1979 elections, the dual mandate was very pervasive — thirteen of the fifteen Irish MEPs held seats in the Dail. This figure fell to five before the 1984 elections but rose to eight after the elections. Political parties have tended to nominate sitting TDs for the European elections because they have a strong political base in part of the Euro-constituency and a national profile. The political parties have been reluctant to establish rules on the dual mandate. Fianna Fáil agreed in 1984 that elected MEPs would have to decide between a political career in the European Parliament or the national parliament in the next general election. In 1987 four of the five dual mandate Fianna Fáil MEPs opted to stay in Europe. Fine Gael had a similar policy but allowed two MEPs to

Table 21.2 *The 1989 European elections*

Party	Seats	Gains/loss	% votes		
			Euro 1989	Euro 1984	General Election 1989
Fianna Fáil	6	−2	31.5	39.2	44.1
Fine Gael	4	−2	21.6	32.2	29.3
Progressive Democrats	1	+1	11.9	—	5.5
Labour	1	+1	9.5	8.4	9.5
Workers' party	1	+1	7.5	4.3	5.0
Independents	2	+1	11.9	10.7	—

Source: The Irish Times, 19 and 20 June 1989.

go forward for re-election to the Dail because of fears of losing the seats. Both MEPs failed to hold their Dail seats which suggests that the electorate did not approve of the continuation of the dual mandate. In the 1989 elections only two dual mandate candidates were successful, one of whom, Mr P. De Rossa will have the task of leading his party and sitting in both the Dail and the European Parliament.

The Oireachtas

The Irish Parliament consists of two houses, an upper house called the Seanad and the directly elected lower house, the Dail. Accession to the Community eroded the exclusive law-making power of the Oireachtas. The opposition parties in the Dail use traditional parliamentary devices, notably debates and parliamentary questions to elicit information about Ireland's approach to Community policies. In addition, the Taoiseach makes a statement to the Dail after each European Council and the Government produces a twice-yearly report entitled *Developments in the European Communities* which is laid before the Oireachtas. The reports are usually late and debated infrequently by the houses of the Oireachtas, thus limiting their effectiveness as a means of control over the Executive's EC policy. The last report that was issued in January 1988 (31st Report).

In 1973, a Joint Committee on the Secondary Legislation of the European Communities was established to oversee the implementation of EC law in Ireland. Over the years, its terms of reference have been widened to include all Community legislation and policy proposals from the initial Commission document to the emergence of secondary legislation in Ireland. In 1982 the committee was also asked to examine relations between the Oireachtas and the European Parliament with particular emphasis on the 'dual mandate'. This remains part of the terms of reference although the matter has never been reported on. The committee has the power to recommend the annulment of a statutory instrument made under the 1972 European Communities Act — the Oireachtas may then pass a resolution within one year annulling the secondary legislation (Chapter 23). Because of the wide legislative powers delegated to the Executive in the 1972 Act, the committee feels that it has a

> duty to see that in the exercise of those powers, the constitutional position of the Oireachtas as the sole legislative authority is maintained against any attempt, whether conscious or not, by the executive to dilute that position. (Joint Committee Report, Report on 78 Statutory Instruments, 7 November 1984, p. 8)

Statutory instruments which are not subject to judicial review on constitutional grounds receive considerable attention from the committee.

There have been five committees since 1973 because they are coterminous with the life of the Parliament. This inhibited the work of the committee during a period of governmental instability in 1981–2 when there were three elections. Between 1981 and June 1983, the committee did not publish any reports. The level of published material emanating from the committee has declined. The first and second committees published fifty-nine and ninety-four reports respectively. This was followed by a valley period of two years when no reports were published. The fourth committee issued thirty-six reports and the fifth committee had issued seven reports before the Dail was dissolved in May 1989.

Ireland does not have a tradition of parliamentary committees; parliamentary culture makes the Dail a talking parliament rather than a working one. This gave the Joint Committee novel features when it was established. It took a number of years to set up working procedures, links with government departments and adequate staffing. The traditional anonymity of the civil service made public servants loath to appear before the committee in the early stages. An expansion of the parliamentary committee system in 1983 when a large number of select committees were set up brought officials into more contact with members of the Oireachtas. The Joint Committee is facing a severe staffing problem arising from public sector cutbacks; at present it has only two full-time staff in the secretariat — at a time when the volume of EC legislation is increasing dramatically.

The committee has been critical of the implementation of EC legislation by the Executive in a number of respects. First, the committee has proposed changes to specific statutory instruments. Second, the committee does not wish to see domestic legislation undermined by EC law without revision of primary legislation. While it accepts that most Community directives will be implemented by secondary legislation, it expresses the opinion that major areas of law, notably, company law, insurance and consumer law require national legislation. This view is reiterated again and again by the committee. Third, the committee is critical of the practice of incorporating the text of a directive verbatim into Irish law. According to the committee, it is 'the duty of Departments to identify the objectives of a Directive, and then to arrange for the provision considered necessary to achieve those objectives, to be expressed in the legal language normally used in this country' (Report on 78 Statutory Instruments, 1984, Appendix 6). The committee argues that the terminology used to implement a directive should be 'readily susceptible of interpretation in accordance with the rules applied in Irish courts' (Report on 19 Statutory Instruments, 20 January 1988, p. 7). Fourth, the terms of reference of the committee exclude directives which are implemented by change in administrative practice.

The committee's capacity to control the Executive is hampered by limited administrative resources and the technical nature of much EC legislation. None the less, officials are aware of the committee and will take its suggestions on board. Parliamentarians serving on the committee are afforded an opportunity to develop a knowledge of EC policies and law. The standard of debate in the Dail on EC issues is poor; very few deputies specialize in a policy area unless they have responsibility as spokesmen. The role of the Joint Committee and the management of EC business in the Oireachtas may need to be reviewed in the light of the expanding corpus of EC law which will have to be implemented in the run-up to 1992.

Bibliography

Collins, N. (1986), 'Ireland', in J. Lodge (ed.) (1984), *Direct Elections to the European Parliament*, London: Macmillan.
Irish Council of the European Movement (1989), Proceedings of the Conference on the NESC Report, October.
The Irish Times.
Report on the 78 Statutory Instruments (1984), Joint Committee on the Secondary Legislation of the European Communities.
Report on the 19 Statutory Instruments (1988), Joint Committee on the Secondary Legislation of the European Communities.

Chapter 22

The political system assessed

Brigid Laffan

It is more appropriate to talk of the consequences of EC membership for the political and governmental system than to talk of costs and benefits as such. As a relatively new member-state Ireland has had to adopt an additional and complicating layer to its domestic polity. The influence of EC membership is more evident in the administrative and governmental system than in the wider political system. Administrative procedures have evolved to manage the continuous flow of Community business through the Council hierarchy and thereafter to implementation and enforcement at domestic level. The management of Community business reflects Ireland's policy style, which tends to focus on the short term to the neglect of longer-term issues. Interdepartmental co-ordination of EC business is less institutionalized than in other EC member-states with domestic ministries retaining considerable autonomy. The fact that the interdepartmental EC committee failed to meet during a critical time (1984/5) in the development of the Community is symptomatic of a weakening in the management of EC business within central government at this time. The new Government (1987) responded by appointing a Minister of State for the Co-ordination of EC business in the Taoiseach's Department and a senior committee of ministers and secretaries in autumn 1987 to oversee the implementation of the Delors package and the internal market programme. The new procedures strengthen the role of the Prime Minister's Office in co-ordinating 'high policy' issues and ensuring that priorities are established. However, it does not address problems of co-ordination lower down the administrative hierarchy. The NESC report on EC membership stresses the need for Ireland to develop a strategic view on the future development of the Community and sets out the main lines of such an approach. The NESC report does not, however, tackle the major institutional and constitutional issues implicit in the largely federalist approach it adopts to the future of the Community. The composition of the NESC as a tripartite body would exclude it from dealing with the political consequences of its recommendations. The absence of a political debate about the future of the

Community institutions and the nature of the decision-making centre that must accompany economic and monetary union leaves Irish negotiators ill-prepared for the forthcoming intergovernmental conference. This is compounded during the first half of 1990 by the burden of the presidency, which must receive all of the Government's and the administration's attention until the end of June 1990.

EC membership exacerbates an already overloaded policy-making process at central government level. Extensive public sector cutbacks in the 1980s with an embargo on recruitment has left many parts of the bureaucracy struggling under the pressure of domestic and EC policies. The immediacy of EC negotiations has led to the neglect of pressing domestic problems. There is also evidence that central government is finding it more difficult to implement the vast corpus of EC law that has been passed by the Council. Adaptation to EC membership has absorbed the energies of civil servants and senior politicians and has made it more difficult to tackle the structural weaknesses in central government. Thus membership has contributed to pressure on the policy-making process.

Although Irish political parties do not fit easily into the pattern of political families found in continental Europe, they have managed to find themselves a niche in the European Parliament. Fine Gael, the Labour party, the Progressive Democrats and the Workers' party are members of traditional party groupings. Only Fianna Fáil, the largest Irish party, was forced to join an alliance with the Gaullists in what is essentially a two-country grouping. Involvement in the extra-national groupings adds a new flavour to Irish politics; for Fine Gael, involvement in the Christian Democratic Union brought a European dimension into the party and exposed party activists to ideas from other European countries. Ireland's minimal representation (fifteen seats) in the European Parliament means that Irish MEPs are not core actors in their groupings, except perhaps for Fianna Fáil which has six out of the twenty deputies in the European Democratic Alliance. This group is, however, a marginal group in the Parliament.

Irish political parties adopt an à la carte approach to their respective political groupings. They adapt group manifestos for the European elections and try to highlight the advantages of membership of their respective groupings. Because of their travel commitments MEPs are not very active in the parliamentary parties at national level. Unless they hold the dual mandate they have no right of audience in the national Parliament and may visit only as 'distinguished strangers'. There is therefore little opportunity for MEPs to influence the development of policy at national level. One gain from EC membership through European elections was the transfer for considerable monies to the parties for the 1989 and 1984 European elections. This aided the two major parties to upgrade staffing levels at their headquarters. Irish political parties in general have not devoted enough attention to ensuring that candidates for the European elections are of sufficiently high calibre for the European Parliament. In the post-SEA era the Parliament has a growing influence in the Community's decision-making process, an influence that will increase after the next intergovernmental conference. More attention must be paid in Ireland to the cinderella of European institutions.

The Oireachtas adapted to EC membership by setting up a watch-dog committee to scrutinize EC policies and Irish secondary legislation. This committee had some novel features when it was established in 1973 and provided a model for the Parliament's expanded committee system. The work of the committee is hampered by a paucity of administrative resources. At a time when there is a considerable expansion in the amount of EC law flowing from the Council, the committee is reduced to two staff members. This limits the coverage it can give to the legislative programme of the Commission and the Council. It has been critical of the implementation of a number of EC legal instruments and its comments are taken seriously by the bureaucracy. The impact of the committee on the wider work of the Parliament is limited because its reports are rarely debated in the full house. Irish parliamentarians have by and large not developed expertise on the Community unless they occupy front-bench positions. Debate on EC matters is limited and not of a high quality. Parliamentary control of EC affairs is thus constrained and the executive is largely unfettered in the management of EC business. The same is true for other areas of public policy, as its underdeveloped committee system makes the Irish Parliament weak. Irish political and governmental structures and processes have adapted to rather than been transformed by EC membership. The organization of the state and the party system largely remains the same, although it is possible to discern some influence on those parties which belong to the traditional political families. Party activists and members of the youth sections have benefited from exposure to their counterparts in other countries. Fianna Fáil is not influenced by the alliance with the Gaullists as there are no party—party links.

EC membership and the demands of the Commission for the involvement of regional and local actors in developing plans for structural fund monies became an issue in the internal debate about the powers and functions of local government. Local actors try to use the Commission as a source of pressure in their search for greater decentralization within the Irish state. This has its dangers for the Commission because of its limited capacity to deliver. In the end, the Commission's most important relationship is the one it forges with the central governments of the member-states. Great expectations in Irish local government are frequently dashed in Brussels.

Chapter 23
The legal system[1]
Paul McCutcheon

The Community legal order

From a lawyer's perspective the unique and distinctive characteristic of the European Communities lies in the creation of a supranational legal system. Community law is directly applicable within the municipal legal orders of member-states and enjoys supremacy over conflicting domestic provisions. Ceded to the Communities are legislative, executive and judicial powers which traditionally were the preserve of sovereign nation states. The independence of the Community legal system and the precedence of Community law over national law was stated thus by the Court of Justice in its decision in *Costa* v. *E.N.E.L.* (p. 594):

the law stemming from the Treaty, an independent source of law, could not, because of its special and original nature, be overridden by domestic legal provisions, however framed, without being deprived of its character as Community law and without the legal basis of the Community itself being called into question.

The transfer by States from their domestic legal system to the Community legal system of rights and obligations arising under the Treaty carries with it a permanent limitation of their sovereign rights, against which a subsequent unilateral act incompatible with the concept of the Community cannot prevail.

This was reiterated in *Internationale Handelsgesellschaft* v. *Einfur-und Vorratsstelle fur Getreide und Futtermittel* where the Court stated that the supremacy of Community law includes precedence over fundamental rights provisions of a member-state's constitution and 'the principles of its national constitutional structure'. From the Community perspective, therefore, Community law applies in national legal systems without the necessity of its being incorporated by any domestic legal measure. Moreover, it is clear that domestic legal provisions cannot abrogate or limit, much less invalidate, Community law. In this context, the Court of Justice was even more assertive in *Amministrazione delle Finanze dello Stato* v. *Simmenthal* where it held that a national court must invalidate a domestic legal provision which is in conflict with Community law. Thus, by the time Ireland was to accede to the European Communities it was clear that the Community legal order is autonomous, directly applicable and enjoyed supremacy within the domestic legal system. The validity of Community law derived, not from domestic provisions, but from the Treaties which established the Communities.

The Irish legal system

Being a common law jurisdiction Ireland falls into the mainstream Anglo-American tradition (Byrne and McCutcheon, 1989). In this regard, the Irish legal system is a direct descendent of the English system, both sharing not only common legal principles but, more importantly, similar judicial techniques and legal methodology. Central to its legal system is the operation of precedent by which courts are bound to follow and apply earlier decisions, giving rise to an extensive body of law shaped and fashioned over hundreds of years of legal history. The law is not to be found in comprehensive codes, so familiar to continental lawyers, but in court decisions, commonly if inaccurately referred to as case law. Accordingly, Irish lawyers have developed and employ methodological techniques to deal with this body of law and are accustomed to exhaustive analyses of judicial reasoning from which they ultimately extract their rules. Moreover, judicial procedure differs with legal arguments usually being presented orally rather than in writing. Accession to the Communities presented Ireland, like the United Kingdom, with the fascinating but uncertain prospect of adhering to a legal order, essentially civilian in its origins, which was largely alien to its legal culture and traditions. Unlike the United Kingdom, however, Ireland had the added dimension of possessing a written constitution, the interpretation of which is left to the courts. Parliament is not sovereign in that it is subject to judicial review and is prohibited from enacting unconstitutional legislation. The corollary is that the courts enjoy the power to declare legislation to be constitutionally invalid and, thus, of no legal effect. This power of review has been vigorously exercised by the courts, especially in their imaginative interpretation of the fundamental rights provisions in Articles 40 to 44. Again, Irish constitutional law is judicially created and the constitutional arrangements made to facilitate accession would ultimately be the subject of judicial consideration.

The constitution and incorporation of Community law into the domestic legal system

The nature of the Community legal system and the provisions of the Treaties conflicted with a number of provisions of the Irish Constitution

(Casey, 1987; Forde, 1987; Kelly, 1987). Article 5 of the Constitution describes Ireland as being 'a sovereign, independent, democratic state' while Article 6 provides that powers of government derive from the people and 'are exercisable only by or on the authority of the organs of the State established by [the] Constitution'. The latter is achieved by Article 15.2 which vests the 'sole and exclusive power of making laws' in the Oireachtas, Article 28.2 which vests executive power in the Government and Article 34 which vests judicial power in the courts. Article 34 also confers on the High Court and Supreme Court the power to determine the constitutionality of legislation, while Article 35 guarantees the independence of the judiciary. The cumulative effect of those provisions is to declare the sovereignty of the state, which is vested in the people, and to confer powers of government on the various institutions established by the Constitution itself. Moreover, those powers are limited by the terms of the Constitution, the interpretation of which, as noted above, falls within the preserve of the courts. It is obvious that, unamended, those provisions were fundamentally inconsistent with the legal order envisaged for the Communities. Accordingly, the ratification by the state of the Treaties would require appropriate amendment of the Constitution. Moreover, given the dualist approach which Irish law adopts with respect to international law,[2] and the provision in Article 29.6 that 'no international agreement shall be part of the domestic law of the State save as may be determined by the Oireachtas', a domestic measure was required to incorporate the Treaties into Irish law.

In order to permit Irish ratification of the Treaties and to ensure validity of Community legal measures the Third Amendment to the Constitution was enacted following the 1972 referendum (see p. 188). Rather than amend each pertinent provision of the Constitution individually a general amending clause was inserted as a new provision, Article 29.4.3 which reads:

The State may become a member of the European Coal and Steel Community (established by Treaty signed at Paris on the 18th day of April, 1951), the European Economic Community (established by Treaty signed at Rome on the 25th day of March, 1957) and the European Atomic Energy Community (established by Treaty signed at Rome on the 25th day of March, 1957). No provision of this Constitution invalidates laws enacted, acts done or measures adopted by the State necessitated by the obligations of membership of the Communities or prevents laws enacted, acts done or measures adopted by the Communities, or institutions thereof, from having the force of law in the State.

Apart from its relative textual simplicity, the importance of enacting a general, or composite, amendment is that it has the effect of limiting each constitutional provision which might otherwise have conflicted with the obligations imposed by Community membership. The alternative method of amending each provision individually carried with it the danger that a relevant provision might have been overlooked or that the courts would subsequently have interpreted a hitherto dormant provision in a manner inconsistent with Community membership. Given the principle of harmonious interpretation which Irish courts adopt with respect to the Constitution, namely that its provisions be read as part of an interlocking whole, the Third Amendment achieves with one general provision that which could not be guaranteed by a number of individual and specific provisions (Temple Lang, 1972; Murphy, 1983; McMahon and Murphy, 1989).

A number of points should be made about the Third Amendment. The first is that the opening sentence is merely enabling in that it confers on the state the authority to join the European Communities by ratifying the Treaties therein mentioned. However, that in itself was insufficient to ensure the constitutional propriety of adherence to the Community legal order. Standing alone, one possible interpretation of that sentence is that the state could join the Communities *subject to the provisions of the Constitution*. In other words, the argument that the authority contained in that sentence did not carry with it the authority to override other constitutional provisions would have been open. Equally open would have been the counter-argument that the sentence contained an implicit authorization both to accede to the Communities and all that was legally consequent thereon. But the resolution of that issue would have been a matter for the courts and the adoption of the latter view could not, of course, be guaranteed. Accordingly, constitutional discretion being the better part of valour, the second sentence was included in the amendment. Its effect is to confer constitutional immunity on both national and Community acts and measures which are 'necessitated by' membership of the Communities. Emphasis must be laid on the expression 'necessitated by'. Not all acts and measures enjoy the immunity and the question whether a particular act or measure is 'necessitated' will be one for judicial determination, initially by the Irish courts and ultimately by the Court of Justice. That question will be one of Community law, involving in particular the interpretation of the Treaties, rather than of national law. Whilst this entails an element of uncertainty, probably inevitable in any legal document, the second sentence has the effect of copperfastening, as far as is textually possible, the validity of legal measures within the domestic legal system.[3] However, the further question as to the scope of the amendment and the nature of its authority was left unanswered, and more likely unasked. Did the amendment authorize ratification of future treaties which might alter the composition, structure, competence and nature of the Communities? In the optimistic and innocent days before 1973 that was a matter of purely academic speculation, to be the subject of another day's litigation.

One further step was considered necessary to complete the reception of Community law into the national system. Given the dualist approach adopted by Irish law and, in particular the provisions of Article 29.6 of the Constitution outlined above, it was felt prudent to complete the incorporation process by legislative enactment. Although it might have been argued that the Third Amendment overrode Article 29.6 matters would be placed beyond doubt by an appropriate legislative measure. Discretion again prevailing, this was achieved by the European Communities Act 1972. This brief Act made general provision in section 2 for reception of Community law:

From the 1st day of January, 1973, the treaties governing the European Communities and the existing and future acts adopted by the institutions of those Communities shall be binding on the State and shall be part of the domestic law thereof under the conditions laid down by those treaties.

The effect of that section was to incorporate existing Community law into Irish law and to ensure the incorporation of future directly applicable Community measures. The relationship between the Third Amendment and the 1972 Act was considered by the High Court in *Crotty* v. *An Taoiseach*. The amendment conferred on the state a licence or authority to accede to the Communities on the occurrence of which it would be bound in international law. The Act was passed by virtue of that licence and had it exceeded its terms it would not have enjoyed the constitutional immunity conferred by the amendment. However, legislative and administrative measures adopted in the running of the Communities, whilst enjoying constitutional immunity, become part of domestic law by virtue of the Act. In the Court's words (p. 758): 'If the second sentence of the Third Amendment is the canopy over their heads the European Communities Act 1972 is the perch on which they stand.'

To ensure the incorporation of other Community measures, such as directives, which are not directly applicable ministers were conferred with power to make regulations (that is domestic regulations, not to be confused with Community Regulations) by section 3. The breadth of that power is evident in section 3(2) which provides that:

Regulations under this section may contain such incidental, supplementary and consequential provisions as appear to the Minister making the regulations to be necessary for the purposes of the regulations (including provisions repealing, amending or applying, with or without modification, other law, exclusive of this Act).

It was clear that given the volume of Community secondary legislation which would require incorporation legislative enactment might not prove to be the appropriate implementing device. Hence the power in section 3. In this context, the general constitutional principles governing the delegation of legislative power must be noted. In *Cityview Press Ltd* v. *An Chomhaile Oiliuna* the Supreme Court held that the delegation of such power is permissible only if confined to the *implementation* of principles and policies, which are contained in the parent statute itself, and that the delegation of a wider power is unconstitutional. On this basis it can be persuasively argued that section 3 is invalid as it clearly exceeds the 'principles and policies' test (Hogan and Morgan, 1986: 16—18). The power therein is defined in the broadest terms imaginable, even to the extent of purporting to authorize the amendment of statutes by ministerial regulation. The likely response to that argument, however, is that the Third Amendment saves section 3 as the incorporation of directives into domestic law is necessitated by Community membership. But the relevant provision of the EEC Treaty (Article 189) merely requires that directives be implemented — the means of achieving which are left to the member-states. In this respect it is arguable that the Treaty envisages that the means of implementing directives will conform with domestic constitutional requirements, which in Ireland is the 'principles and policies' test. Which approach the courts might ultimately take remains a matter of speculation and awaits definitive resolution in a suitable case. But the wise course would be to incorporate measures by statute rather than by ministerial regulation where they might otherwise fail on the 'principles and policies' test.

Parliamentary control over the implementation process was originally provided for in section 4 of the 1972 Act, which stated that ministerial regulations would lapse if not confirmed by the Oireachtas within six months of their being made. One such statute, the European Communities (Confirmation of Regulations) Act 1973 was enacted. Were that provision to remain the enactment of confirmation legislation would be necessary at least every six months. However, given its cumbersome and potentially time-consuming nature the confirmation procedure was soon altered. The European Communities (Amendment) Act 1973 amends section 4 of the 1972 Act. It provides that ministerial regulations enjoy permanent statutory effect unless annulled within one year by the Houses of the Oireachtas on the recommendation of the Oireachtas Joint Committee on the Secondary Legislation of the European Communities (Robinson, 1979). It should be noted that the joint committee acts as a filter and the Oireachtas may annul regulations only on its recommendation. The change is significant in that it dilutes parliamentary control by altering the role of the Oireachtas from one of confirmation to that of veto.

Ratification of the Single European Act

Probably the most significant alteration to date to the structure and competences of the Communities was effected by the Single European Act (SEA). Although it attracted only lukewarm support from those committed to closer European integration, the SEA was designed to accelerate the Communities' development and, in particular, the completion of the internal market. It provided for qualified majority voting in certain instances (thereby eliminating the national 'veto'), enumerated new areas of Community competence and provided for the establishment of a new Court of First Instance which would alleviate the burden on the Court of Justice (Murphy, 1985; Pescatore, 1986; McElhenny, 1988). Title III of SEA contained provisions governing European Political Co-operation (EPC) which for the first time was codified. As SEA amended the Treaties domestic measures were required to incorporate it into the member-states' legal systems prior to ratification. Article 33 of SEA envisaged ratification in accordance with member-states' respective constitutional requirements. Despite the articulation of constitutional doubts the Constitution was not amended to permit ratification, although it should be noted that earlier amendments to the Treaties were incorporated into domestic law by statute rather than constitutional amendment. Instead the European Communities (Amendment) Act 1986 was passed by the Oireachtas and incorporated into Irish law the provisions of SEA which amended the Treaties. Title III was not incorporated into domestic law but was approved by a Dail vote (*Dail Debates* 370: 2365–72). Indeed, the entire process was handled in a somewhat tardy manner. Although it was envisaged that SEA would be ratified by the end of 1986, the legislative process which eventually led to the passing of the European Communities (Amendment) Act 1986 began on 9 December 1986 and concluded two days later. This allowed little time for parliamentary debate and ensured that it received only the most perfunctory consideration. That legislative and public discussion was largely discouraged was reflected in the Government's belated publication in November 1986 of an explanatory guide to SEA. However, this proved to be an unwise course as the Supreme Court was subsequently to hold in *Crotty* v. *An Taoiseach* that Title III of SEA infringed the Constitution and ratification was deferred pending the enactment of an appropriate constitutional amendment.

The *Crotty* proceedings began in spectacular fashion (Bradley, 1987; Sherlock 1987a; Temple Lang, 1987; McCutcheon, 1988). On Christmas Eve 1986 Justice Barrington, of the High Court, granted the plaintiff an interlocutory injunction[4] preventing the deposit of the instrument of ratification. This had the effect of delaying ratification at least until the conclusion of the proceedings. This, in itself, was unprecedented as the courts had not previously granted an injunction to prevent ratification of an international agreement. It is important to realize that at this stage the Court was concerned not with the substance of the plaintiff's claim but merely with whether the Government should be restrained from ratifying SEA pending the conclusion of the proceedings. The decision to grant the injunction sought by the plaintiff was based on the argument that once SEA was ratified and the European Communities (Amendment) Act 1986 came into force the obligations stemming from it would be 'necessitated by' membership of the Communities and, therefore, would be immune from constitutional challenge. In other words, were ratification to proceed the opportunity to challenge would probably be foreclosed. As the plaintiff had raised serious constitutional questions they ought to be addressed at this stage. Moreover, the Court concluded that the plaintiff had sufficient standing[5] to bring the proceedings. As a citizen of the state he had a legitimate interest in its legal and constitutional structure. The final issue to be resolved was whether the balance of convenience lay in favour of granting or refusing the injunction. In support of the former was the fact that the plaintiff had identified a potential violation of the Constitution. Were SEA to be ratified, and later declared to be invalid, the state could find itself in the position of being bound in international law by a provision which was invalid in its domestic law. On the other hand, delay in ratification could cause the state embarrassment, especially in its relations with its European partners. But given the provisions of Article 33 of SEA the Court felt it appropriate to grant the injunction.

The merits of the plaintiff's claim were subsequently considered by a divisional court of the High Court, consisting of Justices Hamilton, Barrington and Carroll. The time had now arrived to consider the long-deferred question concerning the nature of the constitutional authority to join the Communities. In this regard the Court's judgment centred on the Third Amendment and the interpretation of its authority. The Court accepted the defence contention that what was authorized was membership of a Community which of its nature is growing and expanding, what it termed a 'dynamic Community'. The Treaties envisaged a gradual development of the Communities and contained provisions for their alteration, and the Third Amendment entitled the state to consent to amendments which are within the 'original objectives' of the Treaties. The Court did not elaborate on those objectives, other than to indicate that they were economic rather than political. It followed that ratification of SEA in itself would not confer immunity on the European Communities (Amendment) Act 1986. The Act would enjoy immunity only if it came within the scope of the constitutional provision which authorized membership in the first place. If a particular measure were to exceed that authority it would lack validity in domestic law. Having disposed of that point the Court proceeded to hold that the plaintiff lacked standing to seek a general review of the 1986 Act as he was unable to show that he was immediately prejudiced by its provisions. And the Court refused to review the provisions of Title III as they had not become part of domestic law.

The plaintiff appealed to the Supreme Court arguing that the 1986 Act was invalid and that the state was prohibited from ratifying SEA due to the provisions of Title III. Chief Justice Finlay delivered the Court's judgment on the first point. It was held that the plaintiff had sufficient standing to pursue his claim as the legislation would affect every citizen. On the substantive issue the Court echoed the judgment of the High Court. The authority to join the Communities was (p. 767):

not only to join the Communities as they stood in 1973, but also to join in amendments of the Treaties so long as such amendments do not alter the essential scope or objectives of the Communities. To hold that [it] does not authorise any form of amendment to the Treaties after 1973 without a further amendment of the Constitution would be too narrow a construction; to construe it as an open ended authority to agree, without further amendment to the Constitution, to any amendment to the treaties would be too broad.

Accordingly, the question was whether an amendment was effected which was outside the scope of that authority. In this regard, the Court focused its attention on the EEC Treaty and examined its essential objectives as they must have been envisaged by the people when they enacted the Third Amendment to the Constitution. In many cases the Treaty of Rome itself contained provisions which required decisions initially to be taken unanimously but after a transitional period they would require only a qualified majority. Thus, it seemed clear to the Court that it was contemplated that the Community is a developing organism with changing mechanisms of decision-making and therefore the Court was satisfied that none of the proposed changes in SEA from unanimity to qualified majority exceeded the constitutional licence.

However, the Court did sound a note of caution by stating that further changes from unanimity to qualified majority voting would not necessarily be constitutionally permissible. In other words, it was only the actual changes made by SEA with which the Court was concerned and future amendments would have to be similarly examined in the light of the objectives of the Treaty. The Court also held that the enumeration of hitherto unspecified areas of Community competence was merely to state separately matters which were implied within the original objectives of the EEC. Equally, the power to establish a court of first instance did not affect the manner in which judicial power had already been ceded to the Communities and, thus, was a permissible alteration of the Treaty of Rome. The Court concluded that none of the amendments to the original Treaties effected by SEA exceeded the state's licence to join the Communities and their incorporation into domestic law by the European Communities (Amendment) Act 1986 was constitutionally permitted.

On the second point the Court held by a three-to-two majority that Title III was inconsistent with the Constitution and that ratification of SEA was precluded for that reason. Majority judgments were delivered by Justices Walsh and Henchy, Justice Hederman being content to agree with his brethren. Reliance had been placed by the defence on the earlier decision of the Court in *Boland* v. *An Taoiseach* where it refused to set aside the 'Sunningdale Agreement'. It was argued that the courts could not interfere with the exercise of the executive power in regard to international relations. Walsh observed that that power was subject to limits imposed by the Constitution and that, in this regard, the Government does not enjoy a 'free hand'. He distinguished *Boland* on the grounds that it concerned a statement of policy rather than a treaty which purported to bind the state in its relations with other countries. For him the question was whether SEA amounted to an attempt by the Government to free itself from constitutional constraints. He concluded that the provisions of Title III involved an unconstitutional surrender by the state of its sovereignty in that it committed the state to adopt certain courses of action which restricted its freedom in foreign policy matters. He also expressed concern about what he thought to be an ambiguity surrounding the provisions in SEA on security and their implications for Irish neutrality, although those remarks could not be considered to be central to his reasoning. Henchy noted that Title III committed the member-states to a course which would eventually lead to European union in the sphere of foreign policy. No longer were they to have separate foreign policies but were obliged, as far as possible, to merge their foreign policies in order to implement EPC with a view to achieving European union. Although that process was to be gradual it was none the less progressive and entailed an immediate surrender of sovereignty on the part of each state. In response to the argument that Title III merely formalizes existing practice he stated (p. 786):

The methods of co-operation between member states, which hitherto have been informal, aspirational or, at most, declarational (as under the Stuttgart Declaration), now pass into the realm of solemnly covenanted commitment to the conduct of foreign policy in a way that will lead to European Political Union, at least in the sphere of foreign policy. In that respect, Title III of the SEA is the threshold leading from what has hitherto been essentially an economic Community to what will also be a political Community.

Chief Justice Finlay and Justice Griffin dissented, arguing that Title III did not attempt to achieve political union, that it preserved the member-states' maximum freedom of action and did not involve a ceding of sovereignty by the state.

The *Crotty* decision was greeted with astonishment by members of the political and legal establishments. It was castigated as having been reached by the 'narrowest of majorities' and as having embarrassed the state in its dealings with its Community partners (*Dail Debates* 371: 2220; *The Irish Times* editorial, 10 April 1987). The majority was criticized as having read Title III in an overly punctilious manner and having attributed to it an interpretation which did not amount to a 'balanced description' of its contents (Temple Lang, 1987; Keatinge, 1987). To an extent, some of the criticism directed at the Court served to deflect attention from the manner in which the Government sought to secure ratification of SEA. However, the immediate consequence was that a constitutional amendment was required to authorize ratification of SEA (see Chapter 19). Whilst there was some debate about the appropriate wording of the amendment (*Dail Debates* 371: 2187–317, 2319–486, 2497–600) a simple single sentence formula was chosen. A referendum was held in May 1987 and a new provision authorizing ratification was added to the Constitution: 'The State may ratify the Single European Act (signed on behalf of the Member States of the Communities at Luxembourg on the 17th day of February 1986).' Following this amendment SEA was ratified by the state and the European Communities (Amendment) Act 1986 came into force.

Aside from its impact on the ratification of SEA and its immediate political consequences *Crotty* is of more profound legal significance. For the first time the courts considered the constitutional position concerning membership of the Communities and their conclusions can be summarized in a number of propositions. The first is that the Third Amendment authorized accession to Communities which of their nature are developing entities. They are not static and the amendment did not seek to freeze them in their 1973 mode. Second, the permitted development of the Communities is to be derived from the original aims and objectives of the Treaties. Amendments which fall within their scope may be ratified by the state without further constitutional amendment. Third, whilst both the High and Supreme Courts were somewhat vague on the point it is clear that they considered those aims and objectives in the main to be economic rather than political. In this regard, all judges agreed that political union could not be achieved without the Constitution being appropriately amended. Fourth, concerning Title III, the majority took its nature as an international treaty seriously, inchoately reflecting the principle *pacta sunt servanda* — that treaties be honoured — and recognized that it created binding commitments which were susceptible to legal analysis (Freestone and Davidson, 1986; Weidenfeld, 1986; Robinson, 1987). It was satisfied that the Government's freedom of action in matters of foreign policy is circumscribed by the Constitution and that it was prevented from yielding sovereignty in that respect. On this point, a difference of emphasis is evident in the judgments of Justices Walsh and Henchy. Walsh focused on the extent to which sovereignty was to be immediately surrendered and, to a much lesser extent, on its implications for Irish neutrality. Henchy, on the other hand, was more concerned with the potential of EPC inevitably to develop into a form of political union, at least in the foreign policy sphere.

The decision in *Crotty*, however, is not without difficulty. It leaves in doubt the exact scope of Community development which may constitutionally be agreed to and the extent to which the state may enter into internationally binding commitments which potentially undermine national sovereignty. All that can definitely be said is that there is a point beyond which the state may not consent to further integration. That point was not reached by the amendments to the Treaties which were effected by SEA but was exceeded by the provisions of Title III. Given the difference between the judgments of Justices Walsh and Henchy on the latter the scope of the amendment which authorized ratification of SEA is unclear. On the Walsh view one interpretation is that the amendment only permits the surrender of sovereignty which would be immediately consequent on ratification. In this sense the amendment is static and any future surrender of sovereignty would require further constitutional amendment. But an alternative interpretation, based on Henchy's judgment, is that the amendment authorizes not only an immediate yielding of sovereignty but also any future surrender which is consistent with Title III's potential. More generally, some of the Supreme Court's observations on sovereignty are ambiguous and potentially call the treaty-making powers of the state into question.[6]

Community law in Irish courts

Having been incorporated into the domestic system Community law must, of course, be applied in Irish legal proceedings. An Irish court may either decide the issue of Community law itself or refer the case under Article 177 of the Treaty of Rome to the Court of Justice for a preliminary ruling. Among the courts which have been called upon to consider questions of Community law are the Supreme Court, High Court, Circuit Court and District Court, the latter two being courts of limited and local jurisdiction. An immediate effect of Community membership has been the expansion of the jurisdiction of the Circuit and District Courts. Given the supremacy of Community law and the direction in the *Simmenthal* decision those courts enjoy the power to invalidate domestic legal provisions which are inconsistent with Community law — they do not enjoy an equivalent power to test the constitutional validity of domestic legislation. Moreover, a number of quasi-judicial tribunals established under statute might have to consider questions of Community law. These could arise either where a party relies directly on a provision of the Treaties or Community secondary legislation or where a tribunal is charged with the task of implementing domestic legislation which has been enacted in response to Community obligations. An example of the latter is an adjudication in the Labour Court, which despite its title is not a 'court' in the strict sense, under the Anti-Discrimination (Pay) Act 1974, enacted to fulfil Community equal pay requirements.

The supremacy of Community law has never been seriously questioned in Irish courts and, indeed, they have been enthusiastic in their reception of Community law. In *Pigs & Bacon Commission* v. *McCarren* Justice Costello typified the prevailing judicial spirit when he wrote that the consequence of section 2 of the European Communities Act 1972 is to give legal effect to Community law within the domestic legal system in *the manner provided by Community law itself*. Moreover, he accepted without qualification the supremacy of Community law over conflicting domestic law. In a similar vein, in *Campus Oil* v. *Minister for Industry and Energy* the Supreme Court disallowed an appeal against a High Court reference under Article 177, *inter alia*, on the grounds that to do so would be contrary to the 'spirit and letter' of that provision. And in *Murphy* v. *Bord*

Telecom Eireann Justice Keane again emphasized that national law must yield primacy to Community law and he refused to interpret a domestic statute literally where that would have led to a conflict with the provisions of the Treaty. That is not to say, however, that Irish courts will always entertain issues of Community law. In *Dreher* v. *Irish Land Commission* Justice Hamilton declined to consider an argument based on the EEC Treaty as the subject matter of the proceedings arose before Irish accession to the Communities. More significantly, the Supreme Court in *Doyle* v. *An Taoiseach* refused to consider a Community law point where the plaintiffs challenged the validity of domestic regulations. It considered that the case could be adequately disposed of by the application of national law. The analogy drawn by the Court was the constitutional law principle which requires constitutional issues to be decided last. The effect of this decision is that if a case can be adequately disposed of by the application of domestic law no need to invoke Community law arises. However, if domestic law and Community law would result in conflicting decisions it goes without saying that Community law would have to prevail. In *Doyle* the plaintiffs' challenge to the regulations in question was based partly on Community law but the Court invalidated them on a domestic law basis and, hence, had no need to consider the Community law issue.

In their implementation of Community law the courts have been quite prepared to refer cases under Article 177 to the Court of Justice. It is estimated that approximately 50 per cent of cases which involve points of Community law are so referred. Indeed, in one case, *Lee* v. *Minister for Agriculture*, the plaintiff was granted legal aid for the proceedings before the Court of Justice. In *Irish Creamery Milk Suppliers Association* v. *Ireland* Justice Barrington rejected the application in Ireland of the restrictive guidelines set out by Lord Denning in the English Court of Appeal decision in *Bulmer* v. *Bollinger* on when to refer a case under Article 177. He did, however, ask the Court of Justice whether it was appropriate to refer a question at interlocutory stage. The Court confirmed, in joined cases 36 and 71/80, that the matter was one for the discretion of national courts. In *Campus Oil* v. *Minister for Industry and Energy* the Supreme Court held that it lacked jurisdiction to entertain an appeal against a reference by the High Court, stating that the discretion conferred by Article 177 is unfettered in Irish law. Whilst that decision has been criticized it does reflect an open approach to the question of references to the Court of Justice and a willingness to defer to the judgment of lower court judges in this regard (O'Keeffe, 1984; Murphy, 1984). By way of contrast in *Aluminium Design Ltd* v. *Alcan Windows Ltd* Justice McWilliam in the High Court declined to refer the case to the Court of Justice as reference had been requested by neither party and an appeal in the Supreme Court from his decision was possible.

It is hardly surprising that most Irish cases which involve questions of Community law concern matters of agriculture and fisheries. Questions of rights of establishment, rights to provide services, competition law, employment equality and social welfare rights have also arisen. However, it should not be assumed that the invocation of Community law has been confined to 'mainstream' issues. Although the right to import inflatable dolls manufactured in a member-state has not yet been of concern to Irish lawyers (unlike their UK counterparts — see *R* v. *Henn and Darby*) they have shown themselves to be no less imaginative. In *Griffith* v. *Fitzpatrick* the applicant's extradition to England was sought on a charge of defrauding the British Intervention Agency. It was argued, unsuccessfully, that the charge disclosed a revenue offence which is non-extraditable under Irish law — it would seem that the gist of that argument was that the offence alleged was one against Community revenues. Even more inventive was the unsuccessful argument, based on the European Communities (Units of Measurement) Regulations 1983, in *The People (DPP)* v. *Mortimer* that the accused's indictment in a 'gun-running' case be quashed on the grounds the charges expressed distances in imperial rather than metric measures! Of greater significance, however, is the potential impact of Community law on the fundamental rights guaranteed by the Constitution and the possible conflict between the two. This question arose tangentially in *Attorney General ex rel SPUC* v. *Open Door Counselling Ltd and Dublin Wellwoman Ltd*. Article 40.3.3 of the Constitution guarantees the right to life of the 'unborn' having due regard to the 'equal right to life of the mother'. The question which arose was whether the defendants were in breach of that provision by assisting women to procure abortions outside the state, principally in the United Kingdom. One of the defence arguments was that a pregnant woman enjoys the right under Articles 59 and 60 of the Treaty to avail of abortion services lawfully provided in a member-state and that there was a 'corollary right' to obtain information about such services; but it was conceded, probably unwisely, that obtaining assistance to travel abroad for an abortion was not a corollary right. The Supreme Court held that no question of Community law arose. What the plaintiffs in the present proceedings sought to prevent was the assisting of women to travel abroad to have their pregnancies terminated and that preventing 'a pregnant woman from becoming aware of the existence of abortion outside the jurisdiction' (p. 28) was not in issue. Thus, by invoking a narrow procedural argument the Court avoided considering the broader question of the right under Community law to receive services or related information. But it was probably inevitable that the issue would arise again and in *SPUC* v. *Coogan and Others* Justice Carroll referred three questions to the Court of Justice: whether the provision of abortion is a 'service' under Article 60 of the Treaty; whether a member-state could prevent the distribution of information on the details of the availability of abortion in another member-state; and whether there is a right in Community law for a person in one member-state, where abortion is prohibited by its constitution and laws, to distribute specific information about clinics in another member-state where abortions are lawfully performed.

Membership of the Community has also had an enriching effect on domestic juridical techniques and methodology. In *Murphy* v. *Bord Telecom Eireann* the High Court had to consider the interpretation of the Anti-Discrimination (Pay) Act 1974. Under the Act, which was enacted in response to the provisions of Article 119 of the Treaty and Council Directive 75/117/EEC, a claimant is entitled to equal pay where work of 'equal value' is performed. In this case the female applicants engaged in work of greater value than that of the comparable male counterparts, a matter which was not expressly governed by the Act. Justice Keane initially felt compelled, employing domestic principles of interpretation, to interpret the Act literally. Accordingly, he dismissed the claim on the basis that the legislature chose not to provide for cases of this type. However, he referred the case to the Court of Justice which ruled that Article 119 confers a right to equal pay where the claimant is engaged in work of greater value than the person with whom the comparison is made. On the resumed hearing Justice Keane modified his original interpretation of the Act and adopted a teleological interpretation by which the Act was interpreted in the light of its underlying purpose rather than its literal wording. This he considered to be necessary in order to avoid a conflict between domestic law, namely the Act, and Community law. He revised his opinion in the original case to the extent, at least, that a domestic provision will be interpreted in a manner to ensure its compliance with Community law. In *Lawlor* v. *Minister for Agriculture* Justice Murphy was more wholehearted in embracing the teleological method of interpretation and he cited the extra-judicial opinions of Professor Kutscher, a former judge of the Court of Justice. Murphy felt bound to adopt that approach not only when interpreting Community law but also domestic law which implements Community measures. It should be noted that those decisions do not mark a radical departure from domestic principles of interpretation in that the teleological method had earlier been endorsed by the Supreme Court in *Nestor* v. *Murphy*, a case which involved domestic law. However, they do display a willingness on the part of Irish courts to be influenced by European juridical methods and, in this respect, they do not share their English counterparts' rigid adherence to traditional common law principles and techniques (see for instance *Buchanan & Co* v. *Babco Ltd*). Moreover, in *Murphy* v. *Bord Telecom Eireann* Keane expressed the view that courts should presume that the Oireachtas intends to act in a manner consistent with Community law and that legislation should be interpreted accordingly. The endorsement of Community law has not been confined to the modification of interpretative techniques but has embraced the citation of Community precedents in cases which involved issues of domestic law exclusively. Thus, in *Murphy* v. *Attorney General* the Supreme Court, considering a question of domestic law, relied on the decision of the Court of Justice in *Defrenne* v. *Sabena (no. 2)*. Whilst in a general sense these developments might seem to be of minor import, membership of the Community has the potential to condition the evolution of Irish legal techniques and to accelerate the emergence of an indigenous methodology which departs significantly from its English progenitor.

Legislation and delegated legislation

Community membership has required the enactment of a considerable volume of domestic legislation and delegated, or secondary, legislation. For the sake of convenience these measures can be considered as falling into two categories. The first gives domestic effect to structural changes to the Communities. Into this category fall the European Communities (Amendment) Act 1977 (1975 Budget Treaty), European Communities (Amendment) Act 1979 (accession of Greece), European Communities (Amendment) Act 1985 (withdrawal of Greenland), European Communities (Amendment) (No. 2) Act 1985 (accession of Spain and Portugal) and, of course, European Communities (Amendment) Act 1986 which incorporates parts of SEA into domestic law. The European Assembly Elections Acts 1977 and 1984 were enacted to govern direct elections to the Parliament and the European Communities (Supplementary Funding) Act 1984 authorized the transfer of state resources to the Communities. The second category consists of legislation which either incorporates directives into national law or forms part of the process of harmonizing laws. Whilst it is beyond the scope of this chapter to consider areas of substantive law which have been affected by Community obligations the enumeration of a selection of statutes will serve to illustrate the breadth of activity in this regard. Examples include:

Anti-Discrimination (Pay) Act 1974 which implements Council Directive 75/117/EEC on equal pay;
Employment Equality Act 1977 which implements Council Directive 76/207/EEC on employment equality;
Protection of Employment Act 1977 implements Council Directive 75/129/EEC on collective redundancies;
Packaged Goods (Quality Control) Act 1980 which implements Council Directives 76/106/EEC and 76/211/EEC;
Companies (Amendment) Act 1983 which implements the Second Directive on Company Law 77/91/EEC;
Protection of Employees (Employers' Insolvency) Act 1984 which implements Council Directive 80/987/EEC;
Jurisdiction of Courts and Enforcement of Foreign Judgments (European Communities) Act 1988 which implements the 'Brussels Judgments Convention';
Central Bank Act 1989 which implements the Second Directive on Banking.

However, the vast bulk of Community secondary legislation is incorporated into Irish law by means of delegated legislation. In general, legislation is the preferred means of incorporation where major reform is necessary whilst delegated legislation is employed for more technical and administrative matters. The most frequently exercised power of delegated legislation is that which is conferred by section 3 of the European Communities Act 1972, the details of which have been noted earlier. Again a sample of such regulations will illustrate the eclectic, not to say exotic, range of subject matter:

European Communities (Imposition of Provisional Anti-dumping Duty on Certain Angles, Shapes and U, I or H Sections of Iron or Steel) (No. 2) Regulations 1978;
European Communities (Lead Content in Petrol) Regulations 1980;
European Communities (Surveillance of Sanitary Fixtures) Regulations 1985;
European Communities (Clinical Mercury-in-Glass Thermometers) Regulations 1986;
European Communities (Non-automatic Weighing Machines) (Amendment) Regulations 1986.

Regulations have also been enacted under other statutory powers, an example being the Food Standard (Certain Sugars) (European Communities) Regulations 1981 which were enacted under section 2 of the Food Standards Act 1974. Finally, it should be noted that some obligations are implemented by the adoption of administrative rather than legal measures. An example is the farm modernization scheme which was introduced to implement Council Directive 72/159/EEC.

Assessment

Lawyers are unaccustomed to engaging in cost—benefit analyses of legal phenomena preferring instead more abstract evaluations. Nevertheless, it can be observed that Community membership has had a major impact on the Irish legal system, possibly far greater than could have been imagined prior to accession. Superficially this can be discerned from the changed legal environment in which they operate. An increased number of practitioners now specialize in European law, the larger law firms have specialized European law departments, several have branch offices in European cities and greater numbers of law students select European law courses as their final year options. Such is the degree of encroachment of Community law into domestic law that no lawyer who specializes in the traditional legal areas can afford to ignore it. At a more elemental level a smooth transition to the new legal order was achieved through the adoption of the constitutional and legal measures necessary to ensure the reception of Community law within the domestic system. This was accompanied, and probably facilitated, by a willingness on the part of lawyers and judges to acknowledge the character of Community law. Hence the courts immediately and unambiguously recognized the supremacy of Community law and frequently invoke the advisory jurisdiction of the Court of Justice. Moreover, legal techniques have been influenced by Community law through the employment of continental interpretative principles and the citation of Community precedents in domestic cases. To this extent, isolationism has been eschewed and Community law has received an enthusiastic welcome.

However, it would be misleading to assume that all the legal incidents of European integration have been achieved harmoniously and without difficulty and have avoided crisis. The events surrounding the ratification of SEA and the consequent decision in *Crotty* might be considered to have been unfortunate but if blame is to be apportioned it must rest with those responsible for the manner in which ratification was processed. However, that case provided the Supreme Court with its first opportunity to consider the legal and constitutional nature of Community membership and, far from being obscurantist, it was 'pro-European' in two senses. The first is that the Court recognized that Community evolution is authorized by the Treaties and, in domestic law, by the terms of the Third Amendment to the Constitution. In essence the Court indicated that it was not prepared unduly to impede Community development. The Court's observations on the extent of the constitutional authorization to accede to the Communities might be criticized on the grounds of their being unhelpfully vague. In this regard, the middle course steered between holding, on one hand, that no amendments to the Treaties are constitutionally permissible and, on the other, that any amendment is permissible begged as many questions at it settled. However, this is hardly surprising as the Court could not have been expected to endorse in advance all that might occur in the process of European integration.

Second, the decision on Title III of SEA involved a recognition of its legally binding character, a matter which the Court took more seriously than some of its critics. In other words, it did not consider the provisions on EPC to be a meaningless, empty formula. A potential for future crisis lies in the effect that Community law will be held to have on existing constitutional provisions, especially in regard to social areas such as procreative rights. At this stage this is very much a matter of speculation, but the reference to the Court of Justice in *SPUC* v. *Coogan* on abortion information will be awaited with keen anticipation by many 'interested' parties and it is not difficult to imagine the vigorous debate which it could generate.[7]

Another area of controversy might prove to be neutrality which has to date been of minor legal concern, despite Justice Walsh's passing comments in *Crotty*. But if the SEA provisions on security develop to the point of encouraging Irish participation in a common European defence system one can be confident that a plaintiff will again invoke the aid of the courts. All in all exciting times are in the offing and it could be that we have yet fully to appreciate the legal price to be paid for membership of the European Communities.

Notes

1. I am indebted to Brigid Laffan, Raymond Friel and Nicholas Rees for their comments on an earlier draft of this chapter. Needless to say they are exempted from responsibility for any errors.
2. The dualist approach is that international law exists independently of national law and a domestic legal measure is required to incorporate it into domestic law. The contrasting monist approach is that international law is applied directly without the necessity of domestic incorporation measures.
3. Of course a litigant can always challenge the validity under Community law of a 'necessitated' measure. But that would be a question of Community law, not Irish law.
4. An injunction is a judicial order which prevents, or less commonly directs, a particular course of action from being adopted or continued. An interlocutory order lasts until the conclusion of legal proceedings and is designed to preserve the status quo. An interlocutory injunction is granted where the applicant can show that there is a serious question of law to be argued and that the balance of convenience lies in favour of its being granted.
5. Standing is a doctrine which, in brief, requires a plaintiff to show that he or she is adversely affected by a legal provision which he or she seeks to challenge (Sherlock, 1987b).
6. Concern was expressed about the constitutionality of the 'Anglo-Irish Agreement' following *Crotty*. Its validity has subsequently been upheld in *McGimpsey v. Ireland*.
7. The scene is already being set for conflict in this area; see 'Family groups fear for moral values in 1992', *Sunday Tribune*, 1 April 1990.

Bibliography

Bradley, K. (1987), 'The referendum on the Single European Act', *European Law Review* **12** (4).
Byrne, R. and McCutcheon, J.P. (1989), *The Irish Legal System*, 2nd edn, Dublin: Butterworths.
Casey, J. (1987), *Constitutional Law in Ireland*, London: Sweet & Maxwell.
Dail Debates, vol. 370.
Forde, M. (1987), *Constitutional Law of Ireland*, Dublin: Mercier Press.
Freestone, D. and Davidson, S. (1986), 'European Community competence and Part III of the Single European Act', *Common Market Law Review* **23**.
Hogan, G. and Morgan, D.G. (1986), *Administrative Law*, London: Sweet & Maxwell.
Keatinge, P. (1987), 'An aspiration or a binding commitment', *Irish Times* **27** May 1987.
Kelly, J.M. (1987), *The Irish Constitution*, 2nd edn + supp., Dublin: Jurist.

McCutcheon, J.P. (1988), 'The Irish supreme court, European Political Co-operation and the Single European Act', *Legal Issues of European Integration* **2**.
McElhenny, M. (1988), 'The United Kingdom, Ireland and the Single European Act', *Northern Ireland Legal Quarterly* **39** (1).
McMahon, B. and Murphy, E. (1989), *European Community Law in Ireland*, Dublin: Butterworths.
Murphy, F. (1983), 'The European Community and the Irish legal system', in Coombes, (ed.), *Ireland and the European Communities: Ten Years of Membership*, Dublin: Gill & Macmillan.
Murphy, F. (1984), *Common Market Law Review* **21**: 741–55.
Murphy, F. (1985), 'The Single European Act', *Irish Jurist* **20**: 239–63.
O'Keeffe, D. (1984), 'Appeals against an order to refer under Article 177 of the EEC Treaty', *European Law Review* **9** (2).
Pescatore, P. (1986), 'Some critical remarks on the "Single European Act"', PE103.892/rev./ann.1.
Robinson, M. (1979), 'Irish parliamentary scrutiny of European secondary legislation', *Common Market Law Review* **16**.
Robinson, M. (1987), 'Towards a European foreign policy – legal aspects', in De Vree *et al.*, *Towards a European Foreign Policy*, Dordrect.
Sherlock, A. (1987a), 'Sovereignty, the Constitution and the Single European Act', *Dublin University Law Journal* **9**.
Sherlock, A. (1987b), 'Understanding Standing: *Locus Standi* in Irish constitutional law', *Public Law*.
Temple Lang, J. (1972), 'Legal and constitutional implications for Ireland of adhesion to the EEC Treaty', *Common Market Law Review* **9**.
Temple Lang, J. (1987), 'The Irish court case which delayed the Single European Act', *Common Market Law Review* **24**.
Weidenfeld, W. (1986), 'The Single European Act', *Aussen Politik* **37** (4).

Cases referred to

Attorney General ex rel SPUC v. *Open Door Counselling Ltd and Dublin Wellwoman Ltd* [1989], *Irish Law Reports Monthly* **19**.
Aluminium Design Ltd v. *Alcan Windows Ltd* [1980], *Journal of the Irish Society for European Law* **82**.
Amministrazione delle Finanze dello Stato v. *Simmenthal* (Case 106/77) [1978], *European Court Reports* **629**.
Boland v. *An Taoiseach* [1974], *Irish Reports* **338**.
Buchanan & Co v. *Babco Ltd* [1978], *Appeal Cases* **141**.
Bulmer v. *Bollinger* [1974], 2 *All England Reports* **1226**.
Campus Oil v. *Minister for Industry and Energy* [1983], *Irish Reports* **82**.
Cityview Press Ltd v. *An Chomhairle Oiliuna* [1980], *Irish Reports* **381**.
Costa v. *ENEL* (Case 6/64) [1964], *European Court Reports* **585**.
Crotty v. *An Taoiseach* [1987], *Irish Reports* **713**.
Defrenne v. *Sabena* (No. 2) (Case 43/75) [1976], *European Court Reports* **455**.
Doyle v. *An Taoiseach* [1986], *Irish Law Reports Monthly* **693**.
Dreher v. *Irish Land Commission* [1980], *Journal of the Irish Society for European Law* **72**.

Griffith v. *Fitzpatrick* [1979], *Journal of the Irish Society for European Law* **35**.
Internationale Handelsgesellschaft v. *Einfur- und Vorratsstelle fur Getreide und Futtermittel* (Case 11/70) [1970], *European Court Reports* **1125**.
Irish Creamery Milk Suppliers Association v. *Ireland* [1979], *Journal of the Irish Society for European Law* **66**.
Lawlor v. *Minister for Agriculture* [1988], *Irish Law Reports Monthly* **400**.
Lee v. *Minister for Agriculture* (Case 152/79) [1980], *European Court Reports* **149**.
McGimpsey v. *Ireland* [1990], *Irish Law Reports Monthly* **441**.
Murphy v. *Attorney General* [1982], *Irish Reports* **241**.
Murphy v. *Bord Telecom Eireann* [1989], *Irish Law Reports Monthly* **53**.
Nestor v. *Murphy* [1979], *Irish Reports* **326**.
People (DPP) v. *Mortimer*, Special Criminal Court, unreported, case 27/1984.
Pigs & Bacon Commission v. *McCarren* [1978], *Journal of the Irish Society for European Law* **87**.
R v. *Henn and Darby* (Case 34/79) [1979], *European Court Reports* **3795**.
SPUC v. *Coogan and Others*, *Irish Times*, 6 March 1990.

PART IV: SOCIAL, EDUCATIONAL AND CULTURAL POLICY

Chapter 24

Introduction to Part IV
Brigid Laffan

The Rome and Paris Treaties included provisions of a broadly social character which taken together form the basis of the European Community's role. Given the emphasis in the Rome Treaty (EEC) on the completion of a customs union and a common market, it is not surprising that most of the provisions on social policy are linked to the creation of a common market and the equalization of competition among the member-states. The Treaties entrusted the Community with a number of different powers in the field of social policy, namely, regulatory or legislative powers, financial powers and the power to consult with the social partners. The social policy articles of the Rome Treaty refer to labour market policy and working conditions, thus excluding extensive areas of what is considered to be social policy in the member-states.

Article 117 elaborates the aim of the Community's social policy which is to 'promote improved living and working conditions for workers' (EEC Treaty, Article 117). The field of action is laid down in Article 118 which says that the Commission has the task of promoting 'close cooperation' between member-states in the following areas of policy:

— Employment.
— Labour law and working conditions.
— Basic and advanced vocational training.
— Social security.
— Prevention of occupational diseases.
— Occupational hygiene.
— The right of association and collective bargaining between employers and workers.

The Commission is empowered to conduct studies, deliver opinions and arrange consultations on these issues among the member-states. The Single European Act supplements Article 118 with Article 118A that refers to the need for improvements in the 'working environment, as regards the health and safety of workers' (Article 21, SEA). The SEA makes provision for the use of qualified majority voting in this area.

Article 118B in the SEA establishes the objective of 'dialogue between management and labour at European level which could, if the two sides consider it desirable, lead to relations based on agreement' (Article 21, SEA). Articles 119 and 120 of the original Treaty require that the member-states apply the principle of equal pay for men and women and that paid holiday schemes should be similar in each member-state. The remaining articles on social policy deal with the operation of the European Social Fund, which was designed to finance vocational training and mobility in the member-states.

Social policy was not a central feature of Community activity in the 1960s. It was not until the end of the transitional period in the Community's development that attention was focused on the 'human face' of the undertaking. In 1974 the Community launched the first social action programme that consisted of a series of specific legislative proposals in a number of areas and was accompanied by the reform of the European Social Fund (ESF). Programmes for health and safety at work and for improving working conditions formed part of the action programme. The Commission began to examine issues relating to public health, environmental protection and consumer rights. A series of directives established the principle of equal pay, equal treatment for the sexes in employment, working conditions and vocational training. The Community's regulatory powers were used to protect the rights of workers in the event of mass redundancy, company mergers and employers' insolvency. The needs of disadvantaged workers such as the handicapped and migrant workers received attention. The Community developed specific programmes on all of these aspects of social policy (Venturini, 1989).

The enactment of the Single European Act and the programme to complete the internal market brings the Community's social policy back into focus. The President of the Commission, Jacques Delors emphasizes the link between the internal market and social policy in the following way: 'if the social cohesion of the common area is not consolidated, then there will be no internal market' (Speech to the ECTU, 1988). The Commission has attempted to strengthen dialogue between the social partners in what is known as the 'Val Duchesse' dialogue. In September 1988 the Commission presented its first communication on the social dimension of the internal market setting out a work programme covering a range of priority issues. This has now been incorporated into the Charter on Fundamental Social Rights adopted by eleven of the twelve member-states of the Community in Strasbourg on 8/9 December 1989. Britain entered a general reserve on the Charter and refused to sign it with its other partners. Although the Charter is something new for the Community, it borrows from the concepts included in the Council of Europe's Social Charter and the International Labour Organization's (ILO) Conventions. The negotiations on the Social Charter were highly contentious because of Britain's hostility to the whole idea of a charter and because of the different views of the representatives of labour, on the one hand, and employers' interests, on the other. The Commission must now translate the aspirations of the Charter into a work programme in 1990. The main concepts of the Charter are as follows: a reaffirmation of the right to free movement of workers and the professions: a commitment to an 'equitable wage' for workers, annual paid leave and an improvement in working conditions as regards collective redundancies and the legal framework of employment; a reaffirmation of trade union rights and a commitment to equal treatment for men and women; provisions on health and safety in the workplace and commitments on vocational training (Social Charter, 1989).

Social policy may not have been a central feature of the original policy bargain in the EC but at least it had a Treaty basis in however limited a form. The same cannot be said of educational policy which gradually assumed a European dimension in the 1980s in response to the problems of unemployment and the implications of educational standards for the free movement of workers. Furthermore, the desire to create a 'People's Europe' led to a number of programmes promoting the mobility of students and academic staff within the countries of the Community. A Community dominated by economic imperatives and political concerns *vis-à-vis* the wider world paid little attention to culture in the 1960s and 1970s. Again, a concern with the identity of Europe and its meaning to the mass public led to the development of an EC dimension to cultural policy in the 1980s. Direct Community action in the field of culture relates to legislation on the theft of works of art, the preservation of the architectural heritage and provisions dealing with the audio-visual media as part of the internal market for services. EC policy in the social, cultural and educational spheres amounts to a series of programmes and laws covering a diverse range of activities even though primary policy competence remains at national level. The creation of a people's Europe by emphasizing solidarity and shared values is part of the process of legitimizing political integration. The common passport and more recently the EC driving licence are symbols of shared citizenship.

Bibliography

Delors, J. (1988), Speech to European Confederation of Trade Unions (ECTU), Brussels.
European Community (1989): Social Charter.
European Economic Community Treaty (1957).
Single European Act (1986), EC *Bulletin*, Supplement 2/1986.
Venturini, P. (1989), *The European Social Dimension*, Luxembourg: EC Commission Document.

Chapter 25

Manpower policy and vocational training

Brigid Laffan

The situation in Ireland

In this chapter it is proposed to highlight the main characteristics of the Irish labour market and the central issues on the manpower policy agenda. In 1988 Ireland had a labour force of 1.3 million. The size of the labour force is influenced by a variety of factors such as the aggregate population, its age structure, and participation rates of particular categories in the labour market. The participation rate of men in the Irish labour force tends to be above the Community average whereas the female rate is one of the lowest. Ireland has traditionally had a surplus of labour economy and has experienced high levels of unemployment for most of its history as an independent state. In the wake of the first oil crisis, Ireland began to experience high levels of unemployment and continues to have an acute problem of unemployment. During the 1970s, Ireland and Belgium had the distinction of heading the Community's unemployment list. Spain's accession to the Community in 1986 added another country with high unemployment (see Table 25.1). In December 1987 Ireland had 250,000 persons registered as unemployed or 19.4 per cent of the labour force (*Social Europe*, 1988: 128). This is considerably above the EC average of 11.8 per cent and second only to Spain, whose unemployment rate reaches 22.0 per cent.

In Ireland, female unemployment is higher than male unemployment: in December 1988 the male unemployment rate was 16.2 per cent (EC average, 7.9 per cent) in contrast to a figure of 19.3 per cent for women (EC average, 13.1 per cent). However, the rate of unemployment among Irish men is double the EC average. High levels of youth unemployment characterized the recessions of the last decade as young people found it increasingly difficult to make the transition from school to working life. Faced with a highly protected labour market and declining job opportunities, young people found themselves marginalized in the workplace in increasing numbers. In 1986 the unemployment rate in the youth labour force (15—24 years) was 25.5 per cent in contrast to 14.5 per cent for

Table 25.1 *Unemployment rates in 1988*

Ireland	18.7
Germany	7.0
France	11.4
Italy	14.8
Netherlands	12.1
Belgium	12.1
Luxembourg	1.8
United Kingdom	9.8
Denmark	8.0
Greece	7.4
Spain	22.0
Portugal	8.6
EC average	11.8

Source: *Social Europe* (no. 3, 1988), p. 128.

the adult labour force. The situation has improved somewhat as the proportion of young people of the total unemployed has decline from 38 per cent in 1986 to 31.5 per cent in 1988 (Eurostat, 1989).

Unemployment became a major issue on the domestic political agenda during the 1970s; successive governments felt obliged to intervene in the labour market with special measures to alleviate unemployment. Initially, the Government resorted to the traditional instruments of labour market policy such as vocational training to absorb the growing numbers of unemployed. As the crisis deepened additional programmes aimed at direct job creation appeared. Since Ireland's membership of the EC in 1973 the extent of state intervention in the labour market increased greatly and the level of public expenditure in this policy sector grew accordingly; expenditure on training rose from IR£ 13 million in 1976 to IR£ 39 billion in 1985 in real terms (*Government White Paper on Manpower Policy*, 1986: 26).

The level of unemployment must be seen in the light of the re-emergence of significant emigration from Ireland. Between 1979 and 1986 95,000 people left Ireland to search for jobs abroad (NESC, 1989: 109). High emigration is a long-standing feature of Irish life. Up to the 1930s, the United States was the primary destination of Irish emigrants. The slump led to a change in the pattern of migration with Great Britain emerging as the most favoured destination. Irish migrants continue to go to Britain in large numbers; in 1987 it is estimated that 68 per cent of Irish migrants went to Britain and a further 5.3 per cent to other EC countries. Surprisingly, almost 14 per cent went to the United States, many as illegal immigrants (Labour Force Survey, 1988). Thus despite the Community's policy of the free movement of workers, a higher proportion of Irish migrants go to the United States than to continental Europe where they could share the same social security protection as nationals. This may be explained by traditional patterns of migration towards the United States and the weak language skills of many Irish people. There are pockets of Irish workers in continental Europe — nurses in Paris, electronic engineers in Philips and Siemans, for example.

The impact of EC policies and the ESF

Irish officials and manpower agencies adopted an active approach to the ESF from the outset. This is consistent with Ireland's approach to the EC budget. As one of the economically weaker states in the Community, Ireland is committed to strengthening the redistributive element of the budget and there were clear expectations of 'hand-outs' from the Community prior to accession. Financial transfers from the ESF be been sizeable: between 1973 and 1987 Ireland received a total of IR£ 869.5. This amounted to 45 per cent of receipts from the various structural funds (Laffan, 1989: 48). Receipts from the ESF have been greater than from the European regional development fund, although the latter is the largest of the structural funds. In 1987, Ireland received approximately 9 per cent of the ESF in contrast to Spain's 11 per cent — a country with a much larger population and a serious problem of unemployment (NESC, 1989: 470). The financial importance of the fund to individual manpower agencies is very significant. In 1986, the main training agency AnCO spent IR£ 133.5 million of which IR£ 55 million or 41 per cent was contributed by the social fund. Equally the training agency for the hotel and catering industry, CERT, received 50 per cent of its budget from the fund in 1986 (*Government White Paper on Manpower Policy*, 1986: 55).

When Ireland joined the Community in 1973 AnCO, now part of FAS, was a small but growing organization. Any infusion of external finance was bound to have a striking and immediate impact on its activities. The number of people employed by AnCO rose from 908 in 1974 to over 2,300 in 1986 and the number of training centres at its disposal rose from three in 1969 to fifteen in 1982. Receipts from the ESF rose from IR£ 2.5 in 1974 to IR£ 55 million in 1986. Thus the influence of the fund manifests itself in AnCO's organizational growth and in the size of the budgetary resources at its disposal. Its range of activities grew considerably both in terms of the kind of training it undertakes and the numbers availing of training. Vocational training activity increased greatly in the 1970s; by 1985 the training agencies processed 44,651 trainees in contrast to 13,832 in 1976. Intake on direct job creation schemes rose from 3,100 in 1977 to 28,400 in 1986 (*Government White Paper on Manpower Policy*, 1986: 27 and 38).

Irish agencies and central administration adapted to the requirements of the fund very quickly after 1973. In Dublin dossiers were processed in such a way that most Irish applications receive finance. Owing to the financial importance of the fund, the beneficiaries are extremely careful to conform to Commission rules; standard operating procedures are fashioned to exploit the opportunities offered by the fund. This requires an intimate knowledge of the tortuous procedures associated with the fund and an appreciation of the nuances of the policy guidelines. There is a high level of knowledge of the fund in Ireland and this knowledge is easily available to potential applicants.

Irish agencies could not have benefited so much from the fund unless its priorities were congruent with the labour market situation in Ireland. Ireland's status as a superpriority region for the purposes of the Community's financial instruments is a major policy gain. Moreover, the fact that the entire country has this status means that there is no competition among different regions for ESF funding. Because there has been considerable overdemand for the limited resources of the fund since the mid-1970s, superpriority status meant that most programmes submitted by Ireland received funding. Being a net beneficiary of all Community funds poses its own problems for Irish policy-makers as there is now increasing competition for structural fund monies since the Iberian enlargement of the Community.

It is important to examine not only the financial impact of the fund, which has been sizeable, but also its policy impact. Young people received the lion's share of social fund monies during the 1980s and especially after the 1983 reform. Although the member-states would have developed programmes to combat youth unemployment with or without Brussels money because of their fear concerning the social and political consequences of long-term unemployment, because this was a new problem on the policy agenda and governments did not have ready-made solutions, the Commission had the opportunity to analyse the issues and search for policy solutions. The European Centre for the Development of Vocational Training (CEDEFOP) in Berlin contributed to the debate. A consensus emerged that 'alternance training' or linked work experience and training provided a useful model to combat youth unemployment. Programmes adopting this model appeared in one member-state after the other. The 'social guarantee' which was approved by the Council of Ministers in 1983 sought to give unemployed school-leavers access to work experience or training for a minimum period after compulsory education. This was instrumental in the development of youth programmes in Ireland. AnCO's community youth training programme (CYPT) and the work experience programme (WEP) run by the National Manpower Service (NMS) adopted an 'alternance training'-type approach.

When Ireland joined the Community in 1973, training facilities for the handicapped were very underdeveloped. The National Rehabilitation Board was given responsibility for co-ordinating demands for social fund finance to Brussels in order to ensure that this source of finance was used. As a result the number of organizations receiving finance for training handicapped persons grew from ten in 1973 to forty in 1983. The quality of training for the handicapped improved as the Commission insisted on systematic training methods and the keeping of trainee records. The availability of social fund finance ensured that the needs of a marginal group in the labour market were addressed.

The training of women received considerable attention in the operation of the social fund after 1977. A special budgetary heading aimed at the training of women was included in the social fund legislation. The number of women trained by AnCo increased steadily during the 1970s from a low of 128 in 1974 to 7,460 in 1983 which represented 33 per cent of all trainees in that year (AnCO Annual Reports, 1974: 3 and 1983: 7). Yet woman are still concentrated in training programmes leading to traditional 'women's jobs'. The *Government White Paper on Manpower Policy* drew attention to the weak representation of women in skills-based courses (*Government White Paper*, 1986: 31). This may be explained partly by cultural attitudes concerning what women should do and partly by the kind of choices open to young girls in schools. AnCO ran a number of positive action programmes to encourage women into non-traditional areas, including training programmes for 'Women into engineering', 'Women into electronics' and 'Women into management'. Return-to-work programmes for women who wish to re-enter the labour market are also run. Programmes of this kind begin the slow process of redressing the imbalance in the provision of training.

The activities of the social fund may be dysfunctional at national level if its priorities lead to the displacement of issues that require attention on the domestic policy agenda. The emphasis placed on youth unemployment in Irish manpower policy during the early 1970s was partly due to the availability of ESF finance for youth programmes. The needs of older unemployed workers were not given sufficient resources and attention. A report of the National Planning Board in 1984 states explicitly that it would be 'misguided to intensify the policies that discriminate in favour of young job seekers' (*National Planning Board Report*, 1984: 24). The establishment of a number of schemes for the long-term unemployed over twenty-five in 1985 began to tackle the needs of older workers.

The role of the structural funds was a major issue during the negotiations on the Single European Act as the peripheral countries, fearful that the internal market might lead to a greater concentration of wealth in the core economies, looked for a strengthening of the EC's role in promoting cohesion. The articles in the SEA dealing with economic and social cohesion call on the Commission to submit proposals to the Council and the European Parliament for a reform of the structural funds. The legislation dealing with the reform was agreed in 1988 and the new rules apply from 1989 onwards. The Community intends to target a high proportion of structural fund monies towards those parts of the Community whose per capita GDP is less than 75 per cent of the Community average (EC Council Regulation, no. 2052/88). Ireland is considered an 'objective 1' region.

Table 25.2 *Human resource measures in the National Plan 1989–93 IR£*

	1988	1989	1990	1991	1992	1993	Total
State	198	184	153	159	165	182	843
EC	113	143	218	229	240	232	1062
Total	311	327	371	388	405	414	1905

Source: National Development Plan 1989–93, p. 82.

Under the new arrangements each 'objective 1' region had to submit a plan to Brussels setting out its priorities for expenditure over five years and indicating the amount of finance that was being sought from the Community. The Irish plan was submitted in March 1989 — the sections in the plan dealing with the regional and agricultural funds are dealt with in the relevant chapters of this volume. In setting out the policy context of the plan, emphasis is placed on the persistently weak demand for labour in Ireland leading to high levels of unemployment and emigration (*National Development Plan*, 1989–93: 11). The plan sets out the objectives that will be pursued for vocational training and educational programmes over the next five years. Greatly increased resources are requested in the plan from the ESF. Table 25.2 sets out the financial allocations for the 'human resource programme' covering vocational training, education and direct job creation.

A plan relating to objectives 3 and 4 under the new rules is being submitted separately and seeks a further IR£ 557 million. The plan envisages a far higher proportion of total expenditure in this area to come from Brussels than heretofore. Whereas in 1988 the state spent IR£ 198 million on vocational training and employment measures in addition to IR£ 113 million from the social fund by 1993 the plan envisages a total of IR£ 232 million from Brussels and IR£ 182 million from the national budget. Thus expenditure from the national budget is set to decline whereas EC monies are set to become an even more important component of manpower policy expenditure in Ireland. The final amounts pledged by Brussels to the five-year plan for Ireland as an 'objective 1' region are contained in what is known as the community support framework adopted by the Commission on the 31 October 1989. Total expenditure on human resource measures for the years 1989–93 will be IR£ 2,209 million, of which IR£ 1,123 is in the form of EC aid.

Assessment

Financial flows from the ESF to Ireland contribute significantly to the level of public expenditure devoted to manpower policies. Without social fund monies manpower policy institutions could not have expanded as they did. The existence of an embryonic training infrastructure prior to membership meant that the necessary institutional framework was in place to enable Irish agencies to make use of ESF funding when it became available. The flow of Brussels money gave these agencies considerable autonomy because they were no longer completely dependent on the Exchequer for all of their finance. ESF monies, unlike regional fund monies, go directly to the beneficiary agencies and are not absorbed into the national budget.

Membership of the Community brought Irish trainers and vocational training experts into contact with their counterparts in other countries through the Commission's advisory committees and the networks created by CEDEFOP in Berlin. The social fund provided finance for innovatory projects that allowed Irish agencies to try out new methods of training and job creation on a pilot basis and also enabled them to learn from the experiences in other countries. A diffusion of policy ideas across borders is a feature of EC activity in this area. Alternance training, the social guarantee, increased training provision for women and the handicapped are all features of the ESF's beneficial effects on manpower and training policy in Ireland.

However, the emphasis in Ireland on maximum receipts from the structural funds led to an undue emphasis on the Commission's eligibility criteria rather than on the training needs of the country. Up to the mid-1980s the needs of older workers were neglected because of the policy bias in the ESF towards young workers. Moreover, ESF training was taking place in a stagnant labour market with the result that many training programmes were mere palliatives in the face of rising unemployment. The extensive flow of funds to the manpower agencies caused conflict with a related policy sector, education. The vocational education sector saw its policy domain eroded by the training agencies as they began to develop courses that would have been the sole prerogative of educational bodies. Insufficient attention was paid to the impact of ESF monies on the balance of policies at national level.

Bibliography

AnCO Annual Reports.
Eurostat (1989), *Unemployment Series*, no. 3.
Government White Paper on Manpower Policy, (1986), Dublin: Pl. 4306.
Labour Force Survey, (1988).
Laffan, B. (1989), 'While you are over there in Brussels, get us a grant: the management of the structural funds in Ireland', *Irish Political Studies*.
National Development Plan, 1989–93.

National Planning Board Report (1984): Proposals for a Plan 1984–1987, Dublin: Pl. 2309.
NESC (1989), *Ireland in the European Community: Performance, Prospects and Strategy*, Dublin: Pl. 6662.
Social Europe, various issues.

Chapter 26

Women
Brigid Laffan

The situation in Ireland

In 1970 the Irish Government commissioned a study on the role of women in Irish society in response to the UN Decade for Women. The report of the Commission was the first major public document that catalogued the numerous anomalies, inequities and injustices experienced by women across the whole range of societal life. The report highlighted the level of restrictions on women's employment, inequities in the tax system, inequalities before the law and unequal pay. The public image of Irish women is that of wife and mother, guardian of the public morals. The report stressed the 'stereotyped role that is assigned to women, the inculcation of attitudes in both boys and girls in their formative years that there are definite and separate roles of the sexes . . . that a woman's role must be predominantly home-centred while a man's life pattern will be predominantly centred on employment' (Commission on the Status of Women, 1970). The 1937 Constitution emphasizes this role for women — Article 41.2 reads as follows:

2.1 In particular the state recognizes that by her life within the home women give to the state a support without which the common good cannot be achieved.
2.2 The state shall therefore endeavour to assume that mothers shall not be obliged by economic necessity to engage in labour to the neglect of their duties in the home.

This restrictive view of the role of women stemmed from a rural, Catholic, authoritarian culture. By the end of the 1960s rapid urbanization and industrialization was breaking down the old cultural norms.

The women's movement spread its tentacles to Ireland although it never became a widespread social movement as it did in the United States and to a lesser extent in Britain. The women's movement had to devote considerable time and effort to extracting legislative change in such areas as family law and labour law because of the large number of inequities and anomalies in Irish law. The movement in Ireland was thus largely reformist and non-revolutionary. The media and particularly a handful of women journalists provided the catalyst for raising women's consciousness. The women's pages in the newspapers and women's programmes on radio documented the response of the state to the demands of the women's groups and provided women with a forum to write about and discuss life as they experienced it. The movement succeeded in placing women's issues firmly on the political agenda during the 1970s. Political parties responded quickly to the greater saliency of women's issues by including sections on 'women's affairs' in their election manifestos. Membership of the European Community coincided with the politicization of women's issues in Ireland and the policies of the European Community became an important source of external pressure on successive governments.

The impact of EC policy

When Ireland joined the Community in 1973 there was no anti-discrimination legislation on the statute books and the marriage bar to employment in the public service had just been lifted. Although the Treaty of Rome contains only one Article concerning women (Article 119) which provides for equal pay for equal work, the Community has developed a number of action programmes involving a variety of measures to protect and promote women's rights. The first directive on equal pay for men and women was adopted in 1975 and became effective in 1976. The directive sought the elimination of all discrimination with regard to remuneration for the 'same work' or 'work of equal value'. In anticipation of the directive, the Irish Parliament passed the Anti-Discrimination Act of 1974 which provided that men and women should receive equal treatment in regard to pay for like work. As the economic situation deteriorated in 1975, the Federated Union of Employers (FUE) put considerable pressure on the Irish Government for a deferral of the implementation of the equal pay legislation in 1976. At a conference on the topic, a director of the FUE argued that there was a strong case for the postponement of the legislation (FUE Conference Papers, 1975: 12). The Government began to back track on the legislation by a decision to implement an amendment which allowed for exceptions to the principle of 'equal pay' if the viability of an enterprise were to be placed in jeopardy by the legislation. The Government also announced that it would be unable to fulfil its commitment to equal pay in the public sector. The Government then applied for a partial derogation from the equal pay directive to the EC Commission in accordance with Article 135 of the EEC Treaty. Women's groups lobbied the Commission in an attempt to ensure that the legislation was not deferred. The Commission refused the derogation so that the 1974 Act came into force on 1 January 1976 (Curtin 1989: 111–12).

The equal pay directive was followed in 1976 by a directive on equal treatment of men and women as regards access to employment, vocational training and working conditions. The Employment Equality Act 1977 and the Unfair Dismissals Act 1977 provide the legal context for the implementation of this directive in Ireland. The 1977 Equality Act and the Unfair Dismissals Act 1977 prohibit discrimination on grounds of sex or marital status in recruitment for employment, in training, in conditions of employment or in the provision of opportunities for promotion. In 1983 the Employment Equality Agency, set up under the 1977 Act, published a code of practice on equality of opportunity in employment that set out guidelines for employers and trade unions on the operation of the equality legislation. The agency has recommended that loopholes in the original Act should be abolished.

In 1978 the Council adopted a directive on 'equal treatment for men and women in matters of social security' (79/7/EEC) that should have entered into force in 1984. The directive covered all statutory schemes which provide protection against sickness, invalidity, old age, accidents at work and occupational diseases and unemployment. The implementation of the directive in Ireland was far from smooth. Legislation was not introduced in the Parliament until 1985 and this legislation did not have full effect until November 1986. The Social Welfare Act (no. 2) of 1985 provided for the implementation of the directive. In introducing the bill, the Minister for Social Welfare set out the main areas of discrimination that the bill sought to tackle. Married women:

— were paid lower rates of benefit in the schemes of disability benefit, unemployment benefit, invalidity pension and occupational injuries benefit;
— were paid unemployment benefit for a maximum duration of 312 days as against 390 days generally;
— were effectively debarred from applying for unemployment assistance;
— had different conditions applied to them in the matter of adult and child dependants. (Dail Debates, 25 June 1985, 359: 1803)

The new legislation was intended to bring the rates of social benefits and entitlement periods to the same level as for men.

Under the old rules the conditions for women were far more restrictive than for men. Discrimination of this kind against married women rests on an assumption widely held in Ireland and enshrined in the Irish Constitution that women are and should be supported by their husbands while they care for the family and home. This notion of dependency suggests that women are not available for work and should thus receive unequal treatment in matters of social security. According to the Minister when introducing the bill the underlying concept of the Irish social welfare code was that: 'the husband was the breadwinner and head of the household and the person to whom the full benefits of the social security system should be available' (Dail Debates, 25 June 1985, 359: 1807).

The new bill sought to change the notion of dependency so that the assumption that any married women living with her husband is automatically a dependant no longer applied. About 46,000 married women benefited from the new legislation at a cost of IR£ 18 million to the exchequer. However, the implementation of the Act was delayed because of staff shortages and an industrial relations problem in the Department of Social Welfare. A more serious problem was caused by the impact of the new bill on the level of social security payments to certain categories of families. In introducing the legislation in 1985 the Minister for Social Welfare accepted that some 20,000 families stood to lose money in the transition to the new legislation. Prior to the new law, a husband used to receive all increases in social security benefits regardless of the wife's income and status. Under the new legislation there is no longer any entitlement if the spouse is either working or drawing benefit. Considerable political difficulties emerged when the Government attempted to apply the 1985 Act during 1986. The Government was forced to provide transitional measures to alleviate the hardship caused to certain families by the new law (Dail Debates, 20 November 1986, 370: 130). This involved a ceiling (IR£ 50 per week) below which no account is taken of the spouse's income and a transitional payment for one year to anyone affected by the new provisions.

In 1986 the Council enlarged the field of application of the principle of equal treatment to occupational social security schemes (Council Directive, 86/378/EEC) and also adopted a new directive on equal treatment for men and women engaged in a self-employed activity and on the protection of self-employed women during pregnancy and maternity (Council Directive, 86/613/EEC). The latter directive did not require implementing legislation in Ireland as existing equality legislation encompassed the scope of the directive. The directive on equal treatment for occupational social security schemes has not yet been implemented; legislation in the form of statutory instruments is being drafted in the Department of Social Welfare.

During the Irish presidency of the Council of Ministers in 1984, the relevant Council adopted a recommendation exhorting the member-states to adopt a 'Positive action in favour of women'. The purpose of the recommendation was to tackle the continuation of discriminatory practices despite equality legislation. The recommendation sets out to:

eliminate or counteract the prejudicial effects on women in employment which arise from existing social attitudes, behaviours and structures based on the idea of a traditional division of roles in society between men and women; and encourage the participation of women in various occupations in those sectors of working life where they are at present under-represented, particularly in the sectors of the future, and at higher levels of responsibility. (Council Recommendation, 84/635/EEC)

At national level the Government sought to implement the positive action programme in the public sector. Initially the strategy of positive

Table 26.1 *Number of cases referred to an equality offier 1976–85*

1976	51
1977	79
1978	88
1979	99
1980	107
1981	57
1982	24
1983	34
1984	30
1985	14
Total	583

Source: Ireland, UN Report 1987, p. 83.

action was recommended to the large state-sponsored bodies who have all adopted formal policies on equality. In 1986 the Government adopted an equal opportunity policy and guidelines for the civil service.

Monitoring of the equality legislation

The two major pieces of equality legislation set out procedures for the processing of complaints. Grievances can be pursued by any individual through the Labour Court, which refers such cases to an equality officer for investigation and a recommendation. This recommendation may be appealed to the Labour Court and on a matter of law to the High Court. The Employment Equality Agency established under the 1977 Act conducts official investigations, issues what are called non-discrimination notices and monitors the implementation of the relevant laws. Table 26.1 lists the number of cases that have been referred to an equality officer. Irish courts may refer cases to the European Court of Justice to tease out the interpretation of EC law and the manner of implementation in Ireland. A number of preliminary rulings have been sought with regard to the equality legislation (Curtin, 1989).

The Commission has used its role as 'guardian of the treaties' to ensure that Irish law conforms to the equality directives. In 1980 the Commission issued a 'formal notice' followed by a 'reasoned opinion' concerning restrictions in the 1977 Act relating to training for midwifery and employment in psychiatric hospitals. In March 1983, the Commission issued a further 'formal notice' concerning the general exemption of the police force and the prison service from the terms of the 1977 Act. Protective legislation which restricted the employment of women for shift work was also found contrary to the equality directive by the Commission. As a result of a series of 'formal notices', the Irish Government has altered national legislation. The Minister for Labour now issues shiftwork licences permitting women to engage in industrial work at night. The employment equality (European Communities) regulations of 1985 abolished the general exemption of the police force and the prison service from the 1977 Act.

The influence of the EC and the position of women today

Ireland's membership of the Community coincided with the arrival of women's issues on the political agenda at domestic level. The growing commitment of the European Community to equality legislation moulded the treatment of women's issues in Ireland, particularly in the legislative field. The need to implement the long line of equality directives led to a series of equality laws in Ireland. A report of the Joint Committee on Secondary Legislation of the European Communities, which is the Parliament's watchdog committee on EC matters, made the following statement with regard to the impact of the EC on women's issues:

The Community has brought about changes in employment practices which might otherwise have taken decades to achieve. Irish women have the Community to thank for the removal of the marriage bar in employment, the introduction of maternity leave, greater opportunities to train at a skilled trade, protection against dismissal on pregnancy, the disappearance of advertisements specifying the sex of an applicant for a job and greater equality in the social welfare code. After farmers, Irish women in employment have probably benefited most from entry to the EEC. (Joint Committee, Report on Proposals Relating to Equality of Opportunity, 17 October 1984, Pl. 2704: 123)

As parliamentary committees are not given to exaggeration, the extract from the report provides a succinct view of the contribution of the EC to equality legislation in Ireland.

Almost two decades of legislation has helped improve the status of women in Irish society but has not overcome all of the barriers facing women as they seek to broaden the definition of 'women's work' and the 'woman's place'. A striking change since the mid-1970s is the increased participation rate of women in the labour force. In 1975, women comprised 27.4 per cent of the total labour force, a figure that rose to 29.4 per cent by 1984. Most of the increase is made up of married women. The proportion of the female labour force consisting of married women increased from 7.5 per cent in 1971 to 20.4 per cent in 1985 (UN Report, 1987: 77). The participation rate of married women in the labour market is still the lowest in the European Community. Nevertheless, fewer married women are leaving employment when they get married.

The equal pay legislation relates to women who are employed in activities that are the same as or similar to those of men. In Ireland as in other EC countries, women are crowded into a limited number of jobs, frequently referred to as 'women's jobs'. For instance, in manufacturing industry almost one-third of women are in textiles, clothing, footwear and leather. In the professional services, about 70 per cent of women are in nursing and teaching. Furthermore, women tend to find themselves in the lower levels of the organizational hierarchy; in industry, banking and the distributive trades, women make up less than 7 per cent of managers and executives. In the public service, women make up less than 4 per cent of the senior civil service. The crowding of women into a limited range of jobs and their weak representation in the higher occupational levels tends to drive women's earnings downwards. The average hourly earnings of women are around two-thirds of those of men and on a weekly basis, the average earnings of women are 60 per cent those of men. This does not mean that widespread wage discrimination is being practised but it does reflect the pattern of female employment. The ratio of women's hourly rate to that of men increased somewhat from 60.7 per cent in 1975 to 67 per cent in 1985, which suggests that the equal pay legislation has had some impact (Blackwell, 1986).

Equal pay legislation on its own will not result in equal treatment of women in employment. Women need better access to educational opportunities and on-the-job training which would enhance women's promotional prospects. More importantly, women need more flexible work arrangements and child care facilities to reduce the double burden of employment and family responsibilities, given that 'home duties' are still considered the domain of the woman.

Assessment

In the area of equal rights, there are all gains and no losses in the Irish context. The Community's legislative programme has provided an incentive to successive Irish governments to develop policies in this area and the Commission's monitoring of the implementation has ensured that directives passed into Irish law. Access to Brussels networks has given agencies like the Employment Equality Agency and the Council for the Status of Women opportunities to mould both EC policy and national policy. The Community is a useful source of added pressure on the Irish Government. Equality legislation on its own will not overcome the difficulties faced by women in the labour market. Only long-term policies in the educational system, special programmes by the training agencies and more flexible working arrangements will alter women's underrepresentation in the labour market and their presence in a number of limited sectors. The work of the ESF is particularly important in this regard. So too are proposed directives on parental leave, on the burden of proof in the area of equal pay and on completing the implementation of the principle of equal treatment for men and women in statutory and occupational social security schemes.

Bibliography

Blackwell, J. (1986), *Women in the Labour Force: A Statistical Digest*, Employment Equality Report, Dublin.
Commission on the Status of Women (1972), Dublin: Pl. 2760.
Curtin, D. (1989), *Irish Equality Law*, London: The Roundhall Press.
Dail Debates.
Federated Union of Employers (1975), Proceedings of Equal Pay Conference (July). First Report on the measures adopted to give effect to the provisions of the UN Convention on the Elimination of all forms of Discrimination against Women (1987), Dublin: Pl. 4775.
Report on Proposals relating to Equality of Opportunity (1984), Joint Committee on the Secondary Legislation of the European Communities, Dublin: Pl. 2704.

Chapter 27

Industrial relations

Brigid Laffan

Industrial relations in Ireland

The Irish system of industrial relations is strongly influenced by the historical links with the United Kingdom. The important laws which govern trade disputes in Ireland were incorporated into Irish law with the foundation of the state in 1922: the Trade Disputes Act of 1906 forms the cornerstone of bargaining behaviour. The trade union movement in Ireland shares a number of characteristics with its British counterpart, notably a multiplicity of unions largely organized on an occupational basis rather than by industry. 'Voluntarism' is the dominant principle of the system of industrial relations. Put simply, the regulation of the system of industrial relations rests with the parties themselves through free collective bargaining. While the state has a function it is not as important as it is in the states of continental Europe. There is little statutory imitation of the institutions which are common on the continent that provide for collective bargaining and worker participation (McCarthy and Von Prondzynsky, 1984: 245).

Worker participation

The Commission has always interpreted Article 118 of the Rome Treaty as giving it responsibility for promoting the interests of workers in the Community. Its proposals for a fifth directive on the harmonization of company law (1972) and a draft statute for a European company (1973) emphasized the Commissions's commitment to worker participation. The fifth directive on limited companies proposed the application of a two-tier structure involving a management committee and a supervisory council including worker participation. Provision for worker participation also appears in the European company statute. The original proposals for the fifth company law directive met with considerable resistance in the Council of Ministers because the proposed two-tier structure was alien to British and Irish practice of a unitary board structure. The original model of worker participation was borrowed from Germany where there is an extensive use of 'co-determination', under which larger firms are required by law to provide one-half representation for workers on company boards. There was also considerable opposition in Britain and Ireland to any system of obligatory participation of workers at director level (McCarthy and Von Prondzynsky, 1984: 249). The Commission proposed an amended version of the fifth company law directive in 1983 (OJ C240/83). New proposals for a European company statute which would provide an alternative to national law are now before the Council; the Commission suggests that companies should be able to choose from among three models of worker participation.

A proposal for a directive on procedures for informing and consulting the employees of undertakings with a complex structure, in particular transnational firms, known as the 'Vredling Directive', was also the subject of considerable opposition in the Council. The demise of this draft directive was orchestrated largely by the United Kingdom and the United States (Lodge, 1989: 312). Opposition to the directive was also voiced in Ireland because of fears concerning its possible adverse effects on multinational investment (McCarthy and Von Prondzynsky, 1984: 250). The desire to protect the investment climate emerged as an issue during the implementation of the fourth company law directive in 1984–6. The Industrial Development Authority (IDA), which is responsible for attracting investment to Ireland, lobbied to ensure that multinational companies in Ireland would be exempt from the publication of mandatory financial accounts (Laffan *et al.*, 1988: 405).

Although the European model of worker participation is alien to Irish tradition, there has been a commitment to greater participation at a political level. The Worker Participation (State Enterprise) Act of 1977 made provision for the election of employee representatives to the board of a number of the large commercial state-sponsored bodies. The development was intended to stimulate similar developments in the private sector. The latter continues its opposition to compulsory worker participation in any form. The Commission's social action programme based on the Social Charter reintroduces the issue of the right of employees to information to the EC agenda.

Job security

Since the Second World War, the International Labour Organization has issued a series of conventions and recommendations that set out minimum standards which states should apply in the employment relationships between citizens (McCarthy and Von Prondzynsky, 1984: 251). Irish legislation covering redundancy payments and unfair dismissal was influenced by these developments. More recently, the European

Community has had a minor influence on Irish legislation in this area. A series of directives have been enacted which strengthen the rights of employees:

- Directive on acquired rights on transfers of undertakings.
- Directive on collective redundancies.
- Directive on the protection of employees in the event of insolvency of their employers.

The objective of the acquired rights directive is to safeguard the rights of employees when a business is transferred or merged with another and the legal identity of the employer changes. This directive was implemented in Ireland by means of a statutory instrument under the 1972 EEC Act. The European Communities Safeguarding of Employees' Rights on Transfer of Undertakings Regulations of 1980 have largely adopted the wording of the original directive (McCarthy and Von Prondzynsky, 1984: 253). The directive on collective redundancies is implemented by means of statute, the Protection of Employment Act of 1977. It requires the exchange of information and consultation between an employer, the Minister for Labour and employee representatives at least thirty days before making a certain number of employees redundant (5 or more in establishments of 21—49 employees and 30 or more in establishments with over 300 employees). It has been argued that the Irish law is less onerous in certain respects than the provisions of the directive (McCarthy and Von Prondzynsky, 1984: 254). The Protection of Employees (Employers' Insolvency) Act of 1984 implements the third EC directive.

Assessment

The impact of EC membership on Irish industrial relations is limited to a number of specific areas, notably worker participation and job security. The nature of the Irish system of industrial relations with its tradition of free collective bargaining causes difficulties for Ireland in accepting Commission proposals on compulsory worker participation. Although successive governments have been committed to worker participation, the private sector remains opposed to any form of compulsory participation. The trade union movement welcomes EC initiatives in this area, although they considered the original Commission proposals on the structure of the company boards too bureaucratic for Irish practice. The Community's participation could be considered a gain for workers and a complicating factor for employers used to a non-compulsory system of industrial relations. The potential impact of the Community is sizeable if the social dimension of the internal market comes to the fore.

Bibliography

Laffan, B., Manning, M. and Kelly, P. (1988), 'Ireland', in H. Siedentopf and J. Ziller (eds), *Making European Policies Work*, London: Sage.

Lodge, J. (ed.) (1989), *The European Community and the Challenge of the Future*, London: Pinter.

McCarthy, C. and Von Prondzynsky, F. (1984), 'The influence of the European Economic Community on Irish industrial relations', in P.J. Drudy and D. McAleese (eds), *Ireland and the European Community*, London: Cambridge University Press.

Chapter 28

Consumer law

Brigid Laffan

EC policy

The European Community adopted its first consumer protection policy framework in 1975 when five basic consumer rights were laid down:

— Protection of health and safety.
— Protection of economic interests.
— Redress.
— Information and education.
— Representation of the right to be heard (Council Resolution, 14 April 1975, OJC 92.1975).

As in other areas of policy, the Community progressed on the basis of consumer protection programmes which combine general principles with specific legislative proposals in the form of directives which have to be implemented at national level.

Irish practice

The growth of consumer consciousness is relatively recent in Ireland. Prior to the late 1970s the primary means of consumer protection was a series of Prices Acts by which the minister concerned could place maximum prices orders on various goods. The Consumer Information Act of 1978 which was the first major piece of legislation since the Merchandise Marks Act of 1887 heralded a recognition by government of the need to strengthen consumer protection . Both these acts prohibit false or misleading descriptions of goods, services and prices.

The 1978 Act made provision for the setting up of an Office of Consumer Affairs as an autonomous office attached to the Department of Industry and Commerce. The office acts as a watchdog for the consumer, deals with complaints from the public and enforces the corpus of consumer legislation. The role of the office has changed somewhat since

1978. In 1988 the Director for Consumer Affairs assumed the responsibility of the Examiner of Restrictive Practices under the Restrictive Practices (Amendment) Act of 1987 and became the Director of Consumer Affairs and Fair Trade. This decision brings all facets of consumer protection under the mantle of one office. The Director of Consumer Affairs and Fair Trade has considerable powers under various acts to enforce legislation through the courts. The consumer lobby in Ireland is not very strong: the Irish Consumers' Association has a membership of 8,000 and publishes a magazine, *Consumer Choice*. During the 1970s the association devoted its energies to lobbying for modern consumer legislation in Ireland and institutions to protect the interests of the consumers.

Impact of EC legislation

The misleading advertising directive

The directive on misleading advertising was implemented in Ireland in June 1988 (SI 134.1988). To a significant extent, the directive covers the same ground as the 1978 Consumer Information Act which allowed the Director of Consumer Affairs and Fair Trade the right to request that a misleading piece of advertising be withdrawn and if this did not happen, the power to seek a Court Order. The EC directive is, however, different to the 1978 Act in a number of respects. First, its definition of advertising is wider than in the Act. Second, the directive seeks to protect not just consumers but also 'persons carrying on a trade or business'. In other words, the interests of competitors are included in the directive. Third, the most novel feature of the directive is that anybody can apply to the High Court for a Court Order to have an advertisement withdrawn or prohibited because it is misleading. The Director of Consumer Affairs can — under a special procedure — issue a request that an advertisement can be withdrawn and if the request is not adhered to, the Director then applies to the Court. This is a speedy remedy frequently used by the Director of Consumer Affairs. Fourth, the Court may require the advertiser to prove the truth of the claims made in a contested advertisement and can require the advertiser to publish a correct advertisement. Although this directive covers much of the same ground as the 1978 Consumer Information Act, it does have some novel features and is used by the Director of Consumer Affairs in conjunction with the earlier Act.

Consumer credit and the doorstep-selling directive

The directives on consumer credit and doorstep-selling are implemented in Ireland by means of ministerial order. Both plugged a major gap in

Irish consumer legislation. The Consumer Credit Order (SI 319.1987) ensures that advertisements about consumer credit, including hire purchase, must include information about the real cost of credit to the consumer. The directive on doorstep-selling allows a consumer seven days in which to cancel a contract made during an unsolicited visit by a trader to his or her home or place of work.

Labelling and packaging directives

A plethora of directives designed to give the consumer information about the goods they may purchase have been passed by the Community. These have been incorporated into Irish law in the form of secondary legislation. According to the Director of Consumer Affairs, Ireland is not well placed to interpret and apply the food labelling directives because there are too many regulatory agencies involved in this area. The Health Boards, the Departments of Agriculture and Industry and Commerce and the Office of Consumer Affairs and Fair Trade all have a role to play in implementing the directives.

The product liability directive

The directive on product liability has not yet been implemented in Ireland although its implementation date passed in July 1988. The directive is concerned with redress for people suffering death, personal injury or damage to property as a result of defective products. The delay in implementation is caused by the fact that the Government, under pressure from consumer interests and the Joint Committee on the Secondary Legislation of the European Communities, asked that it be implemented by means of primary national law instead of the speedier mechanism of secondary legislation. It was felt that as this is a major piece of consumer legislation, it should go through the full legislative process in the Dail. At present, the buyer is protected under the 1893–1980 Sale of Goods Acts. Under these Acts the buyer must prove negligence no matter how serious the fault or how tragic the consequences. Under the directive on product liability, the requirement to prove negligence is removed in many cases of injury caused by defective products. Thus consumers will be able to obtain compensation where at present the problem of proving negligence is too great.

Assessment

Modern consumer legislation is of recent origin in Ireland and has coincided with membership of the European Community. Undoubtedly, EC consumer legislation has increased consumer protection in strengthening the existing corpus of consumer law by filling in gaps in a number of areas. The directive on misleading advertising gives broader definitions than the national Consumer Information Act and allows for new procedures of redress for the Director of Consumer Affairs. The directives on credit information and doorstep-selling filled a gap in existing Irish law. The directive on product liability has not yet been implemented but will allow easier redress for consumers. The Irish Consumers Association has expressed the fear that in the drive to complete the internal market, the interests of the consumer will not be protected sufficiently (Address by Joan Morrison, Consumers' Association of Ireland, October 1989).

Bibliography

Morrison, J. (1989), *Address to Consumers' Association of Ireland.*

Chapter 29

Education

*Dermot Scott**

The European Coal and Steel Community Treaty of 1951 had as its aim the establishment of a common market in coal and steel throughout the six member-states. The opening of the market was expected to lead to expansion by efficient mines and steelworks, and closure of inefficient pits and works. A social dimension of the Treaty was included, to ease the transition of redundant miners and steelworkers to jobs in other sectors by creating new and sound economic activities capable of reabsorbing redundant workers into productive employment, by paying tideover and resettlement allowances, and by retraining (ECSC Treaty, 1951).

Vocational retraining therefore was brought within the Treaty framework from the beginning. It is clear that it was included for economic reasons, as a counterpart to the opening of the market: help would be required to ease the social aspects of the transition, and to retrain workers for a European economy that was short of skilled labour. Vocational training as such was not involved, much less any aspect of education.

The Treaties of Rome, establishing the European Economic Community and the Atomic Energy Community, brought a corresponding emphasis on transitional measures to facilitate redeployment of labour, but this time with provisions for a European Social Fund (ESF) and for the development of a common vocational training policy (EEC Treaty, 1957, Articles 123–8). These provisions may have been deliberately circumscribed in order to exclude education proper from the ambit of the Communities. Meanwhile, intergovernmental co-operation at a European level within the Council of Europe did include the field of education, but this was not subject to the Community's decision-making process.

Unwillingness to allow education to be part of the Community process remains an important factor today, although action is no longer limited

---

* The author is an official of the European Parliament, working in the Information Office in Dublin. The views expressed are personal and do not commit the institution.

to the field of vocational training. Education is felt to be close to the core of national identity and is sometimes a bastion of a particular language, culture or community. Denmark has often been instanced as a country which has maintained a separate language and culture on a small base of territory and population, and in close proximity to dominant neighbours; and Denmark has been hesitant about allowing a Community education policy to develop. Such hesitations have been shared by other countries, and recent instances include the United Kingdom's unwillingness to allow the Lingua programme for improving language skills to operate in second-level schools, and the Irish Government's successful defence in the European Court of Justice of its insistence on an Irish language qualification for all teachers (Court, 1989).

Given such attitudes, it is not surprising that little headway was made in developing an educational component of Community policy for some considerable time. At the end of the 1960s, however, the thaw in Community affairs evident at the 1969 Hague summit also affected the ESF (Laffan, 1985), and produced the first substantive mention of co-operation in the field of education (Council Resolution, 1971). The revision of the fund allowed for the financing of pilot studies to promote innovative programmes of vocational training; but the initial training of young people was excluded.

Community policy in the field of education

The period from 1973 to 1990 has seen the steady growth of measures relevant to the field of education proper. These have been in response to two stimuli: the need to co-operate within the Community to meet the challenge of unemployment; and the need to respond to the imperatives of the single market by facilitating freedom of movement by workers and by providing training in scarce technical skills. Freedom of movement requires both mutual recognition of diplomas and adequate language skills, and these have featured prominently on the Community's agenda. Other areas of concern have been the provision of education for the children of migrant workers and for the handicapped, equal opportunities for boys and girls, consumer education, illiteracy and the transition from school to work. A third stimulus became evident in June 1985, when the Council and Ministers of Education, meeting in Luxembourg, adopted a series of measures to improve teaching about the Community and Europe in schools (Council Resolution, 1985). The stimulus here was a concern to promote a 'People's Europe', in parallel with the single market concept which was being pursued in the negotiations leading up to the Single Act. These measures mark something of a breakthrough.

The most recent developments in the field are mainly at third level, and are aimed at maximizing the interaction of the third-level systems of education, in order to produce a corps of educated Europeans, with skills and contacts built up over the Community as a whole. Thus the ERASMUS programme aims to achieve greater mobility of teachers and students, for students to spend a significant period of study in another member-state as an integral part of their course and for the promotion of co-operation between universities. The COMETT programme aims to encourage synergy between universities and industry, and to provide better joint training programmes for young people, especially in technology, at local, regional and national level. The 'Yes for Europe' programme, though not aimed at higher education, encourages exchanges of young people between different countries of the EC and so has a widely educational purpose.

In sum, the Community began without an educational policy as such. The dynamics of economic integration, first in the coal and steel sectors and later in the economy in general, drove it to elements of social engineering, originally for certain sectors and for a notionally transitional period only. From this intervention grew a broader and more positive approach to vocational training. The growth of social policy in the 1970s brought a number of interventions in the educational area, concerned mainly with problems relating to mobility. Despite some European concern in the 1980s to deregulate the labour market, the increasing pace of economic integration in recent years led to more far-reaching programmes, nearer the core of the educational process. Education is now recognized as being central to the development of European construction, and this is beginning to be reflected in the efforts of the Irish authorities to develop the curriculum.

The Irish educational system

The Irish educational system has a primary tier of schools established in the 1830s by act of Parliament to provide universal free primary education; a post-primary tier consisting of private schools, often under the auspices of a charitable foundation or a religious order, and public schools established either by local authorities (vocational schools), or by the state (community and comprehensive schools). Third-level education is provided by universities, colleges of technology, and institutions providing training in particular skills or disciplines such as education, catering and agriculture.

Each primary school is administered by a board controlled by the local representative of the Roman Catholic, Church of Ireland, Presbyterian or other clergymen. Recently, several schools have been founded with explicit interdenominational structures, but otherwise all primary schools are confessional. However, the training of teachers, their pay and conditions, and the curriculum for primary schools, are controlled by the Government through the Department of Education. The curriculum, which was reformed in the early 1970s, lays emphasis on the acquisition of basic numeracy and literacy, as well as of a basic knowledge of the Irish language (gaelic), and environmental studies — local history and geography, flora and fauna, civic and political affairs, within a child-centred development approach.

Post-primary education is provided by private institutions (secondary schools), or by those under the control of local authorities (vocational schools) or by more recently established institutions (community and comprehensive schools). Although ownership is decentralized, the curriculum is under the central control of the Government and of the Department of Education, and consists of two cycles. The junior cycle consists of the last three years of compulsory school attendance (12—15 years), and the course followed leads to the Intermediate Certificate examination (a reformed course will lead to the Junior Certificate from 1992, see below). The senior cycle, which follows immediately, or after a 'transition year' of various activities and studies, consists of a two-year course leading to the Leaving Certificate examination, which, like the Intermediate Certificate, is a national certificate set and marked by the Department of Education. Since 1984, a vocational preparation and training programme may be provided in schools; in the vocational sector, ESF support has been given for the running costs of vocational and educational training programmes, affecting some 19,000 trainees in 1988. No trainee grants are available at this level.

Universities are private institutions, and are dependent on government policy in so far as they depend on public funds allocated through the Higher Education Authority. In so far as they can raise resources from other sources they are free to spend as they wish. Admission to all university courses, however, is determined almost entirely by the applicant's success in the Leaving Certificate examination, allocation of places in all faculties in all universities being made by a single computer selection and on a strict points system. Universities, however, set their own examinations and set their own standards, though these are subject to checks of interaction with the university system of the United Kingdom, with which Irish universities are historically linked, and of the United States, where many Irish academics pursue further study.

The Dublin Institute of Technology, the Regional Technical Colleges and the other specialized colleges offer certificate and diploma courses in various disciplines, and sometimes a degree course in collaboration with a university. The courses are often set to meet the certification requirements of the appropriate professional body.

The impact of Community membership on Irish education

The chief influences of Community membership on the Irish education system have been adaptation of the syllabus to prepare pupils to take their place in the wider Community, to increase foreign language skills, to adapt third-level technological training to take advantage of support from Community funds, and to participate in Community-wide schemes of co-operative research and exchange of students. In a more general sense, the system has adapted to meet the changing needs of the labour market; in particular, several courses in European studies have been established in third-level institutions, and a Community element included in many other courses.

Schools

An early instance of the impact of Community membership on the curriculum was the inclusion of reference to the Community in the geography syllabus for the senior years in primary schools. Changes at secondary level have been more gradual. The course for the Intermediate Certificate has a geography syllabus which includes the geography of Community member-states, but there is little other explicit coverage of Community affairs. Civics, a compulsory but non-examination subject in the junior cycle, is sometimes the vehicle for teaching about Community affairs, and while the history course for instance can deal with the origins of the Community, it can cover little of its development or about Ireland's accession. It was decided in the mid-1980s to replace the Intermediate and Group (i.e. technical) Certificate examinations by a new, reformed, single certificate examination, the Junior Certificate. The reform of the junior cycle curriculum, announced in September 1988, and introduced progressively from September 1989, made considerable changes in regard to the European dimension; a statement was made in the Junior Certificate guidelines for teachers that the aim of the curriculum was to prepare the young person for the responsibilities of citizenship in the national context and in the context of the wider European Community. Moreover, this aim was highlighted in the foreword, in respect particularly of business studies, history and geography, 'but all subject teaching should incorporate this European dimension' (Junior Certificate, 1989), an undertaking in line with the conclusions of the Ministers for Education meeting within the Council of September 1985 (Council Conclusions, 1985).

The senior cycle at post-primary level leads to the Leaving Certificate examination, which is normally taken in seven subjects, including English, Irish and maths. This syllabus has been in existence for some time, but may be considered for reform following the changes made in the junior cycle. Whether and to what degree a European Community aspect to the senior cycle would be introduced remains to be seen. What seems clear from recent surveys of schoolteachers and school-leavers is that both, and in particular teachers, would welcome a European dimension to the curriculum (Scott and Whelan, 1990).

A further element in the development of the education system at school level has been a perceived need to improve skills in continental languages. This has been a theme of the European Commission, whose communication of 18 April 1988 on the teaching of foreign languages set out its policy. Ireland has also been concerned and especially in regard to the teaching of German, the language of Ireland's major non-English-speaking customer. The comparative figures for pupils taking continental languages in the Leaving Certificate in 1988 were French: 32,000; German: 2,300; Spanish: 1,000; Italian: 68 (ICEM, 1989).

The most clearly expressed concerns have been those of the business community, conscious of the importance of the German market for Irish producers, and of the need to be able to sell into this market in the post-1992 situation. However, other concerns have been expressed, such as the wish to promote the study of less commonly-used languages as an expression of solidarity from a country whose first official language is Irish. The Minister for Education has declared an interest in increasing diversity of language acquisition in schools. However, financial cutbacks in education in the late 1980s have tended to penalize minority subjects, including German, Spanish and Italian, according to teachers' representatives.

Third-level

As we noted at the start, the chief impact of the Community in the area of education has been through the interpretation of training (an economic concern) to cover wider areas, eventually including education itself. This effect has been felt to some degree in the senior cycle of technological education in vocational and community schools, but has had its major effect in the colleges of technology, in Dublin and the regions.

Social fund scholarships have been available since the mid-1970s for students at colleges of technology, for particular programmes; the scheme was expanded with the reform of the fund in 1983. Approximately 19,400 students were using such grants in early 1990: 13,900 for the mid-level technical programme of one to two years' duration, and some 5,500 for the higher-level and business skills programme. The availability of funding has had two effects: to enable students who would otherwise not be able to do so, to follow courses and to bias studies in the direction intended, i.e. towards providing qualified technical staff to fill perceived shortages at Community level. This introduces another possible effect of membership, as yet unproven, that Irish students have been prepared to pursue studies in an area where they see little hope of employment in Ireland, on the grounds that they can find such employment elsewhere in the Community. The survey referred to above showed considerable appreciation of the possibilities of working in the EC, compared to Ireland and the United States.

Within the universities, two major effects may be observed. First, it may be supposed that Community funding, under a wide variety of research programmes, has some influence in defining the priorities for scientific research and therefore to some extent the teaching bias of scientists, particularly at post-graduate level. Some IR£ 24.54 million was allocated to Ireland in 1988 from a variety of Community research programmes, and while not all such funds go to the universities, they may have a considerable influence on the direction of research and teaching within third-level education.

A more measurable effect has been the inclusion of 'European Studies' both as a discipline in its own right, leading to a degree, and as a component course or module in mainstream disciplines such as law, politics, economics, geography and business studies. Four-year degree courses in European Studies are given in University College Cork and in Limerick University, with approximately 150 students graduating each year in Limerick and 20 in Cork. Courses are also given at masters level in each university, while a masters degree course is to be offered by the Centre for European and Public Affairs in University College Dublin, starting in September 1990. An MSc course in European Studies (economic and political aspects of integration) was started in 1977 in a joint venture by Trinity College Dublin and University College Dublin with support from the Commission, but ended in 1989 when, because of staff shortages, insufficient numbers of young civil servants, for whom it was mainly intended, were made available to attend by their departments.

European Studies has also become a course or module in courses offered by regional technical colleges, or other colleges, e.g. the course offered by Cork regional technical college, or the module offered by the school of journalism at Rathmines College of Commerce.

The impact of specific Community programmes

Two of the conclusions of the Council and of the Ministers of 27 September 1985 on enhancing the European dimension had been to promote the teaching of foreign languages as an important factor for strengthening the European Community, and the promotion of measures designed to encourage contacts between pupils from different countries (Council Conclusions, 1985). The Council took these conclusions further, first by adopting in June 1987 the ERASMUS programme — the European Community action scheme for the mobility of students (Council Decision, 1987), and later by adopting the Lingua programme on language teaching (Lingua, 1989).

The effect of the ERASMUS programme in Ireland has been considerable, though applications have far exceeded funds available and the funds have been thinly spread. In 1988/9, Irish universities and colleges of technology co-ordinated fifteen inter-university co-operations, and were involved in some fifty-one programmes altogether. Irish students travelling totalled 193, spending a total of over 1,400 months abroad, most often in France (67 students) or in Germany (62). Most students were in the 19—21 age group; 98 of the total spent 7—9 months abroad, and 22 spent more than 9 months away. Their studies ranged over forty-six courses, from sculpture to languages, economics to microbiology. The total amount of funding for student grants was ECU 122,200 or ECU 736 per head for the 166 students funded, a figure much lower than for many students from other countries. The funds available were greatly increased in 1989/90, to ECU 267,500 and a further large increase is expected in 1990/1. Whether this will be reflected in a higher level of grant, or in a larger number of bursaries, remains to be seen. The report for the year 1989/90 is expected to show a doubling of mobility as against 1988/9, and the inter-university co-operation programmes will have increased from 51 to 120.

The effects of the Lingua programme are as yet impossible to gauge, but the impact on the schools is likely to be less than initially expected. Other relevant programmes have been ARIAN, through which principals of Irish schools have made study visits to schools abroad, and Ireland has in return received visiting school principals from other member-states; PETRA, a joint training and education programme; the 1978—82 and 1983—7 programmes on the transition from education to working life, which were the Department of Education's first major commitment to an EC programme; and various activities related to youth, and to the fight against illiteracy.

Assessment

Membership of the Community has had undoubted effects on education in Ireland. In order to establish precisely what those effects are, the unanswerable question should be asked: how would Irish education have evolved had Ireland not joined the Community? Ireland is a small open economy, the overwhelming proportion of whose trade is with the United Kingdom and the rest of the EC. Had the United Kingdom joined the Community and Ireland stayed outside Ireland would have either had to continue to trade in the same direction but over a tariff barrier, without CAP or structural fund support and with no voice in the Community institutions; or, to have found new markets or lapsed into self-sufficiency. The consequences of such decisions for Irish education are not evident, for Ireland could have either attempted to compensate for exclusion from the EC by enhanced education and training in Community affairs, or attempted to accompany changes in trading and other links by redirecting education with the aim of preparing Irish children for a different place in the world order. In any case, they would have been considerable.

An unambiguous Community education policy has been slow to

evolve. In fact little happened until the mid-1980s, by which time Ireland had accommodated itself to membership and to EPC, and had begun to take account of the renewed interest in integration that culminated in the Single Act. By this time also, Ireland had become accustomed to using the proceeds of the ESF to assist activities in vocational schools and to support courses in regional technical colleges. When in 1985 the ministers decided to develop the European dimension of the curriculum, the Irish authorities were willing and able to react without political risk, particularly as the momentum of political and economic integration picked up.

Irish education has therefore lost some of its autonomy by using Community funds for purposes designated at Community level. It has begun to incorporate a frame of reference wider than the purely national in the aims of its educational system. It is still wrestling with the problems of improving the competence of school-leavers in modern continental languages, without compromising the teaching of Irish, and within the constraints on general public expenditure. It is clear from the results of the survey mentioned above that the situation in 1988 was not satisfactory to Irish teachers, or indeed to school-leavers, since both expressed great interest in the incorporation of a 'European dimension' in second-level education; this demand may well be satisfied at junior-cycle level by the introduction of the new curriculum, and possibly in future by a revised Leaving Certificate course. Meanwhile, adaptation at third-level has been proceeding in line with demand, and with the availability of resources. Overall, the system's relatively small size and high degree of central direction have made adaptation, once decided, easy to accommodate. The question which researchers are now beginning to raise is whether the Community is doing enough to support Irish education, and in particular whether Community funds spent on training could not more effectively be spent on education itself, both from an economic and from a social point of view (Hannan, 1991).

Bibliography

Communication of the Commission of the European Communities on Teaching of Foreign Languages (COM(88)203), 18 April 1988.

Council Conclusions (1985), *Conclusions of the Council and of the Ministers of Education Meeting within the Council of 27 September 1985 on the Enhanced Treatment of the European Dimension in Education.*

Council Decision of 15 June 1987 adopting the European Community action scheme for the mobility of university students (Erasmus) (87/327/EEC).

Council Resolution (1971), *Resolution of the Ministers of Education Meeting within the Council of 16 November 1971, on Co-operation in the Field of Education.*

Court (1989), 'Decision of the Court of Justice', *Official Journal of the European Communities*, C324. 28.12.89.

ECSC Treaty (1951), Treaty establishing the European Coal and Steel Community.

EEC Treaty (1957), Treaty establishing the European Economic Community.

Hannan, D. (1991), *School-leavers' Assessments of Educational Objectives and Outcomes*, Dublin: Economic and Social Research Institute.

ICEM (1988), 'Language for 1992', Dublin: Irish Council of the European Movement.

Junior Certificate (1989), *The Junior Certificate, Guidelines for Teachers*, An Roinn Oideachais, National Council for Curriculum and Assessment, 1989.

Laffan, B. (1985), *The European Social Fund and its Operation in Ireland*, Dublin: Irish Council of the European Movement.

Lingua (1989), Council Decision of 28 July 1989 establishing an action programme to promote foreign language competence in the European Communities (LINGUA) (89/489), *OJ* L239 of 16.8.1989.

Scott, D. and Whelan, B. (1990), *Europe in the Classroom – Surveys of Teachers and School-leavers*, Dublin: Economic and Social Research Institute.

Chapter 30

Culture and media policy

Fintan O'Toole

In at least one sense, the notion of a European Community cultural policy might seem like a contradiction in terms. Culture, if it is about anything, is about participation, democracy, diversification, the cherishing of differences and contradictions. The EC, in its hitherto almost exclusively economic phase, has been about the opposite: centralization, homogenization, more abstract levels of participation, the eradication of difference and contradiction. The cultural dimensions of the Community's life have themselves been notoriously bland: the European Ideal, our common heritage, a vague appeal to Europe itself as a moral and aesthetic category. Even the attempts to celebrate the founding event of modern Europe, the bicentenary of the French Revolution in 1789, served to reveal the shakiness of the sense of a common European heritage. Instead of reaffirming a shared sense of origin, it served only to open up the deep uncertainties as to where modern Europe might take its bearings from. And, at the same time, the expansion of European horizons to the East has served to make the notion of a European culture still more complex, to return it to the realm of high aspirations and low priorities. In this context it is hardly surprising that the impact of EC membership on Irish cultural activity has been negligible.

Culture is not merely about works of art, and it follows that the cultural dimension of the EC is about much more than aesthetics. The Eurocult Conference in 1972 attempted a placing of the cultural question in the broadest context as follows: 'in the course of European history the pursuit of a better quality of life first resulted in political democracy, then led to social democracy and now expresses itself in the demand for cultural democracy' (Finnish National Commission for UNESCO, 1981: 279). With the rolling back of social democracy in much of Europe in the 1980s, the optimism of that formulation now seems rather innocent, but the making of the connection between culture, democracy and social progress remains crucial. Culture is the ground on which people are empowered to participate in their society. Culture is both the social contribution to the formation of the individual person, and the collective tools — values, language, means of communication, ideas of excellence, the imaginative sympathy by which one individual can make sense of the experience of another individual — by which an individual can contribute to the formation of the society. The question of culture and the EC is therefore intimately bound up with the question of democracy and the EC. The failure to develop an EC cultural policy that is more than just proposing a European 'Dallas' to take the place of an American 'Dallas' is the failure to develop an EC regional policy that can deliver real rights of participation to countries and communities across the Community. With inadequate structures for political democracy, with its social democracy under seige, the EC has not been well placed to go on and develop a cultural democracy. In the case of Ireland, one of the least developed of the EC's regions and likely to remain so after 1992, this failure is at its starkest.

There are three important ways in which Ireland has, arguably, become less European in cultural terms since Ireland's entry into the EEC in 1973. To take the main international component of Irish culture, Roman Catholicism, first, it is probably less consciously European than it has been since the middle of the nineteenth century. Irish Catholicism was Ultramontane, and the sense of a connection to France, Spain and Italy which it gave to Irish culture was probably the strongest Eurocentric element in that culture.

Yet, in spite of the immensely strengthened links to Europe which EC membership has entailed, Irish Catholicism is now, for two very different reasons, much less inclined to think of itself as European. On the one hand, from the right, there is a sense that Irish Catholicism is European only through being the last bastion, an embattled outpost of true Catholicism. For conservative Catholics, most of the rest of the EC is seen as post-Christian. In the constitutional debate on abortion, for instance, the EC was identified by conservatives as the threat to Irish abortion laws, as the moral predator against which the doors needed to be barred. And the success of this appeal demonstrated the contradiction that while conservative Ireland sees EC intervention as a good thing when the subject is beef, it does not see EC intervention as a good thing when the subject is the rights of women or homosexuals or secularists. EC influence works at the economic level, but not at the cultural one.

And, on the other hand, from the left wing of the Catholic Church, Catholicism is now identified much more with the Third World, with Latin America or South Africa, than it is with a European ideal. It is a long time since Irish priests abroad were in Salamanca or Louvain: now they are in El Salvador and Soweto. Radical Catholics are more likely to see the EC as a part of the exploiting northern hemisphere than they are to see it as the Christian heartland to which they owe allegiance. Significantly, both elements of Irish Catholic activism, that of the right and of the left, came together to oppose the endorsement of the Single European Act in an admittedly uneasy alliance (Chapter 19). Either way,

Catholicism as a cultural force in Ireland has had its Europeanism weakened since 1973.

The second sense in which the idea of a connection to a common European culture in Ireland has been undermined is related to this. It is the rapid collapse of Irish classicism since Vatican 2. Because it was the language of the Church, but also because it was a non-English form of European learning, Latin once had an enormous place in Irish education, to the extent of being at one stage almost a vernacular language. The decision of Vatican 2 to have Mass said in the local language marked the beginning of the end of the classical European element of Irish educated culture. When Ireland joined the EC Latin and Greek were still standard subjects at Irish second level schools and Latin was still a requirement for entry to universities. In the 1970s and 1980s, both virtually disappeared from the curriculum. Any appeal to the ancient history of classical European culture is now much less likely to strike a chord in Ireland, even among the academically educated, than it would have been in 1973.

And if classicism as a factor for Eurocentrism was in decline, so too — and this is the third weakening of the cultural connection — is modernism. There was always an irony that Ireland was more important to European modernism than European modernism was to Ireland. Yeats, Joyce and Beckett made huge contributions to the development of modernist culture, but the influence of the latter two in Ireland was always in inverse proportion to their modernism, and Yeats was more important as a romantic in the Irish context. But, at least, Europe was the locus for the exile in 'silence, cunning and exile'. It retained an underground existence as a place of light, of imagined freedom from the restrictions of Irish reaction. Two things happened in the 1970s and 1980s. One was that European modernism fell apart before Ireland had ever had a genuinely modernist culture. Irish architecture, for instance, became post-modern before it had become successfully modern. The other was that as Ireland itself became more liberal as a society, the need for Europe as a place of flight for the artist, or even as a mental and spiritual retreat, became much less. Beckett's death in Paris symbolized the end of that era of cunning exile.

The romance of Europe for Irish artists was much diminished. The Irish exile on the Continent was now more likely to be working in a canning factory in Germany than writing a novel in a garret in Paris, and it showed. The Europe of Dermot Bolger's novel *Nightshift* and *The Journey Home*, of his play *The Lament for Arthur Cleary*, of Michael O'Loughlin's poems and stories, is not the Europe of Joyce and Beckett but that of John Berger and Jean Mohr's *A Seventh Man*, the Europe of the *gastarbeiter*, the migrant worker, a shifting alienated Europe of hostels and railway stations and factories. It was the dark side of the European ideal that was reflected in Irish culture, not the grand aspirations. While others were talking of the common European home, Irish writers were writing about the common European homeless, about the Irish as the

Turks and Yugoslavs of the West, all a part of the underground exiled Europe that underlay the nice aspirational one.

Flitting around any attempt to see Ireland as part of a European culture is a profound irony. It is that the European notion of Irish culture, the view of what Ireland is like held in those European countries where such a question matters at all, tends to be one which is at odds with the whole idea of the EC and what it means to Ireland. For the Irish, the EC is about modernization, industrialization, making us more like the rest of Europe. For European metropolitans, however, Ireland is interesting because it is relatively unmodernized, unindustrialized, less like the rest of Europe. The Ireland of Heinrich Boll's *Irish Diary*, an immensely popular book in Germany, now filtered through the Irish pubs of Berlin and Stuttgart, is of value to Europeans to the extent to which it is unEuropean, unaffected by European consumerism and boom values. Yet the effect of the EC for Irish culture in the broadest terms has been to hasten the disappearance of whatever elements of that romanticized culture remained. 'Romantic Ireland's dead and gone, it's with old Mansholt in the grave.' Yet Europe tends to postulate a static Irish culture at the same time as Europe is creating conditions in which the culture must change. It is hardly any wonder that the notion of a genuine engagement between culture and the EC is one which has to evade a lot of contradictions before it can begin to make sense.

There is another irony too. It is that the economic effects of EC membership for Ireland — in particular the increased affluence which followed entry in 1973 — have worked against the integration of Ireland into some kind of EC-wide culture. Where Irish culture has not been Anglocentric on the one hand, or culturally nationalist on the other (in, for example, the aspiration to develop linguistic tariff barriers by reviving the Irish language as the vernacular), it has been dominated by America. American cultural influence has been strong since the nineteenth century, but it has been immeasurably increased by economic affluence. The forms in which affluence expresses itself are American, both because of the specific role of American capital in the development of Ireland's industrial economy and because of the more general appeal of American popular culture through popular music, cinema fashion and television. Irish farmers buoyed up by EEC money in the early 1970s, for instance, built American-style bungalows to live in and danced the night away to country-and-western bands. The money being spent may come from EC intervention, but what it is spent on comes from the opposite direction. Culturally, Ireland remains between Europe and America, and EC membership has failed to shift the balance.

European cinema may be marginally more popular in Ireland now than it was in 1973 — and Wim Wenders is probably right when he claims cinema as 'the European art and language par excellence' (Kearney, 1988: 254) — but the margin is small. And if Wenders is right and 'there has been no better expression of European identity in this century than

European cinema', then what are we to make of the fact that cinema is still one of the weakest art forms in Ireland? Even successful Irish cinema is sometimes spectacularly unsuccessful in other EC countries. *My Left Foot*, for instance, won two Oscars in the United States in 1989, but was rejected for the Cannes Film Festival as being not up to scratch. And the same is true in other forms of popular entertainment: European pop music and television have little impact in Ireland. Ireland has the lowest ratio of home-produced programmes to imported programmes in the European Broadcasting Union, but little of what is imported comes from outside the United States and Britain. And this is unlikely to change with the new broadcasting technologies: effective control of the Irish Direct Broadcasting satellite will rest not with any EC-based partnership but with the Hughes Corporation, an American communications conglomerate. Even in the print media, the American influence is stronger than the European. The first of the three major national newspapers to be largely owned by a foreign company, The Irish Press, is controlled by the American media magnate Ralph Ingersoll and is likely to develop in accordance with American rather than European practice.

It could be argued that much of the problem with the development of Irish cultural policy within the EC lies with successive Irish governments. It is widely recognized that Irish education policy has been slow to emphasize the acquisition of competence in European languages by Irish students, an essential prerequisite to the development of genuine cultural exchange (see Chapter 28). It is also true that there has been little in the way of coherent cultural policy in Ireland, never mind coherent policy on links with other cultures. The only White Paper on cultural policy ever published by an Irish government (*Access and Opportunity*, 1987) has little to say on the subject beyond the usual nod in the direction of 'an awareness of a common cultural heritage as an element of the European identity' as the 1983 Solemn Declaration on European Union puts it. And the 1980s were particularly bad for any sustained Irish involvement in international cultural debate. The Irish National Commission for UNESCO was allowed to lapse. Ireland withdrew from projects which might have stimulated debate on cultural policy in a European context, like the Council of Europe's project on 'regional experiments in cultural development'.

But there has also been a problem with the EC's cultural policy as a whole. In spite of all the talk about a 'common cultural heritage' and the European identity, the EC as a whole has done little to shape the emerging, and innately international technological forces that are beginning to shape that culture and that identity. The irony of new broadcasting technologies throughout Western Europe has been that while those technologies, particularly the combination of satellite and cable networks, offer possibilities of both a Europe-wide broadcasting culture on the one hand and a huge degree of regional diversity on the other, the way in which those technologies have in fact developed has been in the direction of weakening rather than strengthening a common heritage.

The whole idea of a common heritage presupposes a shared, public realm. It supposes, in other words, the existence of EC citizens rather than of EC consumers. But, throughout the EC, the new technologies have been in private hands, and the programming they have produced has gone against the grain of a public service tradition. It has been creating a culture that is homogenous rather than common, standardized rather than shared, appealing to lowest common denominators rather than to the universal elements in diversity. And in this Ireland has followed the EC road, undermining public service broadcasting as it is being undermined in other EC countries. 'While' as Desmond Bell put it, 'the bureaucrats in Brussels enthuse about the possibility of "television without frontiers" within the European Community — the emergence of a common market for media products and services — the reality is that US penetration of the European audio-visual space increases' (Bell, 1988: 224). The 1989 directive on television without frontiers was a very contentious issue in the Council because of disagreement about the balance between public and private sector broadcasting, permitted advertising time, restrictions on programme content and the extent to which programmes ought to be produced within Community member-states. Because of the compromises in this Directive the EC has failed to harness in any positive way the new broadcasting technologies, and this crucially undermines the prospects for developing an effective EC cultural policy. Ireland has merely followed the EC trends. And Ireland has not even involved itself in whatever, admittedly minor, counter-trends there have been, such as the grouping together under the French Channel Seven of British, German, Italian and Swiss programme-makers.

It is true that the levels of cultural exchange in the simple sense of visits by theatre companies, exhibitions, orchestras and so on, between Ireland and EC countries has increased since 1973. But it is equally true that most of this has happened under bilateral rather than EC auspices and that the same statement could be made about non-EC countries. Polish theatre has been more influential in Ireland in recent years than, say, French or German theatre. There are more Irish paintings of the 1980s inspired by India or Australia or the Bahamas or even Borneo than by Bonn or Paris or Brussels. The European city which has had most bearing on contemporary Irish painters is Berlin, because it is, or was, the most peripheral of West European cities, the one closest to the edge. In Irish culture generally, the search for a European identity has been conducted much more in relation to the East than to the West. In Seamus Heaney's view of things, the modern poets of Eastern Europe are the closest to his heart. In Michael O'Loughlin's 'Stalingrad' or Paul Durcan's 'Going Home to Russia' it is Russia which provides the nearest objective correlative for Irish experience. In the versions of Chekhov for Irish theatre produced by Brian Friel, Thomas Kilroy and Frank McGuinness, the Russian sensibility is incorporated into the Irish one. It is as if membership of the EC has increased rather than diminished the Irish sense of periphery, by-passing the settled societies of Western Europe with which Ireland has, in some ways, little in common. At a psychic level, at least, the Europe to which Irish culture tends to see itself as belonging is the Europe of unfinished business, of unhappy revolutions and civil wars, not a self-confident Europe of the post-war boom economies. It follows that for the EC to have a decisive impact on Irish culture the EC itself has to be broadened and redefined.

A hundred years ago, Oscar Wilde was writing a play, *Salome* in French. Yeats and Synge were meeting, not on the Aran Islands, but in Paris, as indeed were Synge and Joyce. Ninety years ago, Tom Kettle was preaching a United States of Europe; Patrick Pearse was applying his experience of bilingualism in Belgium to a blueprint for Irish education; Oliver St John Gogarty was proposing to Hellenize Ireland; George Moore was proselytizing on behalf of French literature; Synge was counterattacking his detractors as people 'who dare not be Europeans for fear the huckster across the street might call them English (Kiberd, 1984: 15—16). Today, most of this would be seen in Ireland as some kind of effete posturing. In that context, it would be foolish to claim that membership of the EC has made Irish culture more European. But it would be equally foolish to see this problem as being concerned solely or even primarily with the arts, with cultural policy, with culture viewed as a matter of artefacts rather than ways of living. The cultural question underlies both Ireland's sense of itself and the EC's sense of what it ought to be. Until there is a serious regional policy, there can be no serious cultural policy. Until there is economic convergence, there can be no cultural convergence. Cultural contact that is not between equals is at best an exercise in exoticism, at worst an exercise in exploitation. Until all voices are heard with equal attention, it is impossible to tell whether or not they are saying the same thing.

Bibliography

Access and Opportunity: A White Paper on Cultural Policy (1987), Dublin: The Stationery Office.

Bell, Desmond (1988), 'Ireland without frontiers? The challenge of the communications revolution', *Across the Frontiers: Ireland in the 1990s*, ed. Richard Kearney, Dublin: Wolfhouse Press, pp. 219—30.

Finnish National Commission for UNESCO (1981), *The Development of Cultural Policies in Europe*, Helsinki.

Kearney, Richard (1988), *Across the Frontiers*, op.cit.

Kiberd, Declan (1984), 'Inventing Ireland', *Ireland: Dependence and Independence*, The Crane Bag, 8, 1, Dublin, pp. 11—23.

Mulholland, J. (1989), 'TV without frontiers — Europe's other star wars', in D. Keogh (ed), *Ireland and the Challenge of European Integration*, Cork: Hibernia University Press.

PART V: CONCLUSIONS

Chapter 31

Weighing up gains and losses

Patrick Keatinge, Brigid Laffan, Rory O'Donnell

In 1972 the Irish electorate was asked in a simple 'yes'/'no' vote to approve the country's accession to the European Community. That choice was necessarily based on conjecture, however well-informed, and may be seen as as much as an act of faith as of calculation. Although the present scrutiny of membership has the advantage of resting on the considerable experience of the last eighteen years, the path to an overall assessment of its effects is still not uniformly well signposted. Indeed, the procedure adopted in this series, whereby the effects of membership are examined separately under four broad headings, bears witness to the complexities inherent in this task. Thus before commencing on the overall 'balance sheet' for Ireland this chapter summarizes the findings concerning each of these general policy sectors.

Economic policy

Of the eleven areas of economic policy surveyed, from all the available research it is clear that four areas of Community economic policy have been of overwhelming significance for Ireland. Most of the economic effects of EC membership have derived from internal market policy, agricultural policy, monetary policy and regional policy, and in this section we briefly restate the gains and losses which have been identified in earlier chapters.

The major benefits of Community membership arose from the internal market and the Common Agricultural Policy. Industrialization was a major economic policy goal since the foundation of the state. For more than three decades this goal was pursued by industrial protectionism, but in the late 1950s it was decided to change course and seek industrial development by means of export led growth and an open economy. In this context EC membership was the logical outcome of the economic policies pursued by successive Irish governments since the 1950s. By providing a superior environment in which Ireland could pursue a path of development which it had chosen anyway, membership represented an important general gain. This general gain has taken a number of concrete forms. Among these are: the enhanced ability to attract foreign firms which have achieved remarkable export levels to the EC market; the availability to Irish consumers and firms of a much wider range of products; and, for those Irish manufacturing and service sector firms capable of using it, access to a large and more varied market than had previously been available.

In the case of agriculture a similar general benefit can be identified. A fundamental problem of Irish economic policy was the need to find an outlet for the country's agricultural produce. The United Kingdom never provided a wholly satisfactory market outlet; the Common Agricultural Policy offered participation in a much larger market and, more significantly, promised a higher level of guaranteed prices. Again this general benefit has materialized in a number of specific gains to segments of Irish agriculture. The CAP facilitated a considerable increase in the output and incomes of about one-third of Irish farmers.

While the internal market provided an important general gain for Ireland a detailed analysis of Ireland's experience since 1973 exposed specific losses also. Indeed, this applies to the chief effect of EC membership — the pattern of specialization which emerged in the Irish economy. Since accession to the EC there has been a very substantial rearrangement of the pattern of manufacturing in Ireland: a secular decline of a long list of exposed industries and their replacement by foreign firms in a narrow range of manufacturing activities. Not only was this inter-industry adjustment larger than that experienced in other member-states but it also brought about a significant change in the structure of indigenous manufacturing industry. In particular, it eliminated many relatively large indigenous firms in internationally traded activities. This change in structure undermined the leading firms in industries where innovative activity or scale are significant, and thus reduced the ability of indigenous manufacturing to generate industrial growth.

In the case of agriculture also certain losses can be identified. While the CAP has supported increased farm increases for some, it has not overcome, and may even have exacerbated, two fundamental problems in Irish agriculture: the persistence of low farm incomes for a sizeable segment, and the slow development of the food industry.

Community monetary policy has to date consisted very largely of the European Monetary System (EMS). Assessing the gains and losses of Ireland's full participation in the EMS poses especially difficult problems. It must be presumed that the alternative for Ireland was continuation on a long standing one-to-one link with sterling. Perceptions of the effects of EMS membership are highly dependent on which economic theory one chooses to adopt and empirical research is unable to decide between them. Only one thing can be stated with certainty: EMS membership has been much more difficult for Ireland than most economists and policy-makers expected in 1979. Other conclusions must be stated more tentatively. It seems likely that EMS membership aided the achievement and maintenance of low inflation. The absence of the United Kingdom from the exchange rate mechanism of the EMS greatly qualified Ireland's management of policy and its gains from membership of the system. Finally, the real appreciation of the Irish currency through the 1980s which was partly the result of EMS membership, probably had some role in the poor performance of the real economy in that decade. This is so in the sense that substantial reduction in price inflation generally takes considerable time and impacts severely on the real economy as well as on prices and costs. A similar disinflation would have occurred, probably earlier, had Ireland rejected EMS membership in favour of a continued link with sterling.

Finally, in two simple senses Ireland has undoubtedly gained from the existence of Community regional policy. First, Ireland has received direct transfers from the European Regional Development Fund (ERDF). Second, Community regional policy has, to date, meshed well with national development and industrial policy. But, Community regional policy has not succeeded in significantly reducing regional disparities in income or unemployment levels across the EC. This is so because the process of economic integration reflects and reinforces existing regional advantages and disadvantages, and, compared to this and other forces making for regional divergence, Community regional policy has been insignificant in scale.

Foreign relations

Membership of the world's largest trading bloc is in itself an important if unquantifiable benefit for a small open economy. Whatever loss of autonomy it may entail with regard to the development of specific trading relationships, the collective influence of the Community in multilateral negotiations is a resource which would otherwise not exist. A more tangible benefit can be found in the fact that the previous overwhelming dependence on the United Kingdom has been much reduced, though it is still large.

Membership has also been a positive factor in the evolution of Ireland's development policy. It has provided an appropriate international standard for the domestic advocates of a bilateral aid programme, both during the establishment of the programme and as a defence against the programme's critics during periods of financial stringency.

In the broader field of foreign policy, participation in European Political Co-operation has given Irish governments access to a sophisticated diplomatic network. This has allowed opportunities for enhanced prestige and the possibility of mobilizing collective influence in certain circumstances, without being required to modify national positions on major issues in a serious way. The state's most persistent foreign policy issue — its relations with the United Kingdom over the Northern Ireland question — has also been assisted, though not resolved, by the two countries' EC membership.

These political gains, however, must be set against the limited constraints imposed by the obligations of membership in foreign policy co-operation. Although national autonomy is preserved by consensus policy-making in EPC, perceptions of loss can arise. The Community's tentative foray into the field of security policy, with a hint of a future military defence policy, has for some sections of Irish opinion cast a shadow over the state's identity as a neutral (meaning 'independent') diplomatic actor.

Political and legal systems

The closer we approach the political realm the less appropriate it may be to assess the effects of membership in terms of clear cut gains and losses. A new and complicating layer of government and politics has been added to national policy-making, involving intensive and extensive relations with Ireland's EC partners and the Community's own institutions.

Its consequences are more easily observed within the executive and administration than in the wider political system. Ministers and officials formally responsible for domestic agencies are drawn into a web of collaboration with their counterparts in other member-states, thereby gaining experience in multilateral negotiations, and Irish policy-makers no longer look exclusively to Whitehall for policy models. The Department of Foreign Affairs is no longer the only source of policy co-ordination, with the Taoiseach's Department being more directly involved in both routine and strategic issues. Despite a strengthening of co-ordination on EC business since 1987, insufficient attention is paid to co-ordination at middle-management level. The demands of EC membership on government and administration have been considerable, with the result that the system of public policy-making is overloaded.

Governmental adaptation to the Community system has not been followed to the same extent in party politics. Although all parties have found a niche in European political groupings, the biggest party, Fianna Fáil, found itself outside the main political families in the European Parliament when it had to resort to an alliance with the French Gaullists. Because this alliance has not developed close party-to-party relations, Fianna Fáil has experienced less external influence than has Fine Gael. In general, parties have paid scant attention to the European Parliament or to its members' role as a link between the Community and national levels. National parliamentary supervision of European policy remains rudimentary and often ineffective.

Social, educational and culture policy

Irish policy-makers have generally favoured the development of the Community's role in this wide-ranging policy domain. The consequences of EC membership vary from issue to issue. In some areas, notably women's rights, consumer law and health and safety in the workplace, Community policies have moulded national policies, whereas in others EC membership simply added a new dimension to national policies. Ireland is an advocate of EC expenditure in this domain, having championed the initial 'Combat poverty' programme in 1975. Moreover, vocational training is a major recipient of Community funding, which allowed for considerable expansion of manpower and training networks, and a noticeable influence on youth employment policies. This did not, however, provide more jobs, and the expansion of training facilities may have been partly at the expense of the educational system.

Women's issues, which arrived on the political agenda at the same time as EC membership was achieved, were also significantly affected by EC directives and the Community's equality programme. Women's groups are firm advocates of the Community's role in this domain, and have forged strong links with the Commission's bureau for women's affairs and with groups in the other member-states. The Commission is regarded as an ally in furthering gender equality in Ireland.

Improved standards of health and safety in the workplace are another specific gain of membership, though more generally the effect on industrial relations has so far been marginal. The question of worker participation, a contentious issue between the social partners in Ireland, is set to re-enter the agenda with discussions of EC directives on the European company and the right of employees in transnational corporations to obtain access to information. Ireland's acceptance in principle of the Social Charter is qualified by the provision that it should not involve increased costs to industry. Ireland's desire to remain attractive as an investment location is part of the hidden agenda in this policy domain.

The effects of membership on educational and cultural policy are more difficult to identify, though the recent organization of educational exchange programmes and mutual recognition of qualifications is likely to be significant in the coming decade. The completion of the internal market will provide renewed focus on the free movement of workers and the professions, and may well alter the pattern of Irish emigration. At present young Irish emigrants are more likely to end up as illegal immigrants in New York or Boston than as legal immigrants in another EC country. This can be explained by the traditional pattern of emigration towards English-speaking countries and the weakness of language teaching in Ireland. There is, however, a steadily growing number of Irish graduates going to continental Europe to work in the research centres of Philips and Siemens.

Towards a balance sheet

An overall assessment of Ireland's membership of the European Community on the basis of these findings must remain impressionistic at best. In each policy category the 'macro unit' — Ireland — has different connotations. It is one thing to contemplate a cost—benefit analysis of effects on the national economy in general terms, but more detailed investigation reveals very different patterns of gain or loss in specific sectors. Introducing the more loosely structured field, or fields, of social, educational and cultural policies does not merely reinforce the emphasis on qualitative rather than quantitative assessments; it serves to underline the impossibility of aggregating national welfare. 'Society' fragments into varying patterns of winners and losers, with different, and sometimes conflicting, values.

With regard to the fields of foreign relations and the political and legal systems, the point of reference is neither economy nor society but the state itself. The effects of integration on the state may be evaluated according to the criterion of efficiency: is it an effective mechanism in adapting to external pressures?; but it is also often judged simply in terms of the survival of the state as an autonomous or sovereign centre of political authority. Thus, even where it is possible to identify gains in the light of welfare criteria, negative consequences cannot be ruled out in the context of reduced autonomy for the body politic.

A further ambiguity is inherent in any analysis of the effects of EC membership on an individual member-state. What appear at first sight as 'costs' may reflect long-term structural characteristics of the country's economy and society and the political culture deriving from them. In the short to medium term, national policy may influence the outcome in a way which negates or masks the effects of involvement in the Community.

In the light of these methodological difficulties the contributors to this series of national studies have agreed to attempt to find an overall assessment of the effects of membership by putting the hypothetical question — what are the likely consequences of the country concerned *leaving* the European Community?

This question is perhaps most readily addressed in the context of the immediate change that would occur in the context of *foreign relations*. On leaving the EC Ireland would be one of the recently increased number of small European states trying to find their bearings in a rapidly changing European states system. At first sight it might seem that policy could be framed with greater formal freedom; the constraints of EPC, questions about neutrality, and the constitutional ambiguities of the *Crotty* judgment would no longer be present. But two negative consequences would quickly become apparent. The state's diplomatic capacity would be much reduced; the costs of information gathering, external representation and, above all, access to major governments might rise significantly. More importantly, a major difficulty would be shared with the other small states at present outside the EC — how to adjust to the increasing economic and political weight of the Community without being able to exert influence from within. It is a moot point whether Ireland could be able to meet this problem more readily in the company of the EFTA states, themselves edging closer to EC membership, or among the newly liberated but economically handicapped states of Central and Eastern Europe. Isolation is more then ever a cul-de-sac; even Albania seems to be eschewing 'the Albanian option'.

So far as *economic policy* is concerned, consideration of the consequences of leaving the EC forces one to study carefully the nature of the economic gains and losses from Community membership. We have stated these gains and losses baldly above. But we must now add that the major costs or losses, from the internal market, the CAP and monetary policy, cannot be ascribed to Community membership in a direct way. The problems experienced in manufacturing, agriculture and the food industry were the product of Ireland's integration into the EC in combination with the policies pursued by successive Irish governments and the long-run structural characteristics of the Irish economy. Recognition of this interaction between economic integration, domestic policy and initial structural characteristics is central to a balanced assessment of Community membership and of the likely gains and losses from leaving the Community. There can be little doubt that the losses from secession would far outweigh the gains.

Three considerations underlie this statement. First, although there have been major failures in Irish economic policy-making, it cannot be said that Ireland adopted the policies it did or, more accurately, failed to develop policies, *because of its membership of the EC*. Consequently, it cannot easily be argued that Irish policy-making would be better if Ireland left the Community.

Second, EC membership has brought to light fundamental weaknesses in the Irish economy, especially in the manufacturing sector. But it cannot be said that membership of the Community was the cause of these structural problems. Not only do these problems derive from Ireland's economic history but they continued to give rise to severe social crisis even under the regime of protection, which prevailed till the mid-1960s. The failure of Irish development policy under a regime of protection strongly suggests that leaving the Community, and presumably retreating from the internal market, would do little to overcome the major barriers to industrialization. Indeed, the very similarity between the failure of Irish policy under protection (1932 to 1965) and under free trade (1965 to the present) suggests that the key question is not free trade (EC membership) versus protectionism (leaving the EC). The key question is the structural weaknesses which inhibit economic development. It is these structural weaknesses which must now be addressed by both national and Community policy.

The third consideration which strongly disfavours secession from the EC is a realistic assessment of the policies which would be available to Ireland is she were outside the EC, and an appreciation of the external economic forces which would still operate. Many of the forces which strongly influence the Irish economy are inseparable from the internationalization of economic activity which exists independently of the fact that countries embark on formal integration. Consequently, many of those forces would still affect Ireland if she were outside the Community and, as a very small state, Ireland would have a quite limited capacity to resist or alter them.

Indeed we can go further and say that Ireland has *greater* capacity within the Community and this will be of increasing significance. This is because the projects and policies adopted by the European Community are, in part, *responses* to changes in the world economy and world politics. The 1992 project is a perfect example. The internal market programme should be seen in the context of other changes in the economic environment such as technological change, organizational change, and the emergence of important new producers, in particular from Japan and newly industrialized countries. One of the most significant features of the current wave of technological change and the associated organizational restructuring is that is seems to be *inherently international* or, perhaps more accurately, supranational. National markets, particularly small national markets, would be a hindrance to the full development of the new technologies.

Recognition of these facts allows us to see 1992 and Ireland's Community membership in a new light. The move to complete the internal market can be seen partly as a response to a set of changes which are occurring in any event and which will inevitably increase the international aspect of economic life. In this context the decision to complete the internal market would seem to do two things. It helps to ensure that these new developments in business occur fully in Europe, rather than influencing Europe but partly passing it by. Secondly, it allows the Community to influence the process of economic and social change. Some features of the technology and new organizational patterns are indeed inherent and therefore inevitable — an example would be its internationalism — but many others are not. For example, while the new trends in technology and business undoubtedly demand changes in social relationships within the firm, and between groups and individuals in society, the exact new pattern of social and distributional arrangements is not determined rigidly by the new economic environment. While no single national government in Europe, and least of all the Irish, can greatly influence the economic environment, or fashion the social developments which a rapidly changing economy produces, there seems little doubt that the European Community can.

The consequences of leaving the Community for the *political and legal system* would be dramatic to say the least. The Irish judicial system and the corpus of economic law are enmeshed in the Community's legal order. Departure from the Community would require a constitutional referendum to repeal those sections of the Constitution that were altered to make provision for membership. A referendum would be followed by the repeal of an extensive body of primary and secondary law that has been enacted to take account of EC directives.

The political system could no doubt adapt to a post-EC world, but it would be the poorer for it. Irish politicians and civil servants have gained from participation in the multilateral fora that characterize the Community. For a small state overshadowed by a near and more powerful neighbour, a seat at the table is of immense psychological and material value. The steady diffusion of policy ideas across borders enriches public policy-making. Given that the Community has emerged as the core regional organization in Europe, membership of the club enhances the national political system.

The consequences for the *social, educational and cultural domain* would be less dramatic. Irish agencies would no longer benefit from budgetary transfers from the social fund. Nor would Irish specialists be included in the debates on vocational training, health and safety in the workplace, consumer law and equality policies. The professionals involved in these policy networks regard the EC dimension as a useful addition to the national policy debate, and welcome their participation in the cross-national networks created by the Community. Emerging policies on educational exchange offer Irish students and academics the possibility to attend courses in other countries, thereby forging links with colleagues that enrich their student and professional lives. Departure from the Community would narrow Irish horizons once again.

In sum, therefore, the option of leaving the Community would appear to resolve few if any of the deep-seated dilemmas across the whole spectrum of public policy which are facing Irish governments. The critics of membership have not presented attractive alternatives. The Community has been no panacea, but participation in a formal framework of integration has provided an opportunity to influence the collective response to a range of forces which even the strongest national governments cannot control on their own. The degree of order, stability and predictability which regional integration can bring is not limitless, but it is none the less all the more important in the context of the major changes which now confront all European countries, whether inside or outside the European Community.

The new agenda

Assessing the gains and losses of EC membership is a particularly elusive exercise at this juncture because the quality of integration itself — the choices it raises and the demands it imposes — is not a fixed target.

German unification, the collapse of Communism in Eastern Europe, and the Community's own moves towards Economic and Monetary Union all lend urgency to a renewed debate on the broad goals of the EC and the implications for the member-states. The emergence of proposals for Political Union during the Irish presidency in the first six months of 1990 thus served to concentrate attention on a new agenda for Community integration.

What are the issues that Irish policy-makers must address from an Irish viewpoint? First, the most recent Treaty change in the Community, the Single European Act (SEA), was badly handled by the political establishment. The Government, after much prevarication, published a White Paper on the implications of the SEA but decided against a referendum, only to find that the *Crotty* judgment gave rise to a referendum anyway. On this occasion the Government must be seen to keep the Oireachtas fully informed by means of debates and the publication of discussion documents, and should hold a referendum on any treaty changes so as to pre-empt another challenge through the courts. Second, Irish policy-makers should pay serious attention to the design of the system both for an EMU and Political Union. Ireland has no great tradition of contributing to the debate on institutional changes in the Community. Apart from some early discussion on the European Parliament in the 1970s and the chairing of the *ad hoc* committee on institutional affairs by Senator James Dooge, Ireland has merely reacted to ideas emerging from other countries and the Community institutions. Only one paper was submitted to the intergovernmental conference in 1985 and that was on cohesion. This time it may be politically prudent, to ensure the broadest domestic support for any possible treaty amendment, to clarify Ireland's positions more fully at an earlier stage.

So far as European Political Co-operation is concerned, this may require an examination of just what 'security' implies in a European system which is no longer based primarily on ideological confrontation between standing military alliances. Neutrality has been significant as a (rather inexpensive) badge of sovereign independence, but it does also encapsulate quite specific attitudes towards the role of military force. These merit reconsideration in any new system of European security, as does the definition of what is a permissible topic for policy harmonization within EPC. Moreover, security is increasingly concerned with matters of judicial and policing co-operation, which may impinge on national sensitivities about extradition.

However, Political Union is likely to focus mainly on the powers of the various institutions, notably the balance between the Parliament and the Council. The early indications are that Ireland would not favour co-decision for the EP at this stage because of its weak representation in that assembly. More generally, the concept of subsidiarity — that policy functions should be undertaken at the lowest level of government and administration which can discharge them effectively — is likely to be at the forefront of discussion. Hence the way it is applied will be of immense importance to Ireland. There is a tendency to use subsidiarity as a means of appeasing those forces that fear a centralizing and powerful Community. In other words, subsidiarity can be used to minimize the impact of political union and EMU on national sovereignty. Thus, for Ireland and for the other lesser developed states, subsidiarity may lead to an EMU without the proper flanking policies that would assure that there is balance and equity in the new economic and political order.

It is therefore of the utmost importance that Ireland makes a substantial contribution to the intergovernmental conference on EMU. This is so because the recent debate on EMU has been dominated by two issues of questionable real significance: loss of sovereignty and the nature of the European Central Bank. These two matters have crowded out more important issues and have thereby prolonged the tendency of both member-states and the Community to ignore the full requirements and implications of economic integration. Two issues, in particular, need to be highlighted: first, the assignment of economic policy powers in a genuine economic and monetary union and, second, the determination of the macroeconomic priorities of the Community. We briefly consider each of these in turn.

The first issue concerns the very nature of economic and monetary union. We would accept the definition of EMU that has been adopted by the National Economic and Social Council. This involves not only monetary and macroeconomic policy union, but also Community-level management of a wide range of interventionist and market regulating policies currently undertaken by the member-states — and, in general, all allocation of policy functions to the Community, the member-state, and the local authority based roughly on some rational principles of public finance. The creation of such a European economic and monetary union would require a re-assignment of policy powers between the local, national and Community tiers and a considerable extension of the fiscal role of the Community and the Community budget. The arguments for seeking to build such an EMU are strong, given the possible improvement in microeconomic performance, macroeconomic performance and, most significantly, the likely regional pattern of income and economic activity. Both Ireland and the Community as a whole would have a lot to gain from moving towards an economic and monetary union of the sort specified above. This would ensure that the 1992 programme creates a genuine common market, would secure the monetary stability and macroeconomic progress established in recent years, and would greatly enhance the Community's ability to bring about convergence in living standards.

The problem is that much of the recent discussion of EMU has focused narrowly on the technicalities of monetary union or a single currency, and paid insufficient attention to either economic union or the design of an overall policy framework for the Community. For example, the

Delors Report on Economic and Monetary Union introduced the principle of subsidiarity as meaning that policy functions will be carried out at national level so long as they have no adverse repercussions on the cohesion and functioning of the EMU, but then applied it in a way which ignored the extent to which national policies do in fact create spillover effects. A rigorous application of the principle of subsidiarity, and the economics of integrations, would indicate that many more functions will have to be shared between the Community and the national tiers of government than was envisaged by the Delors Committee.

The Delors Report recognizes that historical experience suggests that economic and monetary integration can, in the absence of countervailing policies, have a negative impact on peripheral regions. But virtually the only policies proposed to deal with this are the existing structural measures. A realistic view shows that convergence will *not* be attained by the internal market plus the existing structural funds. Finally, in specifying the system of macroeconomic management for a European EMU the Delors Committee completely ignored the role which the central budget plays in maintaining macroeconomic balance in existing economic and monetary unions.

Overall, the Delors Committee and most of the subsequent debate has not pursued the analysis of economic and monetary union to its logical conclusion, and has thus taken insufficient account of the requirements and implications of genuine economic integration. The task facing Ireland in the intergovernmental conference is to widen the argument to include a more adequate analysis of the role of public finance in economic and monetary integration.

The second issue which has unfortunately dominated recent discussion of EMU is the desirable constitutional blueprint for the European Central Bank (CB). This issue is, of course, of some significance and, by and large, there are strong arguments for a constitutionally independent CB. But what matters most is not the legal constitution of the CB but the power relationship between it and the 'government'. Whatever the constitutional position of the CB, it will have absolute power so long as Europe has no system or body capable of setting the macroeconomic policy priorities of the Community. Progress on the monetary front without progress in this field also will mean that the macroeconomic policy of the Community will be set by default, because the CB, however constituted, will be up against a vacuum. Of course the establishment of a body with the capacity and legitimacy to set the macroeconomic priorities of the Community requires not only economic but political integration. Indeed, this gap in the debate on EMU, created by the misguided attempt to assuage rather than confront fears of loss of sovereignty and by the excessive concentration on the constitutional design of the CB, has served to conceal deep and unavoidable connections between economic, monetary and political integration. Ireland's interest lies in these connections being laid bare and hence it must act, in the intergovernmental conference, to remove the veil.

Finally, it will be necessary, for the first time in Ireland's experience of EC membership, to confront the question of the appropriate territorial limits of an integrated 'Europe'. Previous enlargements of the EC, including that in which Ireland participated, have been within the confines of the Cold War *West* European system. Even these enlargements, by increasing the political and economic heterogeneity of the Community, have checked the pace of integration. The opening to the East not only raises the spectre of more difficult enlargements, it poses the question whether the EC, with its present political arrangements, can work as effectively with more than twice the present number of members.

Appendix

Glossary of Irish names

Bunreacht na hÉireann	The Constitution of Ireland.
Dáil (full title, *Dáil Éireann*)	The popularly elected legislative assembly.
Éire (Ireland)	In the Constitution, the name of the state.
Fianna Fáil ('Soldiers of Destiny')	The title of the largest party, founded in 1926.
Fine Gael ('Tribe of the Gaels')	The successor of Cumann na nGaedheal ('League of Gaels'). At present the second largest party.
Oireachtas	Parliament.
Seanad (full title, *Seanad Éireann*)	Senate.
Sinn Féin ('We Ourselves')	At the time of independence a coalition of separatist groups. The name is currently used by extremist nationalists.
Taoiseach	Prime Minister.
Teachta Dála	Member of the Dáil. Abbreviated to TD.

Index

African, Caribbean and Pacific countries
  172–3, 175, 176, 178, 180
agricultural policy xiv, xvi, 6, 42–58
  in EC 60, 70, 166
  effects of EC in Ireland 46–8, 279, 280
  in Ireland 4, 44–5, 167
  see also Common Agricultural Policy
agricultural trade, Irish 46, 47, 58, 166, 169
agriculture xix
  in Ireland 15, 42–58, 124
air pollution 120, 121, 122
air transport 93, 105, 106, 109–10, 112
AIRBUS programme 137
Anglo-Irish relations 148, 156–7, 161–4
  passim, 168, 187, 198, 282
approximation,
  fiscal 127, 131–4, 135
  of laws 92, 130
  see also harmonization
ARIAN programme 267
Austria 158, 161

Barrington, Justice 215, 216, 221
Barry, Peter 198
Beckett, Samuel 272
Belgium 3, 16, 26, 80, 166, 236
Bell, Desmond 275
Berger, John 272
Blaney, Neil 202
Bolger, Dermot 272
Boll, Heinrich 273
Bretton Woods system xix, 76, 79, 180
BRITE programme 138, 142
budgetary policy 39, 70, 71–2, 73, 74

Carroll, Justice 216, 222
cartels 90–91, 93, 97
Cecchini Report 11
CERN programme 137
China, People's Republic of 152
Christian Democrat group, European
  Parliament 199, 207
'cold shower effect' 26–7, 33, 35

collective bargaining 233–4, 252
COMETT (Community Action Programme
  for Education and Training for
  Technology) 262
Common Agricultural Policy xii, xix, 42,
  46–8, 60, 70, 72, 73, 74, 120, 166,
  199
  Guidance and Guarantee Fund see
    European Agricultural Guidance and
    Guarantee Fund
  Ireland and 46–58, 180, 198, 280, 285
  levies, subsidies 46, 52, 56, 58
  quotas 47, 58, 72
Common External Tariff 38
Common Market 3–4, 8–9, 90, 93, 97,
  98, 127, 134, 165, 233, 289
Common Market Study Group 188
Common Transport Policy 104, 105,
  110–11
  see also transport policy
competition 3, 10, 35, 72, 233
  EC policy 90–2, 97, 98
  impact of EC policy in Ireland 90, 93–6,
  102
Conference on Disarmament in Europe 162
Conference on Security and Co-operation
  in Europe (CSCE) 152, 153, 158, 162,
  163
consumer protection xiv, 234
  EC policy 256
  effect of EC legislation in Ireland 257–9,
  283
  in Ireland 256–7
COST programme 137
Costello, Justice 220
Council of Europe 151, 158, 164
Council of Ministers 191, 208, 239, 247,
  288
Cox, Pat 200
Crotty v. an Taoiseach 215–18, 219, 226,
  284, 288
cultural policy 270–6
  EC policies 235, 270, 271, 274

impact of EC policies in Ireland 271–6, 283, 287
  in Ireland 271–6
customs union 8–9, 12, 165, 166, 233
Cyprus 151, 166

Dail Eirann 175, 190, 198, 201, 203, 204, 215
de Gaulle, President Charles xix
De Rossa, P 199, 202, 203
Delors, Jacques 234
Delors Report 186, 206, 290
Denmark xviii, 17, 62, 80, 172, 187, 261
Denning, Lord 221
development policy xiv, xvi
  in EC 172–3, 176
  impact of EC policy in Ireland 175–82, 281
  in Ireland 147, 155, 173–5, 181–2, 285
Disaster Relief 173
Dukes, Alan 198
Dooge, Senator 161, 288
Durcan, Paul 275

East–West relations 152–3, 166
economic and monetary union 69, 70, 74, 75, 76, 88, 186, 194, 288, 289–90
economic policy xii, xiv, xvi, 3, 285
  in EC 3–4, 39, 40, 289
  effects of EC policies in Ireland 285
  Irish xix, 4–5, 7, 39–40, 44, 85, 99, 187, 280, 285
economies of scale 10, 92
economy, Irish 12–15, 40, 84, 167, 168, 285–6
  effect of EC membership 28–30, 38, 55–7, 85–7, 285
educational policy xii, xiv, 283
  in EC 235, 260–2, 267
  impact of EC membership 263–8, 283, 287
  in Ireland 262–3, 274
electronics industry 103, 139
emigration 4, 167, 237–8, 283
energy policy xiv
  in EC 99, 114–15, 117, 120
  impact of EC membership 116–17
  in Ireland 114, 115–16
environment policy xii, xiv
  in EC 4, 60, 117, 119–20, 122, 234
  effects of EC policy in Ireland 119, 122–5
  in Ireland 119, 121–2, 176
environmental protection 234
ERASMUS programme 262, 266
ESPRIT programme 137, 138, 140, 142
EURAM programme 138
Europe-12 Research and Action Committee xiii, xv, xvi, 6
European Agricultural Guidance and Guarantee Fund 47, 56, 62, 66
European Atomic Energy Community (EURATOM) 114–15, 136, 211, 260
European Bureau (Ireland) 192
European Central Bank 289, 290
European Centre for the Development of Vocational Training 239, 242
European Coal and Steel Community xi, 97, 136, 156, 211, 260
European Commission 63, 64, 65, 68–9, 99, 105, 186, 194, 195, 196, 208, 234, 265, 283
European Communities Committee (Ireland) 192, 193
European Court of Justice 149–50, 209, 261
European Currency Unit (ECU) 79
European Democratic Alliance 199, 207
European Development Fund 176, 177, 178
  see also European Regional Development Fund
European Free Trade Association (EFTA) xix, 151–2, 169, 170, 285
European Investment Bank 62, 80, 108, 115, 117, 177
European Monetary System 38, 53, 76–88, 280
  Ireland and 82–5, 280–1
European Parliament 63, 105, 157, 186, 194, 198, 199–200, 202, 203, 207–8, 288
European People's Party (Christian Democratic group) 199
European Political Co-operation xii, 149–58 *passim*, 160, 162, 163, 188, 191, 202, 215, 219, 281, 282, 288
European Regional Development Fund 63–8, 108, 111, 117, 195, 238, 281
  quotas 63, 65
European Social Fund 62, 66, 234, 238–42 *passim*, 260, 263, 265, 268
European Space Agency 137
exchange rates 76–7, 78, 79–81, 82–4, 85–6, 87
Exchange Rate Mechanism 77
Export Profit Tax Relief 130, 131
external trade xii, xiii, xvi, 147, 165–71
  EC policies 165–7
  effects of EC policies in Ireland 168–71
  in Ireland 167–8

Fianna Fáil xix, 188, 197–203 *passim*, 207, 208, 282
Fine Gael xix, 162, 188, 197–203 *passim*, 207, 282
Finland 158

INDEX

Finlay, Chief Justice 216, 218
fiscal policy,
   in EC 3, 6, 70, 74, 98, 126, 127–30, 134
   impact of EC policies in Ireland 131–5
FitzGerald, Dr Garrett 198, 199
food industry 55, 58, 280
foreign policy xiv, xvi
   in EC 147, 149
   impact of EC policies in Ireland 150, 158, 281
   in Ireland 147–8, 149–58, 174, 177, 180, 181
foreign relations xii, xiii, xiv, xvi, xx
   EC and 147
   effect of EC membership in Ireland 281–2, 284
   Irish 147–8
France 3, 26, 27, 65, 80, 166
Friel, Brian 275

Gains and losses from EC membership, xi, xii, xx, 5–6, 279–91
in the field of
   agricultural policy 46–8, 55–8, 279, 280
   competition policy 90, 93–6
   the economy 6, 39–40, 279–81, 285
   fiscal/taxation policy 131–4
   foreign relations 281–2, 284
   industrial policy 97, 101–3
   the internal market 7, 32, 36, 39–40, 103, 279
   monetary policies 85–8, 280–1
   political and legal systems 282
   regional affairs 68–70, 74, 281
   social, educational and cultural policy 283
   technology policy 139–43
   transport policy 108, 111–12
   women's rights 250
General Agreement on Tariffs and Trade (GATT) 56, 166, 167
German question xiii, 288
Germany, Federal Republic of xii, xiii, 3, 12, 65, 77, 78, 80, 82, 153
Gogarty, Oliver St John 276
government and administration, Irish 190–6
   and community business 191–2, 193–5
   effects of EC membership 191
   local and regional government 195–6
Great Britain *see* United Kingdom
Greece xviii, 37, 42, 65, 69, 151, 166
Green Party (Ireland) 202
Griffin, Justice 218
Grubel Lloyd index 28

Haagerup Report 157
Hamilton, Justice 216, 221

harmonization,
   of company law 252
   fiscal 127, 128, 130, 131–3, 134, 135
   of technical standards 92, 95, 96
Haughey, Charles J 191, 192, 198
Heaney, Seamus 275
Hederman, Justice 217
Helsinki Final Act 152
Henchy, Justice 217–20 *passim*
human rights 152
Hume, John 200

Industrial Development Authority (IDA) (Ireland) 61, 100, 102, 122, 253
industrial policy,
   in EC 4, 39, 74, 91, 92, 97–9
   impact of EC policies on Ireland 97, 101–3
   in Ireland 4, 7, 23, 39, 61, 69, 97, 99–101, 103, 130, 167, 279–80
industrial relations,
   in Ireland 252–4
   results of EC membership on 254
industrial specialization 27, 33, 36, 37, 38–9, 280
industrial structure 10, 11–12, 26, 30–2, 33, 34, 39, 69, 280, 285
inflation 77, 79, 80, 82–5 *passim*, 87, 281
infrastructure projects 67, 70, 74
Ingersoll, Ralph 274
integration xvi, xx, 3, 5, 72, 268, 287
   economic 8–12, 15, 25, 27, 35–8, 39, 98, 289–90
interest rates 78–9, 81, 84, 86, 87
internal market xi, xii, xiii, xvi, 6, 7–40, 60, 64, 70, 73, 74, 90, 98, 100, 126, 127, 135, 186, 202, 283
   effects of in Ireland 7, 32, 36, 39, 103, 206, 214, 234, 279, 280, 285, 286
International Development Association (UN Agency) 173
International Energy Agency (OECD agency) 115
International Labour Organization 253
International Monetary Fund 179
international terrorism 163
Irish Dairy Board 45
Irish Distillers company 94
Irish Sovereignty Movement 188
Irish Supreme Court 160, 213, 215, 216, 219–23 *passim*, 226
Italy 3, 12, 26, 27, 80

Japan 92, 98, 102, 169, 170, 286
Joint Committee on Secondary Legislatin of the European Communities (Ireland) 203–5, 208, 249
Joyce, James 272, 276

Keane, Justice 221, 223
Kettle, Tom 276
Kilroy, Thomas 275
Kutscher, Professor 223

Labour Party (Ireland) 197–203 *passim*, 207
legal systems xiii, xiv, xvi
 in EC 209–10
 impact of EC policies on Ireland 210–14, 225–7
  Community law in Irish courts 220–24
  domestic and delegated legislation 213, 224–5
  and Single European Act 214–20
 Irish legal system 210
  Constitution 210–13
Lemass, Sean 191
less-developed countries 172, 176, 177, 178, 180
Lingua programme 261, 266, 267
Lomé Conventions 166, 169, 170, 172–3, 176, 178, 179, 180
Luxembourg xiii, xviii, 3, 80
Lynch, Jack 200

McGuinness, Frank 275
macroeconomic co-ordination 70–4 *passim*, 78, 87, 126, 289
McWilliam, Justice 221
Maher, T J 200, 202
manpower 233, 236–42
 in Ireland 236–8
manufacturing industry, Irish 18–26, 27, 34
 effects of EC membership 20, 23, 35, 36, 38
 industrial structure *see main entry*
media, media policies 271, 274, 275
modernism, modernist culture 272
Mohr, Jean 272
monetary compensatory amounts (under CAP) 56
monetary policy xiv, xvi, 3, 6, 87
 in EC 39, 60, 76, 79–82, 280
 effects of EC policies on Ireland 76, 82–4, 85–8, 279, 285
 Irish policies 39, 76–9, 80
Moore, George 276
Multi-Fibre Arrangements 99, 167, 180
multinationals 101, 103, 141
Murphy, Justice 223

National Board for Science and Technology (Ireland) 138, 140
National Development Plan (Ireland) 106, 111, 191, 196, 201
National Economic and Social Council (Ireland) 72, 100, 194, 198, 206, 289
national identity xvi, xx, 187–9
 see also sovereignty
NATO xix, 148, 152, 153, 160, 163
Netherlands xii, 3, 16, 80
New Community Instrument 115
New International Economic Order 174, 180
North–South relations 154, 174, 177, 180–1
Northern Ireland xiii, xviii, xx, 42, 105, 148, 156–8, 163, 200, 282
Norway 158

Occupational health matters 233
Official Development Assistance (Ireland) 174, 175, 176, 177–8
oil crisis, 1973 xix, 12, 115, 116, 236
Oireachtas (parliament) 203–5, 211, 214, 215, 223, 288
 see also Dail Eirann
O'Loughlin, Michael 272, 275
O'Malley, Desmond 197
Organization of Economic Co-operation and Development (OECD) 85, 115, 138, 176
 Development Assistance Committee 176, 178
Organization of Petroleum Exporting Countries (OPEC) 170

Pearce, Patrick 276
PETRA programme 267
political and legal systems xiii, xiv, xvi, 185
 EC policies 185–6
 impact on Ireland of EC membership 206–8, 282, 284, 286–7
 see also legal systems
political process (Ireland) 199–205
 parliament 203–5
 political parties 197–203, 207, 282
 system assessed 206–8
 see also Dail Eirann; Fianna Fáil; Fine Gail; Oireachtas
Portugal xii, xviii, 37, 42, 65, 69, 151
product differentiation 10, 11, 12
Progressive Democrat Party (Ireland) 162, 197, 200, 202, 203, 207
proportional representation 200

RACE programme 138, 142
rail transport 108–9, 112
regional policy xiv, xvi, 6, 60–75
 in EC 4, 60, 62–8, 69–70, 90, 91, 92
 impact on Ireland of EC membership 65–8, 73, 74, 279, 281
 Irish regional policy 61–2, 74

road investment, in Ireland 108
road transport 106–8
Roman Catholicism 271–2

Science and technology *see* technology policies
SCIENCE programme 138
sea transport 105, 106, 110, 112
sectoral policies, in EC 98–9, 102–3
security policy xii, xiv, xvi, 147
　in EC 160, 164, 282, 288
　impact on Ireland of EC membership 162–4
　in Ireland 152, 161–2
Single European Act xi, xx, 4, 60, 64–5, 92, 105, 119, 120, 128, 137, 147, 149, 155, 160, 161, 186, 188, 191, 194, 195, 198, 199, 202, 214–20, 226, 233–4, 240, 271, 288
'Snake' arrangement 76, 79
social policies xii, xiv, xvi, 260
　Charter on Fundamental Social Rights 234–5, 283
　in EC 60, 233–5, 262
　impact on Ireland of EC membership 238–40, 283, 287
social security 233, 247
soil improvement 120
Southern Africa 154
sovereignty xiv, xvi, 187–9, 211, 289
　impact on Ireland of EC membership 188, 209
　in Ireland 211, 219–20
Soviet Union 152, 166, 169
Spain 37, 42, 65, 69, 151, 166, 236, 238
SPRINT programme 142
state aids 91–2, 94–5, 95–6, 97, 99, 101, 102
state monopolies 92
STRIDE programme 142
structural policies, in EC 70, 71, 73, 74
Sub-Saharan Africa 173, 179
Sweden 158
Switzerland 158
Synge, J M 276

Taxation policies 3, 6, 126
　corporation taxes 129–30
　in EC 126, 127–30, 134
　excise duties 129
　impact on Ireland of EC membership 131–5
　Irish policies 130–1
　VAT 127–8, 131, 132–3
Taoiseach 175, 190, 191, 192, 194, 199, 200, 203, 206, 282
technical efficiency 26–7, 33, 35
technical standards 92, 95, 96

technology policies xiv
　in EC 4, 60, 72, 92, 98, 102–3, 136–8, 142
　impact on Ireland of EC membership 139–43
　Irish policies 138–9
telecommunications industry 103
trade,
　external xii, xiii, xvi; *see also main heading*
　impact on Ireland of EC membership 32–8, 169, 170, 171
　internal 60
　international 8–9, 33
　intra-industry 10, 11, 26, 27–30, 33, 35, 37
　Irish trade 15–18, 28–30, 169–71, 180
　　agricultural 46, 47, 58, 166, 169
trade preferences 166, 169, 170, 172
transport, in Ireland 105–6
transport infrastructure 110–11, 112
transport policy xiv, xvi, 93, 99
　in EC 104–5, 107, 109, 110–11
　impact on Ireland of EC membership 108, 111–12
　regulation and deregulation 72
Treaty of Accession 71
Treaty of Paris 97, 99, 211, 233
Treaty of Rome 3, 4, 62, 64, 71, 72, 90–1, 92, 97, 101, 104, 109,. 119, 120, 130, 131, 136, 137, 165, 186, 211, 214, 217, 220, 233, 245, 252, 260

Underdeveloped Areas Act (Ireland) 61
unemployment 4, 236–7
United Kingdom xii, xiii, xix, 4, 12, 17, 37, 42, 44, 46, 58, 62, 77, 82, 85, 86, 128, 140, 148, 156, 157 161, 167, 168, 170, 172, 187, 210, 234, 237, 244, 252, 253, 261, 267, 280, 281
　see also Anglo-Irish relations
United Nations 148, 151, 154, 155, 158, 163, 173, 176, 177
　UNIFIL 163
United States 92, 98, 102, 137, 140, 148, 153, 154, 167, 169, 237, 244, 253, 273

'Val Duchesse' dialogue 234
vocational training,
　in EC 233, 234, 260–1, 287
　in Ireland 236–42, 262, 268, 283

Walsh, Justice 217, 219, 226
water quality 120, 122
Wenders, Wim 273
Western European Union 160, 163
Wilde, Oscar 276
women's rights 176, 177, 240, 244–50

impact on Ireland of EC membership 245–50, 283
Irish policies 244–5
Workers' Party (Ireland) 197, 199, 200, 202, 203, 207
working conditions 233, 234, 235, 252–4, 283, 287
World Bank 173, 176, 177, 179
World Food Programme 173

Yaounde Convention 166
Yeats, W B 272, 276